Rural Development

Rural Development

Principles, Policies and Management

(Second Edition)

Katar Singh

Sage Publications
New Delhi • Thousand Oaks • London

This edition first published in 1999 by

Sage Publications India Pvt Ltd
32 M-Block Market, Greater Kailash-I
New Delhi-110 048

Sage Publications Inc.
2455 Teller Road
Thousand Oaks, California 91320

Sage Publications Ltd
6 Bonhill Street
London EC2A 4PU

Third Printing 2001

Published by Tejeshwar Singh for Sage Publications India Pvt Ltd, typeset by Siva Math Setters, Chennai and printed at Chaman Enterprises, Delhi.

Library of Congress Cataloging-in-Publication Data

Singh, Katar, 1939–
    Rural development: principles, policies, and management/by
Katar Singh. —2nd ed.
        p. cm. (c). (pbk.)
    Includes bibliographical references and index.
    1. Rural development. 2. Rural development projects—India—
Case studies, I. Title.

HN49. C6S56 307.1'412—dc21   1999   98–32121

ISBN: 0–7619–9308–8 (US-hb)   81–7036–772–7 (India-hb)
         0–7619–9309–6 (US-pb)   81–7036–773–5 (India-pb)

Sage Production Team: Dhiren Bahl, Radha Dev Raj and Santosh Rawat

To
the fond memory
of
my beloved parents

Contents

List of Tables

List of Figures

Preface to the Second Edition

Students and teachers of rural development received the first edition of the book very well. It had a long innings of over a decade. Recently, some of my colleagues and students suggested that I revise and update the book, and I also realised the need to do so. However, I did not find the time nor had a strong will to start the work. I also thought that some younger teacher would do a better job of writing a new textbook on the subject. But, as far as I know, no good textbook on the subject has since appeared. However, it was not this that got me started. The real impetus to revise the book came from no less a person than Mr Tejeshwar Singh, Managing Director, Sage Publications, who wrote to me in October 1997 urging me to revise the book. I wrote back to Mr Singh in the affirmative and set a deadline for the end of January 1998 for myself. In the first week of January 1998 I received, along with New Year's greetings, an enquiry from him about the status of the book. As I was not able to make much headway until then due to my various other preoccupations, I had to seek an extension of the deadline, which was granted. Thereafter, he religiously sent me reminders until I finally wrote to him that the revision work was almost over, and that the manuscript would be couriered to him by the end of June. I kept my word this time. So the real credit for this edition of the book must go to Mr Tejeshwar Singh, and I am thankful to him for this, as also for his comments, and his personal interest in this project.

I have updated, substantially revised and augmented Chapters 2, 3, 4, 11, 14 and 15, and dropped Chapter 8, as in my opinion, it did not serve any useful purpose, and merged Chapters 17 and 18 into one chapter on Implementation, Monitoring and Evaluation. The remaining chapters were also revised and updated wherever necessary. So this second edition of the book comprises 16 chapters. While revising them, I took into consideration the comments made by various reviewers of the first edition, the suggestions made by Mr Tejeshwar Singh, and the feedback that I received from my students and colleagues at the Institute of Rural Management (IRMA). The revised edition retains all the strengths of the first one, is trimmed of unnecessary matter, and adds quite a few new things to most chapters. Like the first edition, this one also is primarily addressed to students, teachers, trainers and researchers interested in rural development, and practitioners working in rural development organisations. I hope readers will find it better than the first one.

Many persons helped me in revising and updating the book. My wife, Vimala Singh, willingly (and many times unwillingly), allowed me to work long hours on holidays and in the evenings after office hours on weekdays. My son, Dr Anil Shishodia, being an economics teacher himself, helped me with data and other relevant literature, besides proofreading and correcting many chapters. As in the case of the first edition, my personal assistant, Mrs Lissy Verghese, aptly handled various secretarial and administrative chores, painstakingly word-processed the manuscript and saw to it that I met the deadline. Mr Eric Leo, my secretary, also helped a lot in word processing, making figures, tables and printing the text. Mr Oliver Macwan carefully word-processed all the tables included in Chapter 2. I am grateful to them all and thank them for their ungrudging and willing help and cooperation, without which it would have been very difficult for me to complete the revision of the book. Last but not least, I am highly thankful to Ms Omita Goyal, Managing Editor, and Ms Jaya Chowdhury, Chief Desk Editor, Sage Publications, for processing the manuscript expeditiously and bringing out the book in such a short period of time.

Anand   Katar Singh
6 August 1998

Preface to the First Edition

This book is the outcome of more than two decades of my professional experience in teaching, training, research and extension activities in the field of agricultural and rural development. From July 1961 when I started my professional career as Senior Research Assistant in charge of a research-cum-extension project in farm planning, I have had diverse experiences ranging from handling 'nuts and bolts' type jobs to building conceptual and quantitative models of development. Most of the material presented in the book is based on my own ideas, observations and research, and has been tested in some form or the other in my undergraduate and postgraduate classes and in various short-term training programmes at both the G.B. Pant University of Agriculture and Technology, Pantnagar, and the Institute of Rural Management, Anand (IRMA).

The book consists of eighteen chapters which are grouped into three parts. Part I comprises five chapters which are devoted to an exposition of the meaning, objectives, measures, hypotheses and determinants of rural development. Part II contains eight chapters which deal with rural development policies, policy models, policy instruments and selected rural development programmes followed in India. Part III includes five chapters which together cover various organisational and managerial aspects of rural development such as planning, organising, financing, implementing, monitoring and evaluation. Thus, the book is a comprehensive treatise on rural development covering all the three important aspects of the subject—principles, policies and management.

This book is written for all those interested in contributing towards, and acquiring knowledge about, rural development. More specifically, this book is addressed to teachers, trainers, researchers, students and agencies interested in rural development. In particular, it examines the meaning of rural development, its pace and level, the lessons learned from India's experience with various rural development programmes, and how these programmes should be managed.

In writing this book and in the development of my thoughts and ideas about agricultural and rural development, I have benefited a great deal from my interaction with my teachers, colleagues, students, people in the rural areas, policy makers, planners, bankers and from the writings of many development theorists. To name them all would be impossible and to mention a few invidious. I extend my sincere thanks to them all. My greatest debt is to my parents, Late Shrimati Anandi Singh and Late Shri Rajvir Singh, who taught me, through their work and attitude, the basics of farm and household development and management. My formal education has served only to corroborate and enrich what I learnt from them. I thank my wife, Vimala Singh, who kept me free from various household responsibilities and spent many lonely evenings and holidays ungrudgingly while I worked on this book.

I am extremely grateful to Shri R.N. Haldipur, Director, IRMA, who granted the permission and provided the necessary facilities and a congenial environment for writing this book, and whose advice and encouragement during the course of this work was invaluable. My sincere thanks are also due to Dr G.V.K. Rao, former member, Planning Commission and currently a member of IRMA's Board of Governors, for his valuable advice and suggestions to improve the book.

Finally, I want to thank my secretary, Mrs Lissy Varghese, who so willingly and carefully typed the final as well as earlier drafts of this book. Her cheerfulness, meticulous work and patience made writing easier, quicker and more of a pleasure.

Anand   Katar Singh
February 1986

Introduction

The term Rural Development is a subset of the broader term 'Development'. Howsoever we define it, development is a universally cherished goal of individuals, families, communities and nations all over the world. Development is also natural in the sense that all forms of life on Planet Earth have an inherent urge to survive and develop. Given these two attributes, i.e., its universal supremacy as a goal and its natural occurrence, development deserves a scientific study and analysis. Hence it is not surprising that the subject of development has been studied by scholars of all faiths, ideologies and disciplines. So much has been written and said about rural development, that one finds it difficult to justify yet another book on this subject. However, it is my conviction that there is need for a textbook on rural development—a book that churns out valuable insights and practicable lessons from the vast literature that is available on the subject. This book is intended to be a book of that sort. That such a book was needed was amply evident from the first edition of the book that had a long innings of over a decade. Having said this, I now proceed to examine some of the commonly used connotations and definitions of development in general, and rural development in particular. The objective is to arrive at a definition that is easy to understand and use.

Concepts and Connotations of Rural Development

Development is a subjective and value-loaded concept, and hence there cannot be a consensus as to its meaning. The term is used differently in diverse contexts. It basically means 'unfolding', 'revealing', or 'opening up' something which is latent. When applied to human beings, it therefore means 'unfolding' or 'opening up' their potential powers. Generally speaking, the term development implies a change that is desirable. Since what is desirable at a particular time, place and in a particular culture may not be desirable at other places, or at other times at the same place and in the same cultural milieu, it is impossible to think of a universally acceptable definition of development. At best, development in the context of society could be conceptualised as a set of desirable societal objectives which society seeks to achieve. Thus defined, development is cherished by all individuals, communities and nations, irrespective of their culture, religion and spatial location.

These days, sustainable development has become a buzzword. According to the World Commission on Environment and Development (WCED 1987: 43), 'sustainable development is development that meets the needs of the present without compromising the ability of future generations to meet their own needs.' In simple words, sustainable development is a process in which the set of desirable societal objectives, or the development index, does not decrease over time. Constancy of natural capital stock, including natural resources and the environment, is a necessary condition for sustainable development. The set of 'sufficient conditions' includes an appropriate institutional framework and governance system for implementation of sustainable development policy.

The term rural development connotes overall development of rural areas[1] with a view to improve the quality of life of rural people. In this sense, it is a comprehensive and multidimensional concept, and encompasses the development of agriculture and allied activities, village and cottage industries and crafts, socio-economic infrastructure, community services and facilities, and, above all, the human resources in rural areas. *As a phenomenon*, rural development is the end-result of interactions between various physical, technological, economic, sociocultural and institutional factors. *As a strategy*, it is designed to improve the economic and social well-being of a specific group of people—the rural poor. *As a discipline*, it is multi-disciplinary in nature, representing an intersection of agricultural, social, behavioural, engineering and management sciences. In the words of Robert Chambers (1983: 147):

> Rural Development is a strategy to enable a specific group of people, poor rural women and men, to gain for themselves and their children more of what they want and need. It involves helping the poorest

[1] Areas outside the jurisdiction of municipal corporations and committees and notified town area committees.

among those who seek a livelihood in the rural areas to demand and control more of the benefits of rural development. The group includes small scale farmers, tenants, and the landless.

Thus the term rural development may be used to imply any one of the above-mentioned connotations. To avoid ineffective floundering among the myriad definitions, we shall define rural development as: 'A process leading to sustainable improvement in the quality of life of rural people, especially the poor.'

In addition to economic growth, this process typically involves changes in popular attitudes, and in many cases even in customs and beliefs. In a nutshell, the process of rural development must represent the entire gamut of change by which a social system moves away from a state of life perceived as 'unsatisfactory' towards a materially and spiritually better condition of life. The process of rural development may be compared with a train in which each coach pushes the one ahead of it, and is in turn pushed by the one behind, but it takes a powerful engine to make the whole train move. The secret of success in rural development lies in identifying, and, if needed, developing a suitable engine to attach to the train. There are no universally valid guidelines to identify appropriate engines of rural development, if at all they exist. It is a choice that is influenced by time, space and culture.

Basic Elements of Rural Development

Whatever the geographic location, culture and historical stage of development of a society, there are at least three basic elements which are considered to constitute the 'true' meaning of rural development. They are as follows (Todaro 1977: 16–18):

1. **Basic Necessities of Life.** People have certain basic needs, without which it would be impossible (or very difficult) for them to survive. The basic necessities include food, clothes, shelter, basic literacy, primary health care and security of life and property. When any one or all of them are absent or in critically short supply, we may state that a condition of 'absolute underdevelopment' exists. Provision of the basic necessities of life to everybody is the primary responsibility of all economies, whether they are capitalist, socialist, or mixed. In this sense, we may claim that economic growth (increased per capita availability of basic necessities) is

a necessary condition for improvement of the 'quality of life' of rural people, which is rural development.

2. **Self-Respect.** Every person and every nation seeks some sort of self-respect, dignity, or honour. Absence or denial of self-respect indicates lack of development.

3. **Freedom.** In this context, freedom refers to political or ideological freedom, economic freedom and freedom from social servitude. As long as a society is bound by the servitude of men to nature, ignorance, other men, institutions, and dogmatic beliefs, it cannot claim to have achieved the goal of 'development'. Servitude in any form reflects a state of underdevelopment.

The new economic view of development considers reduction or elimination of poverty, inequality and unemployment as an important index of development. Seers (1969: 3) succinctly tackled the basic question of the meaning of development when he wrote:

The questions to ask about a country's development are therefore: What has been happening to poverty? What has been happening to unemployment? What has been happening to inequality? If all three of these have declined from high levels, then, beyond doubt, this has been a period of development of the country concerned. If one or two of these central problems have been growing worse, especially if all three have, it would be strange to call the result 'development' even if per capita income doubled.

Growth versus Development

While economic growth is an essential component of development, it is not the only one, as development is not a purely economic phenomenon. In the ultimate sense, it must encompass more than the material and financial sides of people's lives. Development should, therefore, be perceived as a multidimensional process, involving the reorganisation and reorientation of both economic and social systems. In addition to improvements in the level and distribution of incomes and output, it involves radical changes in institutional, social and administrative structures. Finally, although development is usually defined in a national context, its widespread realisation may necessitate fundamental modifications of the international economic, social and political systems as well.

The Vedic prayer '*sarve sukhinaha bhavantu, sarve santu nira-mayaha*', i.e., 'may everybody (in this universe) be happy and healthy', highlights the global and multidimensional nature of development.

Why Rural Development

Since time immemorial, India has been, still continues to be, and will remain in the foreseeable future, a land of village communities. As a matter of fact, the village was the basic unit of administration as far back as the Vedic Age; there is a reference to *gramini* (village leader) in the *Rig Veda*. The predominantly rural character of India's national economy is reflected in the very high proportion of its population living in rural areas: it was 89 per cent in 1901, 83 per cent in 1951, 80 per cent in 1971 and 74 per cent in 1991. With more than 700 million of its people living in rural areas, and with the rural sector contributing about 29 per cent of its gross domestic product, no strategy of socio-economic development for India that neglects rural people and rural areas can be successful. The rural character of the economy, and the need for regeneration of rural life, was stressed by Mahatma Gandhi (Anonymous 1978: 2, 31). He wrote in *Harijan* (4 April 1936):

India is to be found not in its few cities but in its 7,00,000 villages. But we town dwellers have believed that India is to be found in its towns and the villages were created to minister to our needs. We have hardly paused to enquire if those poor folk get sufficient to eat and clothe themselves with and whether they have a roof to shelter themselves from sun and rain.

He further wrote in *Harijan* (29 August 1936), 'I would say that if the village perishes, India would perish too. It will be no more India. Her own mission in the world will get lost. The revival of village life is possible only when it is no more exploited.'

Rural development is, therefore, an absolute and urgent necessity in India now, and will continue to be so in future. It is the sine qua non of development of India.

Rising Expectations and Development

The common man in India, as also in other developing countries, expects a higher standard of living for himself, his family, his community and his nation. Particular expectations, of course, differ from person to person and from region to region, but the expectation of a marked improvement in material conditions of life is general throughout the world. People want and expect to have better diet, clothes, houses, education, a secure life and freedom from servitude. This is the revolution of expectations that has swept over the Third World countries.

There are many explanations for this phenomenon. First, the demonstration effect of the rural elite, urban rich and foreign tourists engaging in ostentatious consumption of exotic and luxurious goods has distorted the consumption and utility functions of the poor. Second, films, radio, television and advertising have exposed the masses to modern gadgets and lifestyles, and have thus aroused their expectations. Third, local and national politicians have assured the rural poor of the modern amenities of life, if they would vote for them. Fourth, the central governments have declared time and again that the eradication of poverty is their major policy goal. Through these media, the common man has first learned about the new products, gadgets and services, then come to want them, and now to demand them.

The economies of most developing countries (including India) cannot possibly fulfil these expectations in the immediate future, and there is bound to be a collision between rising expectations and economic reality. The outcome will vary from country to country, but it will certainly involve disillusionment, demoralisation, agitation and political upheaval. It is this that makes rapid agricultural and economic development a national imperative.

Development and Change

Development is both a cause and a consequence of change. There is a two-way relationship between them, i.e., development influences, and is influenced by, a change. The change implies a physical, technological, economic, social, cultural, attitudinal, organisational, or political change. Whereas all manifestations of development can be traced to some change somewhere, sometimes not all changes lead to development; a change may be either for the better (development), or the worse (retrogression).

In the context of rural development, a 'change' may be considered to be an instrument which can be used to promote rural development. In India, the introduction of technological changes in the mid-sixties (new high-yielding varieties of crops, fertilisers, improved farm machinery and pesticides) led to the so-called Green Revolution in agriculture. Similarly, technological innovations, such as modern milk processing and feed processing plants, artificial insemination of dairy animals, and organisational innovations such as the Anand-pattern dairy cooperatives introduced in India on a large scale in the early seventies under the Operation Flood programme, contributed significantly to the modernisation and development of the dairy industry of the country. Elsewhere, such as in Taiwan and the People's Republic of China, agricultural development was largely a result of institutional reforms, especially land reforms and technological advances. Karl Marx was one of the great advocates of revolutionary (socio-economic) change as an instrument of development.

A change may occur naturally or autonomously, or may be induced. A development manager may accelerate the pace of development by both inducing a desirable change in a given system, and by properly directing the autonomous change. It is important that the likely impacts of a contemplated change on various segments of society be carefully evaluated *ex ante* (before the change is introduced).

Human Beings as the Cause and Consequence of Development

Human beings are both the cause and consequence of development: it is the human factor that is the pivot of the process of development. Though the study of a human being is basic to the study of development, it cannot be of a human being in isolation, but rather of human beings in relation to their fellows, or of humans in society and in their environment.

It is the creation of conditions, both material and spiritual, which enable the human being as an individual, and the human being as a species, to be at her/his best. Those who control a human being's livelihood, control a human being. A person's freedom is illusory when he/she depends upon others for the right to work and the right to eat. Equally, a nation is not independent if its economic resources are controlled by another nation. Political independence is meaningless, if a nation does not control the means by which its citizens can earn their living.

In other words, human development follows from economic development, only if the latter is achieved on the basis of the equality and human dignity of all those involved. Human dignity cannot be given to a human being by the kindness of others; indeed, it can be destroyed by kindness which emanates from an act of charity, for human dignity involves equality, freedom and relations of mutual respect among humans; it depends on responsibility, and on a conscious participation in the life of the society in which a human being lives and works.

The whole structure of national societies and of international society is therefore relevant to the development of people. There are few societies which can be said to serve this purpose; there are few, if any, which both accept and are organised to serve social justice, in what has been called the Revolution of Rising Expectations.

The greatest advances in technology and economic growth have been achieved under capitalism. But the decisions pertaining to what goods shall be produced, and how they shall be produced, are made by a small number of people who have control over land and capital. The determining factor in their decision making is whether the activity will yield profit, power, or prestige to them, as owners of land or capital. The needs of humankind are secondary, if they are considered at all.

There is no profit in producing cheap houses, so they are not produced; there is 'no money' for schools and hospitals, but enough for five star hotels and luxury apartments. The result is a few people living in luxury, using the wealth produced by humans for their own grandeur and to ensure their own power. At the same time, masses of men, women and children are reduced to beggary, squalor, and to the humiliation of that disease—the soul-destroying insecurity which arises out of their enforced poverty.

Let us be quite clear that, if we are interested in a human being as an individual, we must express this by our interest in the society of which those individuals are members, for humans are shaped by the circumstances in which they live. If they are treated like animals, they will *act* like animals. If they are denied dignity, they will act accordingly. If they are treated solely as a dispensable means of production, they will become soulless 'hands', to whom life is a matter of doing as little work as possible, and then escaping into the illusion of happiness and pride through vice.

Some Dilemmas in Development

Literature on development abounds in a variety of dilemmas and dogmas, such as rural versus urban development, agricultural versus industrial development, primacy of capital versus labour, and natural/autonomous versus induced/planned development. A brief critique of these dilemmas seems in order to clarify some of the issues.

Rural versus Urban Development

Economic development in Western countries has been associated with growing urbanisation, as reflected in the increasing proportion of the urban population. Hence, there is a tendency among economists to consider urbanisation as an index of development. Growing urbanisation is obviously the consequence of the growing concentration of infrastructural networks and capital-intensive industrial enterprises in urban centres. This type of concentration has resulted in the existence of what is known in the literature on the economics of development as 'dualism', or coexistence of two separate economic subsystems in an economy, in many developing countries. On one hand, there exists in the economy a small but highly modern and developed urban subsector, which absorbs most of the material, financial and educated and talented manpower resources; on the other hand, a very large but traditional and underdeveloped rural subsector, characterised by widespread poverty, unemployment and low productivity, which forms the majority of the population. In many developing countries, both the subsectors coexist, but without those linkages between them that were once the main factors which contributed to the development of today's developed countries.

At the other extreme, there is another dogma rapidly emerging in many developing countries, that rural development is a prerequisite for overall development, and hence it deserves the highest priority in terms of allocation of resources. In their enthusiasm to promote the cause of rural development, the proponents of this school of thought usually tend to either disregard or underplay the linkages between the rural and the urban subsectors of the economy. What is needed is a new approach to development, which explicitly recognises the interlinkages and complementarity between the rural and the urban subsectors, and provides for integrating them completely.

Agricultural versus Industrial Development

Closely analogous to the rural versus urban development dilemma, is the dogma that industrialisation alone can modernise agriculture and thereby raise agricultural productivity, wage rates and provide employment to labour displaced by mechanisation of agriculture. This has led many development economists to associate development with industrialisation. Following this dogma, many developing countries have established highly capital-intensive and sophisticated industrial enterprises, similar to those in developed countries. Such efforts, however, have often led to bitter disappointment when the desired results failed to materialise. Such projects are mere showcases, whose contribution to development is negligible, and sometimes even negative, because they are built at the expense of enterprises that meet the basic needs of people. Nations with high agricultural potential spend enormous resources on agricultural imports and depend heavily on imported technology, capital and management. At the same time, local agriculture stagnates and nutritional standards remain far lower than in the advanced countries. Distribution of income is tilted in favour of industrialists against farmers, workers and consumers.

At the other extreme is agricultural fundamentalism, which holds that in the initial stages of development when per capita incomes are low, agriculture alone can serve as an instrument of development, and that increased agricultural productivity is a prerequisite to increased income and industrialisation. The proponents of this dogma argue for allocation of more resources and attention to agriculture, rather than to industry. They do not, however, realise that agriculture cannot develop alone, and that concomitant development of industry and supporting infrastructure is essential not only for the growth of the national economy, but for the advancement of agriculture itself. The non-agricultural sector must be developed to the extent that it is able to provide the agricultural sector with new farm inputs and services vital to its development, as also to absorb the manpower rendered surplus as a result of increased labour productivity in agriculture.

Agricultural fundamentalism has generally resulted in growth without development, mainly because of lack of linkages between the agricultural and non-agricultural sectors, and partly because of distribution of income being skewed in favour of big landlords.

The establishment of small and less capital-intensive industrial enterprises in rural areas, along with introduction of new technology in agriculture, is likely to establish linkages between agriculture and industry. The Israeli strategy of integrating agricultural and industrial sectors is worth emulating. In Israel, industrial enterprises were set up in rural areas, along with the introduction of more efficient methods of agricultural production. Initially, the industrial enterprises included mostly services and industries connected with agriculture, such as feed mix plants, factories for processing agricultural produce and for production of tools and various accessories. Most of these enterprises are owned, either fully or in part, by the farmers themselves. In course of time, the scope of industrial enterprises was widened to include activities completely unconnected with agriculture, such as jewellery manufacture and ceramics (Weitz 1971: Ch. 9).

Capital versus Labour Dogma

This is a legacy inherited by today's development economists from their predecessors in the developed countries, who considered capital to be the key instrument of development. The Harrod–Domar model represents a typical example of this dogma. In this model, the rate of growth is expressed as the product of the savings rate and the output-capital ratio. Under the assumptions that capital and labour cannot be substituted for each other, and that labour is in surplus supply, capital becomes the overriding constraint on economic growth. This dogma received a further fillip from those techno-economists who held that all new technology is embodied in capital.

Capital fundamentalism has been blindly accepted by development economists and planners in the developing countries. This has led to the promulgation of a number of policies in these countries, all aimed at increasing savings, redistributing income from the workers to the capitalists, granting monopoly rights to national and multinational corporations, transferring resources from the private to the public sector, increasing dependence on foreign aid and loans, and underpricing capital, particularly foreign exchange, for capital goods. This has resulted in a number of adverse effects on the economies of these nations. For example, underpricing foreign exchange for capital goods has killed the incentive to develop labour-intensive technologies adapted to domestic needs and circumstances, and has led to premature and excessive mechanisation in a number of sectors, resulting in unemployment of labour and underutilisation of other domestic resources.

Capital fundamentalism has extended to cover human capital formation as well. Higher education is highly subsidised in most developing countries, with the result that millions of college and university graduates are added annually to the pool of the unemployed white-collar proletariat. In India, enormous investment has been made in the institutes of higher learning, particularly in the fields of engineering, technology, agriculture, medicine and management. Many of the graduates of these institutes usually do not like the work environment and compensation rates prevailing in the country, and seek jobs abroad. Thus, the scarce resources invested in their education and training are lost to the country. It seems that at this stage of India's economic and technological development, we need more institutes to train barefoot agricultural and other technicians, engineers, doctors and rural managers, rather than institutes for highly advanced training. Similarly, one wonders why we should produce more college and university graduates in disciplines like arts, science, commerce, agriculture and veterinary science than we need. The demand for higher education could be brought down to match the availability of jobs, by pricing it at its real resources cost, which is markedly higher than the present cost. In the USA and other Western countries, most students terminate their studies at the high school level and become self-employed. But their training is broad-based and highly practical and relevant to their context, with the result that high school graduates are able and confident to set up and manage their own small business or take up wage-paid jobs. We should learn from this experience, and make our education less capital-intensive and more relevant to our requirements. We need to thoroughly overhaul our present education policy, which has become outdated and irrelevant in the context of our changed environment. More emphasis needs to be placed on vocationalisation of education.

Autonomous versus Induced Development

In every country, some development takes place naturally or autonomously over time, but its level and pace may not be adequate to maintain a reasonably satisfactory standard of living. In such situations, some sort of intervention is needed to speed up the pace of natural development. Development planning is one of the forms of intervention that has become a fad in many developing countries of the world, and is considered a magic door to development. In fact, even the advanced countries have come to realise the need for some sort of planning or government intervention in the economic processes. It seems that there is a growing consensus around the statement that any planning is better than no planning at all, and decentralised planning is better than centralised planning.

However, we need to realise that planning can make a positive contribution only if it facilitates the achievement of development objectives more rapidly and more efficiently than if development followed natural forces. It is now becoming increasingly apparent that the development effort cannot be left to the government alone; it must be shared by private, cooperative, corporate and other non-governmental organisations and agencies, and above all by the people themselves. Planning by the government should complement and supplement the efforts of individuals and non-governmental organisations.

So what *is* development?

- Is everything *new* development?
- Is *modernisation* development? Modernisation will usually mean such changes as seem more efficient, more productive.
- Is *economic growth* development?
- Is *social change* development?

2

Rural Economy of India

Introduction

India is one of the oldest surviving civilisations, and the biggest democracy in the world. It has a rich and diverse cultural heritage, and it has two of the world's 18 hot spots of biodiversity. It ranks second after China in the world in terms of population, first in terms of cattle and buffalo population, and sixth in terms of geographical area. It has the world's third-largest reservoir of technically-trained manpower, and is now one of the seven nuclear weapons states. Its mainland covers an area of 3.29 million sq. km or 329 million hectares (ha), measures about 3,214 km from north to south between the extreme latitudes, and about 2,933 km from east to west between the extreme longitudes. Over the last 50 years since Independence, India has achieved impressive progress in the fields of science and technology, and it is now self-sufficient in foodgrains and milk production. On the negative side, India has not yet been able to fully develop and harness its human and natural resources for the benefit of its people, and it has yet to solve its pernicious problems of illiteracy, poverty, unemployment and vulnerability to natural calamities.

India's economy is predominantly rural in character. This is evident from the fact that, in 1991, nearly 74 per cent of its population lived in some 5,80,000 villages, and about two-thirds of its workforce was engaged in agriculture and allied activities in rural areas. Agriculture and allied activities contributed about 29 per cent of India's gross domestic product (GDP) at factor cost at the current prices in 1994–95.

In a predominantly agrarian country like India, rural development is a sine qua non of national development, and agricultural development a prerequisite for rural development. Therefore, in such a country, agricultural development should form the foundation for national development.

The role of agriculture in economic development has been recognised and discussed since the time of the Physiocrats. According to the Physiocrats, it was only the agricultural sector which produced an economic surplus over costs of production, and therefore it played the most strategic role in economic development. They considered commerce and manufacturing as non-productive, in the sense that the value of the raw materials handled by these sectors was enhanced only enough to pay for the labour and capital used in the process of production.

The Classical writers also recognised the importance of agriculture in economic development. It is now believed that the agricultural sector formed the core element of Adam Smith's basic growth model. He thought that the production of an agricultural surplus to support non-farm production was essential for economic development.

In this chapter, we present an overview of the rural economy of India, with special emphasis on the role of agriculture in India's national development. We begin with a description of the size and structure of India's rural economy, and its salient characteristics.

Size and Structure of the Rural Economy

India's economy can be thought of as comprising two main sectors, namely, the rural sector and the non-rural sector. The rural sector is, in turn, composed of two main subsectors, i.e., the agricultural subsector and the non-agricultural subsector. The agricultural subsector comprises agriculture and allied economic activities such as crop husbandry, animal husbandry and dairying, fisheries, poultry and forestry. The non-agricultural subsector consists of economic activities relating to industry, business and services. Industry here refers to cottage and village industries, *khadi*, handloom, handicrafts, etc.; business refers to microenterprises, trading of general goods, small shops, petty traders, etc., whereas services refer to transport, communications, banking, input supply, marketing of farm and non-farm produce, etc. The main stakeholders of the rural sector include farmers, agricultural and non-agricultural labourers, artisans, traders, moneylenders, and those engaged in providing such services as transport, communications, processing, banking and education and extension.

The size of the rural sector could be measured in terms of the rural population, the population of livestock, the extent of land, forest and other natural resources, production inputs used and output produced. According to the 1991 Population Census, India's rural population was

62.87 crore[1] which accounted for 74.3 per cent of the country's total population. Of the total population of the country, 11.76 crore were cultivators and 7.03 crore agricultural labourers. India is endowed with livestock resources of high genetic diversity, and ranks first in the world in terms of the population of cattle and buffaloes. According to the 1992 Livestock Census, the country had 20.45 crore cattle, 8.35 crore buffaloes, 5.08 crore sheep, 11.53 crore goats, 1.28 crore pigs, 0.3 crore pack animals and 30.7 crore poultry birds (GOI 1998a: 318). As far as land is concerned, land utilisation statistics are available for about 305 million ha, which is 92.7 per cent of the total geographical area of about 329 million ha. In 1993–94, the net area sown in the country was 142.10 million ha, gross cropped area 186.42 million ha, net irrigated area 51.45 million ha, and cropping intensity 131.19 per cent. About 22 million ha of land was under non-agricultural use.

Forests are a very valuable renewable resource, providing a vital life support system. With the fast growing population, the demand on forests has progressively increased. Interpretation of Landsat imagery indicates that out of 75 million ha of area recorded as forest, only 64 million ha sustains the actual forest cover, and out of this only 35 million ha has adequate cover, which accounts for only about 11 per cent of the total geographical area of the country at present. The National Forest Policy (1988) stipulates that the country as a whole should aim at keeping about one-third of the geographical area under forest cover. With all its biological and genetic diversity, forests are nature's gift to humanity. The forests being degraded by the ever increasing biotic pressure need to be rehabilitated by afforestation, not only for environmental considerations, but also for meeting the local demand for firewood, small timber, fodder and for defence and industry.

Water is vital for realising the full potential of agriculture. India is very well-endowed with water resources. With an average annual rainfall of about 120 cm in the country, and surface flow of about 188 million ha metres, India has vast water resources. However, the total utilisable water is 114 million ha metres, comprising 69 million ha metres as surface water and 45 million ha metres as ground water. Further, the Central Ground Water Board provisionally puts the revised estimate of ground water at 80 million ha, as against the previous estimate of 45 million. Pending firming up of these estimates, the ultimate irrigation potential is taken as 114 million ha. With sustained and systematic development

---

[1] 1 crore = 10 million = 100 lakh.

of water resources, irrigation potential in the country has increased from 22.6 million ha in 1951 to 89.3 million ha at the end of 1996–97.

Fisheries play an important role in the rural economy of India, by way of augmenting food supply, generating employment and earning foreign exchange. India has a marine coastline of 12,700 km, maritime area of 4.52 lakh sq. km and an Exclusive Economic Zone of 200 lakh sq. km (Singh 1994: 10).

The level of use of energy is an important determinant of rural development. The rural sector is starved of energy. It will be a challenging task to meet the growing demand for energy from households, industry, transport, agriculture and business. The pattern of demand for energy is also changing over time. Analysis of total commercial energy consumption shows that there is an increasing trend in the consumption of petroleum products, natural gas and electricity. Measures will have to be initiated for reducing the energy intensity in different sectors through changes in technology and processes. Interfuel and intrafuel substitution will have to be optimised. The main emphasis will have to be on maximising the use of renewable sources of energy, with affordable cost to low income groups in rural and urban areas. Major stress should be laid on efficiency, conservation and demand management to bring down the energy elasticity of output.

Table 2.1 presents data on the use of major inputs in India's agriculture, and Table 2.2 on the production of foodgrains, milk and fish. As shown in Table 2.1, in 1995–96, the total quantity of certified quality seeds distributed was about 6.9 lakh tonnes, total fertiliser consumption in terms of NPK nutrients 139 lakh tonnes, the average per ha consumption of NPK nutrients 75 kg in the country, and the area under high-yielding varieties of paddy, wheat, *jowar*, *bajra*, maize and *ragi* 72.11 million ha. In 1997–98, the flow of institutional credit to agriculture in the country was 34,274 crores, total production of foodgrains 19.4 crore tonnes, milk 7.1 crore tonnes, and fish 53.46 lakh tonnes (GOI 1998a: 114–23).

The Characteristics of the Rural Sector

Some of the salient characteristics of the rural sector are presented in Tables 2.1–2.8, and briefly described in the following sections.

Excessive Dependence on Nature

Agricultural production, being biological in nature, depends more on weather and other climatic factors than non-agricultural production. For

Table 2.1
Use of Selected Agricultural Inputs in Agriculture in India

Input	Unit	1950–51	1960–61	1970–71	1980–81	1990–91	1995–96
1. Distribution of certified quality seeds	Lakh qt	—	—	—	25.01	57.10	68.80
2. Consumption of (N + P + K) nutrients	Lakh tonnes	0.69	2.92	21.77	55.16	125.46	138.76
3. Consumption of NPK nutrients	kg/ha	NEG	1.90	13.13	31.83	67.49	74.81 (E)
4. Consumption of pesticides	'000 tonnes	2.35	8.62	24.32	45.00	75.00	61.26
5. Total area under HYVs	Million ha	—	1.89 +	15.38	43.08	64.98	72.11

Source: GOI. 1997. *Agricultural Statistics at a Glance.* New Delhi: Directorate of Economics and Statistics. Department of Agriculture and Cooperation, Ministry of Agriculture, Government of India, pp. 97–98.

(E)   = Estimated.

HYV = High Yielding Varieties of crops.

qt   = quintal = 100 kg.

NEG = Negligible.

+   = Relates to 1966–67.

Table 2.2
Production of Foodgrains, Milk and Fish in India

Year	Foodgrains (million tonnes)	Milk (million tonnes)	Fish (lakh tonnes)
1950–51	50.82	17.0	7.52
1955–56	66.85	19.0	NA
1960–61	82.02	20.0	11.60
1965–66	72.35	20.47 (1966–67)	NA
1970–71	108.42	20.79	17.56
1975–76	121.03	NA	NA
1980–81	129.59	31.6	24.42
1985–86	150.44	45.0	28.67
1990–91	176.39	53.9	38.56
1995–96	185.05	66.0	49.49
1996–97	199.30	68.5	51.40
1997–98	194.00	71.0	53.6

Sources:

1. GOI. 1997. *Agricultural Statistics at a Glance.* New Delhi: Directorate of Economics and Statistics, Department of Agriculture and Cooperation, Ministry of Agriculture, Government of India, pp. 9, 122.

2. GOI. 1998. *Economic Survey 1997–98.* New Delhi: Ministry of Finance, Government of India, pp. 114, 122–23.

example, in India about 64 per cent of the net area sown in 1993–94 was rainfed, where crop production wholly depends on the quantum and distribution of rainfall over the growing season. Given the wide fluctuations in rainfall in India from year to year and area to area, crop production and hence farm incomes vary widely. In a nutshell, Indian agriculture is vulnerable to natural calamities, such as droughts, floods, hailstorms, and cyclones. This means that the degree of nature-induced risk and uncertainty in agriculture is higher than in the non-agricultural sector, and so also the need for insurance against such risks. But sadly, the coverage of crop insurance is very limited, and therefore most farmers have to bear the burden of risk and uncertainty themselves, and become broke in the process.

Preponderance of Small Uneconomic Land and Livestock Holdings

In 1990–91, there were over 10.6 crore operational landholdings in India, of which 8.35 crore (78 per cent) were marginal and small farmers operating two ha or less of land (Table 2.3). Similarly, it is estimated that most of some 7 crore households in India owning milch animals are small holders having one or two animals. The average size of operational landholdings in India was 1.55 ha in 1990–91, and it has been declining over time. It declined from 2.69 ha in 1960–61 to 1.82 ha in 1980–81, and to 1.55 ha in 1990–91. The land and livestock holdings are not only small in size, but also widely scattered all over the countryside. Landholdings are also fragmented particularly in those states where consolidation of landholdings has not yet been done. The process of subdivision and fragmentation of landholdings continues unabated generation after generation under the existing land inheritance laws. The small and fragmented landholdings are a great obstacle to economical use of farm labour and machinery. The subdivision and fragmentation of landholdings needs to be stopped through appropriate legislative measures.

Almost all the marginal and small farmers are poor, producing very little marketable surplus. It is estimated that the farmers having less than four ha of land are not financially viable, if they depend wholly on the income from the land. Thus, over 90 per cent of farmers in India are not financially viable. Development of this huge number of farmers is quite a big challenge for policy makers and planners.

Low Capital-Labour Ratio

India's rural sector is starved of capital and overcrowded with human labour. Consequently, the amount of capital available per worker, i.e., the

Table 2.3
Distribution of Operational Land Holdings in India

Category of holding (ha)	No. of holdings ('000) (%)		Area operated ('000 ha) (%)		Average size of holdings (ha)	
	1985–86	1990–91*	1985–86	1990–91*	1985–86	1990–91*
Marginal	56,147	63,389	22,042	24,894	0.39	0.39
(less than 1)	(57.8)	(59.4)	(13.4)	(15.1)		
Small	17,922	20,092	25,708	28,827	1.43	1.43
(1–2)	(18.4)	(18.8)	(15.6)	(17.4)		
Semi-Medium	13,252	13,923	36,666	38,375	2.77	2.76
(2–4)	(13.6)	(13.1)	(22.3)	(23.2)		
Medium	7,916	7,580	47,144	44,752	5.96	5.90
(4–10)	(8.2)	(7.1)	(28.6)	(27.0)		
Large	1,918	1,654	33,002	28,659	17.21	17.33
(10 and above)	(2.0)	(1.6)	(20.1)	(17.3)		
All	97,155	1,06,637	1,64,562	1,65,507	1.69	1.55
holdings	(100.0)	(100.0)	(100.0)	(100.0)		

Source: GOI. 1997. *Agricultural Statistics at a Glance*, p. 115. March. New Delhi: Directorate of Economics and Statistics, Department of Agriculture and Cooperation, Ministry of Agriculture, Government of India.
Notes: Figures in brackets indicate the percentage of respective columns to totals. Percentages are on the basis of absolute values.
*Provisional.

capital-labour ratio, is low, and this is one of the main reasons of low productivity in the sector. To improve this ratio, it is necessary to step up both public and private investment in the sector, and to facilitate through appropriate policies the absorption of surplus workers in the non-agricultural sector. Sadly, both public and private investment in agriculture have been declining in real terms, but in recent years some buoyancy has been observed in private investment. The decline in public investment is attributed to diversion of resources from investment to current expenditure on output price and input subsidies.

Low Factor Productivity

Low crop yields have been the bane of India's rural sector since long (Table 2.4). As mentioned in the preceding section, the low factor productivity is mainly due to inadequate capital in the form of production

Table 2.4

Average Yield Rates of Principal Crops in Selected Countries, 1995

Country	Yield (kg/ha)			
	Cereals	Wheat	Paddy	Maize
India	2,134	2,482	2,879	1,633
China	4,494	3,541	6,017	4,913
Japan	6,449	3,625	6,012	10,500
S. Korea	5,864	2,857	6,179	3,913
Chile	4,533	3,550	NA	9,500
USA	4,647	2,410	6,274	7,121
World	2,729	2,453	3,689	3,776

Source: FAO. 1996. *Production Year Book 1995. Vol. 49.* Rome: Food and Agriculture Organisation, United Nations Organisation, pp. 15–20.

inputs, raw materials, and improved machinery and equipment available per worker/unit of enterprise. For example, the low average crop yields in India as compared to those in developed countries like Japan, Israel and China are due to low inputs of fertilisers and plant protection chemicals. Similarly, the low average milk yield per milch animal in India is due mainly to the low quantity of concentrated feed and the poor quality of fodder fed to the animals. What is required to improve the resource productivity in India's rural sector is to close the technology gap and reduce the redundant labour force.

Long Gestation and Low Rate of Turnover

It takes a relatively longer period of time for investment in agricultural enterprises to yield benefits than in many non-agricultural enterprises. For example, it takes three to four months for most crops to mature, four to six years to raise a young buffalo calf to a stage when she starts yielding milk, and 5–10 years before fruit saplings start bearing fruit. Besides, the annual flow of net returns from investment in most agricultural enterprises is also low. This results in a low rate of turnover, or alternatively, it takes longer to recover the investment made.

High Incidence of Poverty and Unemployment

The incidence of both poverty and unemployment is higher in the rural sector than in the urban sector. For example, in 1993–94, about 37 per cent of the rural population was below the poverty line, as compared to about 32 per cent in urban areas. In absolute terms, of the total population of 32 crore living below the poverty line in 1993–94 in the country, 24.4 crore (76 per cent) were in the rural areas. Similarly, the number of unemployed persons per 1,000 population (on the basis of both 'usual status' and 'current weekly status') is higher in rural areas than in urban areas. It is then no surprise that the average per capita income in rural areas is also markedly lower than in the urban areas. For example, over the period July–December 1991, the average consumer expenditure per person per month (a proxy for per capita income) in rural areas was about Rs 244 as compared to Rs 370 in urban areas (Table 2.5).

Preponderance of Illiterate and Unskilled Workforce

Although the average literacy rate in the country as a whole is miserably low, in rural areas it is pathetic: in 1991 it was about 45 per cent, as compared to 73 per cent for the urban population (Table 2.5). With 55 per cent of rural people being illiterate, it is very difficult to find income generating activities for their level. Besides, most of the rural people do not have the skills required for doing wage-paid employment in the non-agricultural sector. So the illiteracy and the lack of skills among the majority of rural people are serious constraints on their socio-economic development. It is a pity that while, at one extreme, in India we have world-class scientists, engineers, managers and academicians, we have, on the other extreme, dozens of crores of illiterates amongst us. This is a glaring example of the socio-economic and technological dualism that we have in India. India can make nuclear bombs, but cannot make and run the required number of schools for everyone.

Lack of Basic Infrastructure

Indian villages miserably lack such basic infrastructure as schools, health care centres (leave aside hospitals), all-weather roads, means of transport and communication, drinking water facilities, and electricity for domestic and agricultural purposes. It has been established through empirical studies that basic infrastructure is an important determinant of development. As a matter of fact, the 'Growth Centre' theory of development is based on this premise. Although in many states good progress has been made recently under the Minimum Needs Programme and other programmes to provide the bare minimum infrastructure, there are crores of people living in remote tribal and hilly areas where not much has been done.

Table 2.5
Selected Demographic and Socio-economic Indicators in India

Item	Year	Unit	Rural	Urban	All India
Demographic indicators					
Total population[1]	1991	Million	629 (74.3%)	217 (25.7%)	846 (100%)
Decennial growth rate	1981–91	%	19.6	35.6	23.4
Sex ratio	1991	Females/1,000 Males	939	894	927
Crude birth rate	1994	Per 1,000 population	30.5	23.1	28.6
Crude death rate	1994	Per 1,000 population	10.1	6.5	9.2
Infant mortality rate	1994	Per 1,000 live births	79	51	73
Socio-economic indicators					
Literacy rate	1991	%	44.69	73.08	52.21
Scheduled Caste population	1991	million	112 (18%)	26 (12%)	138 (16.3%)
Scheduled Tribe population	1991	million	63 (10%)	5 (2.3%)	68 (8.1%)
Average household size	1991	no.	5.0	4.7	—
Housing status	1991				
Kachcha		%	33.8	9.6	27.4
Semi-*pucca*		%	35.7	17.7	31.0
Pucca		%	30.6	72.8	41.6
Total workers	1991	million	249	65	314
Percentage of people below poverty line	1993–94	%	37.3	32.4	36.0
Consumer expenditure per person per month	July–Dec. 1991	Rs			
Food			153.59	207.77	—
Non-food			89.91	162.57	—
Total			243.50	370.34	—

Source: National Institute of Rural Development (NIRD). 1996. *Rural Development Statistics 1994–95.* Hyderabad, pp. i–iv.
Note:
1. Including estimates for Jammu and Kashmir.

The Role of the Agricultural Subsector

The rural sector constitutes the basic foundation of India's economy. No programme of national development can ever succeed unless it is built upon this foundation. More specifically, the rural sector in general, and its agricultural subsector in particular, contributes to the growth and development of India's economy in the following ways.

Contribution to GDP

The agricultural subsector occupies a place of pride in India's economy, and will continue to do so in the foreseeable future. Table 2.6 presents data on the share of agriculture in India's Gross Domestic Product (GDP) at factor cost, at the current and the 1980–81 prices. Agriculture contributed 34.7 per cent of the GDP at current prices in 1980–81, but its share declined to 28.7 per cent in 1994–95. As a matter of fact, the share of agriculture has been gradually declining ever since 1950–51, when it was 56.46 per cent. The declining share of agriculture in GDP does not, however, mean a retrogression of agriculture, it only means that the secondary and tertiary sectors of the economy are expanding at a higher rate. And this is what one would anticipate as the process of economic development moves forward. This has happened in developed countries all over the world. In general, the more developed a country, the smaller is the share of agriculture in its national income. For example, in 1995, the share of agriculture in GDP was only 2 per cent in the UK, 3 per cent in USA, and 4 per cent in Japan (World Bank 1997: 236–37). We could conclude by emphasising that as agriculture is the most important sector of India's economy, development must act directly on agriculture, if the majority of the country's people are to be affected by development.

Mainstay of Livelihood and Employment

A peculiar feature of India's economy is a very high proportion of the country's population living in rural areas: in 1951, it was about 83 per cent and in 1991 about 74 per cent (Table 2.7). Similarly, though the share of the agricultural sector in GDP has been declining over time, the proportion of the population dependent upon agriculture has been more or less stagnant around 60 per cent since 1961. According to the 1991 Population Census, 59 per cent of the total workers in the country were engaged in agriculture, of whom 35.2 per cent were cultivators and 23.8 per cent agricultural labourers. This means that agriculture is the main source of livelihood and employment for

Table 2.6
Share of Agriculture and Allied Activities in India's
Gross Domestic Product (GDP) at Factor Cost
(Rs crores)

Year	Total GDP		Agricultural GDP		Percentage share of agriculture	
	At current prices	At 1980–81 prices	At current prices	At 1980–81 prices	At current prices	At 1980–81 prices
1980–81	1,22,427	1,22,427	42,466	42,466	34.7	34.7
1985–86	2,33,799	1,56,566	69,964	49,855	29.9	31.8
1990–91	4,77,814	2,12,253	1,35,162	60,991	28.3	28.7
1991–92	5,52,768	2,13,983	1,59,299	59,398	28.8	27.8
1992–93	6,30,182	2,24,887	1,77,910	63,335	28.2	28.2
1993–94[1]	7,23,103	2,36,064	2,04,962	65,493	28.3	27.7
1994–95[2]	8,54,103	2,51,010	2,45,139	68,851	28.7	27.4

Source: GOI. 1997. *Agricultural Statistics at a Glance.* New Delhi: Directorate of Economics and Statistics, Department of Agriculture and Cooperation, Ministry of Agriculture, Government of India, p. 6.

Notes:

1. Provisional.
2. Quick estimates.

about two-thirds of India's population. In developed countries like the UK, USA, Germany and Japan, the proportion of the population dependent upon agriculture has been declining continuously; in 1995, it was 2.1 per cent in the UK, 2.6 per cent in USA, 3.0 per cent in Germany, and 5.5 per cent in Japan, as compared to 61.6 per cent in India (FAO 1996: 26–35). The higher percentage of the population dependent upon agriculture indicates the inability of the industrial and services sectors to absorb the incremental rural population. The obvious remedy in such cases is to expand the industrial and services sectors at a faster rate.

Source of Raw Materials

Agriculture is the principal source of raw materials for India's leading industries, such as sugar, cotton, jute, textiles, leather, tobacco and edible oils. Many other industries like fruit preservation and processing, *dal* mills, handloom weaving, *gur* making and oil crushing, also depend upon agriculture as a source of raw materials. The rate of growth in all these industries is thus dependent on the rate of growth in the agricultural sector, and agricultural development is a prerequisite for their development.

Table 2.7
Distribution of India's Population by Category of Workers, 1991
(In crores)

Particular	Rural	Urban	Total
1. Total Population	62.28	21.58	83.86
2. Total Workers	24.90	6.51	31.41
3. Marginal Workers	2.67	0.15	2.82
4. Main Workers	22.23	6.36	28.59
(i) Cultivators	10.76	0.31	11.07
(ii) Agricultural labourers	7.03	0.43	7.46
(iii) Livestock, forestry, etc.	0.49	0.11	0.60
(iv) Mining and quarrying	0.10	0.07	0.18
(v) Manufacturing, processing, servicing and repairs in:			
(a) household industry	0.48	0.20	0.68
(b) other than household industry	0.79	1.40	2.19
(vi) Construction	0.23	0.32	0.55
(vii) Trade and commerce	0.73	1.40	2.13
(viii) Transport, storage and communications	0.27	0.53	0.80
(ix) Other services	1.33	1.60	2.93

Source: GOI. 1998. *India 1998.* New Delhi: Publications Division, Ministry of Information and Broadcasting, Government of India, p. 249.

Table 2.8
Value of India's Export of Agricultural Commodities
(Rs crores)

Year	Country's total exports	Agricultural exports	Percentage share of agriculture
1992–93	53,688	7,884	14.7
1993–94	69,751	10,811	15.5
1994–95	82,674	11,051	13.4
1995–96	106,353	17,496	16.5
1996–97	118,817	21,021	17.7

Source: GOI. 1998. *Economic Survey 1997–98.* New Delhi: Ministry of Finance, Government of India, p. 123.

Source of Foreign Exchange

Agriculture is an important source of earning foreign exchange, which is needed for importing capital goods for the rapidly expanding industrial sector. In the year 1996–97, the value of agricultural exports was Rs 21,021 crore, which accounted for about 18 per cent of the total value of exports from India (Table 2.8). Agriculture makes its contribution to the net foreign exchange earning through the displacement of current and potential imports, and through expanded exports.

Market for Industrial Goods and Services

The agricultural sector provides a ready and big market for many goods manufactured and services provided by the secondary and tertiary sectors. Such goods include pesticides, insecticides, farm machinery, pumping sets, cattle and poultry feed, fish feed, pipelines, fencing material, veterinary medicines and vehicles. Rural people also buy consumer goods manufactured by the industrial sector. In fact, now many big companies have their eyes on rural markets for their products and services. Thus, increased farm income and purchasing power is a valuable stimulus to industrial development. It has been argued by a number of economists that insufficient purchasing power in rural areas is the basic problem in industrial development in low-income countries. If industrial development is in fact throttled by the lack of a mass market, the solution is to increase rural purchasing power. But there is clearly a conflict between the need for enhancing agriculture's contribution to the capital requirements for overall development, and the emphasis on increased farm purchasing power as a stimulus to industrialisation, and there is no easy reconciliation of this conflict.

Source of Cheap Food

Economic development is characterised by a substantial increase in the demand for food. Apart from autonomous changes in demand, the annual rate of increase in the demand for food is given by $D = p + \eta g$, where p and g are the rates of growth of population and per capita income respectively, and η is the income elasticity of demand for food. With the annual compound population growth rate of 2.14 per cent per annum registered in India during the decade 1981–91, and with a modest rise of 3 per cent in real per capita income per annum, the annual rate of increase in demand for food in India is around 4 per cent (assuming the income elasticity of demand for food to be 0.6). If food supplies fail to expand in pace with the growth of demand, the result is likely to be a substantial rise in food prices, leading to political discontent and pressure on wage rates, with consequent adverse effects on industrial profits, investment and economic growth. The inflationary impact of a given percentage increase in food prices is much more severe in a developing country like India, than in a high-income economy. This is a simple consequence of the dominant position of food as a wage good in low-income countries, where 60 to 80 per cent of the total consumption expenditure is devoted to food, compared with 20 to 25 per cent in developed economies. There are thus severe penalties attached to the failure of adequate food production in developing countries.

The Role of the Non-agricultural Subsector

In most developing countries (including India), the rural labour force has been growing rapidly, but employment opportunities dwindling. As the land available for expansion of agriculture becomes increasingly scarce, opportunities for non-farm employment must expand, if deepening rural poverty is to be avoided. Given the expected growth and composition of large-scale urban industries, they are unlikely to be able to absorb the rising tide of workers migrating from the countryside to the cities. Looking toward the twenty-first century, we must slow the process of the urban spread, with its high social and environmental costs, such as congestion, pollution and skyrocketing land costs. Expansion of the rural non-agricultural sector, with its emphasis on labour-intensive and small-scale enterprises, widens income opportunities for the poor, including small farmers, the landless and women, enabling them to even out extreme fluctuations in their incomes.

The relative importance of the rural non-agricultural subsector, and the composition of the various economic activities included in the sector, differ widely from region to region in India. Broadly defined, this subsector includes economic activities outside agriculture, carried out in villages and varying in size from households to small factories. Some examples of these activities are cottage, tiny, village and small-scale manufacturing and processing industries, trade, transportation, construction and services of various kinds. Household industries have declined over time, whereas small-scale, non-household industries have expanded. Cottage enterprises based on part-time family labour are relatively less efficient than small-scale, full-time, specialised rural industries; as the cost of labour rises, enterprises with no scope for division of labour continue to lose their cost advantage. The rural towns that serve as trading and distribution centres for both urban and agricultural goods subsequently attract manufacturing activities.

The linkages between the rural non-agricultural and agricultural sub-sectors are critical for rural development. The growth in farm income provides an expanding market for consumption goods and agricultural inputs produced by the non-agricultural subsector, while agricultural raw materials are processed in the rural non-agricultural subsector. The relative strengths of the consumption and production linkages depend on the pace and pattern of growth in agricultural income, and the production technology used in agriculture. The higher the per capita income growth, the higher the share of non-food consumption in rural expenditure, and hence the greater the stimulus to the growth of the rural non-agricultural subsector. The share of locally produced consumption goods (as against imports from urban areas or abroad) in consumption expenditure depends on the distribution of income in agriculture. It is higher among the medium or small farmers, than among the rich.

In India, cottage and village industries have been an important occupation of landless and other poor people in villages for ages. As a matter of fact, agriculture and rural industries are complementary to each other. The Khadi and Village Industries Commission (KVIC) has identified 95 village industries for government support. These industries are divided into the following seven categories:

1. Mineral-based industries.
2. Forest-based industries.
3. Agro-based industries.
4. Polymer- and chemicals-based industries.
5. Engineering- and non-conventional energy-based industries.
6. Textile industry other than *khadi*.
7. Service industry.

The non-agricultural subsector of India's rural sector also occupies an important place in India's economy, as a source of income and employment opportunities for the landless. In 1991, out of 24.9 crore rural workers, about 3.9 crore (16 per cent) were engaged in the non-agricultural subsector. According to the Report of the Study Group on the Non-Farm Sector in India (1994), the non-agricultural subsector could generate an additional 2.65 crore jobs by the year 2001, if the employment in this subsector continues to grow at the rate of 5.4 per cent per annum—the rate at which it grew over the period 1977–78 to 1987–88.

The total number of small-scale industries increased from 4.2 lakh in 1973–74 to 28.6 lakh as on 31 December 1996; the value of production increased from Rs 7,200 crore in 1973–74 to Rs 4,12,636 crore in 1996–97, and the total amount of employment generated in 1996–97 stood at 160 lakh persons. The value of exports from the SSI sector stood at Rs 39,249 crore in 1996–97 (GOI 1998a: 109–10). The sector recorded a growth rate of 15.8 per cent in 1996–97 over the previous year. The sector contributes over 40 per cent to the gross turnover in the manufacturing sector, about 45 per cent of manufacturing exports and about 35 per cent of the total exports. In order to give a further boost to this sector, several policy initiatives have been taken by the Government of India, including a scheme of integrated infrastructural development, concessional rate of excise duty to non-registered units, quality certification scheme to acquire ISO 9000, raising project outlay from Rs 30 lakhs to Rs 50 lakh in the single window scheme, and adequate and timely supply of credit as per the Nayak Committee recommendations. Besides, the investment limit for SSI units has been increased from Rs 60 lakh to Rs 3 crore, for the tiny sector from Rs 5 lakh to Rs 25 lakh, and the composite loan limit for SSI units from Rs 50,000 to Rs 2 lakh.

The Nayak Committee (1992), set up to examine the adequacy of institutional credit to the SSI sector and related aspects, observed that it would be safe to presume that the bulk of the financial needs of the rural segment of the SSI sector was met from private sources, including moneylenders. In regard to the overall SSI sector, it observed that: (a) there has been a dispersal of SSI units away from the metropolitan areas and large cities; (b) in spite of the increased flow of credit, the share of the tiny sector and village industries has been dismally low; and (c) establishment of forward and backward linkages to ensure the success of enterprises has not kept pace with the increase in the flow of credit. Credit is only one of the essential inputs for industrialisation, and only if other supporting facilities, including adequate and timely availability of raw materials, skilled labour and marketing support, are provided on an assured basis, will entrepreneurs be able to prepare viable proposals and obtain institutional finance. The Nayak Committee recommended, among other things, the creation of a separate fund for modernisation, research and marketing, venture capital assistance for promoting viable projects by technocrat entrepreneurs, and detailed data collection for village and tiny industries.

Lack of adequate infrastructure is a major impediment to the development of industries in the rural areas. Electricity, transport, communications and availability of ancillary and allied services, viz., suppliers of raw materials and other inputs, semi-skilled and skilled labourers to attend to the problems of machinery, marketing and credit support agencies, etc., are essential for the growth of industries. In their absence, production activities of tiny units tend to concentrate around the peripheries of urban centres. The Sivaraman Committee has suggested that the responsibility for providing infrastructural and extension support to the development of industries in rural areas (including providing raw material supply) be assigned to the state governments. In the absence of responsive and committed agencies for providing these essential services, banks find the task of supporting the development of rural industries frustrating.

The income generated from various activities in this subsector is more evenly distributed than that generated in the large-scale manufacturing subsector. Besides, due to the low capital requirement per worker, the subsector can generate more jobs with a given amount of capital than the corresponding large-scale factory industries.

Challenges and Opportunities

Achieving food security has so far been the overriding goal of agricultural policy in India. The introduction and rapid spread of high yielding varieties in the late sixties and early seventies resulted in a steady growth of output of foodgrains. Public investment in infrastructure, research and extension, along with crop production strategies, have significantly helped to expand foodgrain production and stocks. Foodgrain production, which was 8.2 crore tonnes in 1960–61, has increased to 19.4 crore tonnes in 1997–98. With proper management of various inputs (including water and fertilisers), India can produce enough food not only for its people, but also for export. It could be the potential granary of the world—the country which the world should look up to for feeding its rising population. The present crop yields in India are very low as compared to those in developed countries. For example, in 1995 the average cereal yield in India was only 2,134 kg per ha, as compared to 6,449 kg in Japan and 5,864 kg in South Korea. The yield gap could be bridged only through a comprehensive integrated National Agricultural Policy emphasising, *inter alia*, increased public and private investment in agriculture, widespread use of appropriate new technologies, and producer-oriented price policies and professionally-managed programmes. If the average cereal yield in India can be increased to the level of the world average, India can become the world's number one nation in terms of foodgrain production. Therefore, the biggest challenge before India is how to increase its crop yields to the world average level.

Landholdings in India are not only small in size, but also widely scattered all over the countryside. Landholdings are also fragmented in those states where consolidation of landholdings has not yet been done. The process of subdivision and fragmentation of landholdings continues unabated generation after generation, under the existing land inheritance laws. Small and fragmented landholdings are a great obstacle to economical use of farm labour and machinery. The subdivision and fragmentation of landholdings needs to be stopped through appropriate legislative measures, such that landholdings below an economically-viable level are not allowed to be subdivided further. Effecting such a reform in the structure of landholdings is a great challenge for policy makers.

Liberalisation has opened up new opportunities for Indian farmers to benefit from higher world prices for their produce, and lower prices for some of the inputs. Export orientation has brought in its wake the need for high-tech projects and for exploring international markets for exportable commodities. The assessment of credit demand, appraisal, and instruments of financing the high-tech projects are all difficult tasks. Meeting the credit needs of this emerging export-oriented high-tech sector requires concomitant institutional innovations, for which a beginning has been made with the establishment of agricultural development finance companies.

Of late, there has been a spectacular growth in public awareness about the adverse environmental impacts of economic growth and development. This has come from increasing air and water pollution, soil erosion, depletion of ground water aquifers, denudation and degradation of forests, and increasing waterlogging and soil salinity in canal command areas. In view of this, a new paradigm of sustainable development is emerging. This paradigm does not favour blind pursuit of economic growth at the cost of environmental degradation. A serious challenge before rural development planners today is how to achieve a faster rate of development, while keeping the natural resources and quality of the environment intact.

Similarly, the rural non-agricultural subsector will have to expand at a much faster rate, to provide income and employment opportunities to surplus rural people. This is also possible if a well-thought-out long-term national policy for the rural non-farm sector development is formulated and implemented effectively.

Concluding Remarks

The rural sector occupies an important place in India's economy. About 74 per cent of India's population lives in its 5,80,000 or so villages, and about two-thirds of the country's population is dependent on agriculture and allied activities for its livelihood. Agriculture and allied activities contributed about 29 per cent of India's gross domestic product at factor cost in 1994–95 at current prices. It is also an important source of foreign exchange and raw materials for India's major agro-industries, and a large market for industrial products. Thus, the rural sector forms the basic foundation of India's economy. No programme of national development can ever succeed if it is not built on this foundation.

Sadly, despite the impressive progress that India has made since Independence in the field of science and technology, the rural sector and people remain grossly underdeveloped, with about 55 per cent of the rural people being illiterate and 24.4 crore (37 per cent of India's population) living below the poverty line in 1993–94. The sector is characterised, *inter alia*, by the preponderance of small and scattered rural enterprises, lack of basic infrastructure, low productivity, excessive dependence on weather and climatic factors and a consequently high degree of risk and uncertainty. There is need to reduce the weather-induced risk in agriculture through appropriate crop insurance schemes. It is also necessary to consolidate scattered and fragmented landholdings and prevent their further subdivision and fragmentation through appropriate legislative measures, so that farm labour and machinery could be used more cost effectively.

There is need for the government to accord a very high priority, next only to defence, to rural development and to formulate a comprehensive national rural development policy, guaranteeing a reasonably satisfactory level of living to everyone in the sector, and liberating them from their servitude to ignorance, the rich, the elite and nature. Both public and private investment in the sector needs to be stepped up in order to increase the factor productivity in the sector, and improve the quality of life of rural people. Public investment is needed for creating and strengthening basic infrastructure, and private investment for expanding income and employment generating activities.

The non-agricultural subsector of the rural sector has been increasing at a faster rate than the agricultural subsector in the recent past, and has a vast potential to provide employment opportunities to rural people in the future. Looking towards the twenty-first century, we must slow the process of the urban spread, with its high social and environmental costs such as congestion, pollution and skyrocketing land costs. Expansion of the rural non-agricultural sector, with its emphasis on labour-intensive and small-scale enterprises, widens income opportunities for the poor, including small farmers, the landless and women, enabling them to even out extreme fluctuations in their incomes.

3

Measures of Development

Statistical measurement of the level and pace of rural development is important for a number of reasons. Quantitative measures of rural development are needed to indicate the extent of economic and social well-being of rural people, to serve as a benchmark for future planning, to serve as instruments of monitoring, evaluation and control of ongoing programmes, to facilitate spatial and temporal comparisons of development and to serve as criteria for advancing loans. Needless to emphasise, if the measures are to be meaningful, they must be consistent with the objectives of rural development.

The main objectives of rural development in all societies, irrespective of their economic, political and sociocultural systems are: (*a*) to increase the availability and improve the distribution of life-sustaining goods, such as food, clothes, shelter, health and security; (*b*) to raise per capita purchasing power and improve its distribution by providing better education, productive and remunerative jobs and cultural amenities; and (*c*) to expand the range of economic and social choices to individuals by freeing them from servitude and dependence. Therefore, a measure of rural development should provide, at the minimum, an indication of per capita availability of life-sustaining goods or per capita income in rural areas, as well as some idea of the distribution of income, assets and other means of socio-economic welfare. There is at present no single indicator of rural development which adequately captures its multifaceted nature. A variety of indicators have been used by economists to reflect the multiplicity of goals which characterise rural development. For the sake of orderly presentation, we categorise the indicators into two classes, namely, measures of the level of rural development, and measures of distribution of income. A critique of some of these indicators is presented in the following sections.

Measures of the Level of Rural Development

The following measures are commonly used (or can be used) to measure the level of rural development at a particular time in a particular place, as well as over time and across space.

Per Capita Real Gross National Product (GNP)

Gross National Product is the market value of all final goods and services produced in a year, and attributable to the factors of production supplied by the normal residents of the country concerned. Real GNP is the GNP adjusted for changes in prices, and is computed by dividing GNP by the general price index. Per capita real GNP is the most widely used measure of the economic well-being of people. If computed for rural people separately, it could be used as a measure of the economic component of rural development. More real GNP per capita means that, on the average, we are economically better off. But in reality, GNP has the following weaknesses as a measure of economic well-being:

- It does not include the value of physical and mental satisfaction that people derive from leisure.
- It does not include the value of non-paid housewives' services, and home labour such as gardening, painting and care of pets and domestic animals. If a bachelor marries his maid, the GNP is reduced, because he no longer pays for her services.
- It does not assign any negative values to those side-effects of economic activities that reduce the total satisfaction from the output of those activities. The examples of such side-effects are air pollution, water pollution, noise and other disagreeable aspects that accompany industrialisation.
- It does not give any negative weight to the 'disamenities' of living in dirty, noisy and crowded cities and slums, compared to more clean, open and pleasant surroundings. Nor does it assign any positive weight to such environmental amenities as clean air and water, and a pollution-free environment.
- It is not only difficult, but also time-consuming and expensive, to determine per capita income of rural people, most of whom are self-employed and, being illiterate, do not keep any written records of their income and expenditure. It takes quite an experienced and well-trained rural researcher/investigator to find out the true per capita income of rural people.

Clearly, the GNP does not include every thing that contributes to human happiness, and does not exclude every thing that diminishes it. But despite all its weaknesses, per capita real GNP is the only quantitative indicator of the economic component of rural development available for intra-national and international comparisons over time and over space.

Per Capita Consumption Expenditure

Given the weaknesses of per capita income as a measure of rural development, per capita *consumption expenditure* of rural people is considered a better measure of rural development for several reasons, including relative ease in recall by the respondent, of expenditure incurred and the general tendency of rural people not to hide any expenditure, as compared to income. Per capita consumption expenditure is a reasonably good proxy variable for per capita income. The National Sample Survey Organisation (NSSO) conducts sample surveys all over India at regular intervals to estimate the consumption expenditure for both urban and rural people. The estimates are considered reasonably reliable. Besides, other estimates of consumption expenditure are also available for selected areas, from research reports of institutions and scholars. Like nominal income, nominal consumption expenditure also should be adjusted for changes in the general price index over time and across space, to make it useful for comparison purposes.

Per Capita Public Expenditure on Community Facilities and Services

The level of rural development in a country is a function of the per capita quantity of various goods and services consumed by its rural population, in a particular reference period of time. It does not matter whether the goods and services consumed are purchased by a person with his personal income, or whether he receives them without specific expenditure on his part. Certain services, facilities and civic amenities, such as schools, hospitals, roads, parks, police protection and street lights, are provided by the government free or at a nominal cost to its people. The availability of these facilities and services represents 'real income', and therefore constitutes part of the level of living. Per capita public expenditure on such services and amenities is a good measure of socio-economic welfare. For comparisons over time and space, this measure should also be adjusted for changes/differences in the general price index. This measure, used in conjunction with per capita income or expenditure, constitutes a reasonably satisfactory measure of rural development. However, estimates of this variable/measure are not made by any organisation/agency in India. Therefore, one has to collect the requisite information from the office records of village panchayats and other village/block level organisations to estimate this measure and use it.

Physical Quality of Life Index (PQLI)

This measure was developed by Morris and McAlpin (1982: 1–30) to determine the impact of development projects on their target groups. The measure is called the Physical Quality of Life Index (PQLI). It supplements per capita real GNP, which is the most widely used measure of economic growth. It has three components, namely, infant mortality, life expectancy at age 1, and basic literacy. These three component indicators lend themselves to intra-national and international comparisons, are simple to compute and understand, are fairly sensitive to changes in distribution of benefits of development, do not reflect the values of any specific cultures, and reflect results, not inputs.

In calculations of GNP, various goods and services can be combined via a common element: market price. But the three component indicators of PQLI do not have any common element that values them all. Instead, a simple indexing system is used to combine them into a single-index PQLI. For each indicator, the performance of individual states/countries is evaluated on a scale of zero to 100, where zero represents an absolutely defined 'worst' performance, and 100 represents the 'best' performance. Once the performance for each indicator is scaled to this common measure, a composite index is calculated by averaging the three indicators, *giving equal weight to each of them.* The resulting PQLI, thus, is also scaled zero to 100.

Morris and McAlpin computed the PQLI for 150 countries. The range for each component index was based on the examination of the historical experience of the countries concerned. The literacy index ranged from zero literacy to 100 per cent literacy for the population aged 15 years and over, the infant mortality rate from 229 to seven per thousand births, and life expectancy at age one from 38 to 77 years. Using these ranges and actual data for Nigeria, India and the USA, they computed a PQLI for each of them, as shown in Table 3.1. They argue that PQLI measures the combined effects of nutritional status, public health facilities, family income and social relations.

Table 3.1
Life Expectancy at Age 1, Infant Mortality and Literacy:
Actual Data and Index Numbers (Early 1970s)

Country	Life expectancy at age 1[1]		Infant mortality[2]		Literacy[3]		PQLI[4]
	Years	Index No.	Per 1,000 live births	Index No.	Per cent	Index No.	
Nigeria	49	28	180	22	25	25	25
India	56	46	122	48	34	34	43
USA	72	87	16	96	99	99	94

Source: Morris, David Morris and Michelle B. McAlpin. 1982. *Measuring the Condition of India's Poor: The Physical Quality of Life Index.* New Delhi: Promilla and Company Publishers, p. 16.

Notes:

1. Years of life expectancy are converted to an index number according to the formula

$$\frac{\text{Life expectancy at age 1} - 38}{0.39}$$

2. The infant mortality rate is converted to an index number according to the formula

$$\frac{229 - \text{Infant mortality rate per thousand}}{2.22}$$

3. Literacy index numbers correspond to the actual data.
4. Average of life expectancy at age 1, infant mortality and literacy indices (equally weighted).

Human Development Index (HDI)

Rediscovering the truth that people must be at the centre of all development, the United Nations Development Programme (UNDP) decided to bring out every year, beginning in 1990, a report on the human dimensions of development. The *Human Development Report 1990* was the first such report. The report addresses the question of how economic growth does or does not promote human development. It discusses the meaning and measurement of human development, proposes a new composite index of human development, summarises the record of human development over the past three decades, and sets forth strategies for human development in the 1990s (UNDP 1990).

The *Human Development Report 1990* defined human development as the process of increasing people's options. It stressed that the most critical choices that people should have include the options to lead a long and healthy life, to be knowledgeable, and to find access to the assets, employment and income needed for a decent standard of living.

Development, thus defined, cannot be adequately measured by income alone. The report therefore proposed a new measure of development, the Human Development Index (HDI), composed of three indicators: life expectancy, adult literacy and income expressed in logs. The subsequent *Human Development Reports* have made some refinements in the procedure of defining the component indicators and computing the HDI. The refinements include adjustment of income for differences in purchasing power and disparities in income distribution, combining adult literacy and mean years of schooling into an index of educational attainment, and computing disaggregated HDI for males and females and for different population groups. In addition, HDI has also been supplemented by a human freedom index, and indicators of human security for selected countries for which data are available.

The HDI for 1994 was calculated on a different basis from that in the previous years. Maximum and minimum values were fixed for the four basic variables: life expectancy (85 and 25 years), adult literacy (100 per cent and zero per cent), mean years of schooling (15 and zero years) and income adjusted for differences in purchasing power and expressed in terms of Purchasing Power Parity (PPP) ($40,000 and $200). For income, the threshold value was taken to be the global average real GDP per capita of PPP $5,120. Multiples of income beyond the threshold were discounted using a progressively higher rate (UNDP 1994: 92).

The minimum and maximum values of component variables were fixed without reference to particular countries, i.e., the values were norms. The minima were those observed historically, going back about 30 years, and the maxima were the limits of what could be envisioned in the next 30 years. This permitted more meaningful comparisons across countries and over time.

An index was prepared for each of the component variables of HDI, using the following formula:

$$\text{Component index} = \frac{\text{Actual value} - \text{Minimum value}}{\text{Maximum value} - \text{Minimum value}}$$

Illustration of the Procedure of Computing HDI

For illustration, we take a pair of countries, one industrial (Greece) and one developing (India). Their basic variables are as follows:

Country	Life expectancy (years)	Adult literacy (%)	Mean years of schooling	Income (PPP $)
Greece	77.3	93.8	7.0	7,680
India	59.7	49.8	2.4	1,150

Life Expectancy

$$\text{Greece} \quad \frac{77.3 - 25.0}{85.0 - 25.0} = \frac{52.3}{60.0} = 0.872$$

$$\text{India} \quad \frac{59.7 - 25.0}{85.0 - 25.0} = \frac{34.7}{60.0} = 0.578$$

Adult Literacy

$$\text{Greece} \quad \frac{93.8 - 0.0}{100.0 - 0.0} = \frac{93.8}{100.0} = 0.938$$

$$\text{India} \quad \frac{49.8 - 0.0}{100.0 - 0.0} = \frac{49.8}{100.0} = 0.498$$

Mean Years of Schooling

$$\text{Greece} \quad \frac{7.0 - 0.0}{15.0 - 0.0} = \frac{7.0}{15.0} = 0.467$$

$$\text{India} \quad \frac{2.4 - 0.0}{15.0 - 0.0} = \frac{2.4}{15.0} = 0.160$$

Educational Attainment

$$\text{Greece} = 2(0.938) + 0.467 = 2.343/3 = 0.781$$
$$\text{India} = 2(0.498) + 0.160 = 1.156/3 = 0.385$$

Adjusted Income

Greece's income is above the threshold, but less than twice the threshold. Thus, the adjusted income for Greece was computed as follows:

$$\text{Greece} = 5,120 + 2(7,680 - 5,120)^{1/2}$$
$$= 5,120 + 101$$
$$= 5,221.$$

Table 3.2
*Indices of Life Expectancy, Educational Attainment and Adjusted
Income and HDI for Greece and India*

Country	Indexed life expectancy	Indexed educational attainment	Indexed adjusted income	All three	HDI
Greece	0.872	0.781	0.968	= 2.621	0.874
India	0.578	0.385	0.183	= 1.146	0.382

The indexed adjusted income for Greece was as follows:

$$\text{Greece} = \frac{5{,}221 - 200}{5{,}385 - 200} = \frac{5{,}021}{5{,}185} = 0.968$$

India's income is below the threshold, so it needs adjustment. To calculate the distance for income, we used the maximum adjusted income (5,385) and the minimum (200). The indexed adjusted income for India was as follows:

$$\text{India} = \frac{1{,}150 - 200}{5{,}385 - 200} = \frac{950}{5{,}185} = 0.183$$

The indices for the three component variables, and the HDI thus computed for Greece and India, are presented in Table 3.2.

All countries have made substantial progress in human development. Between 1960 and 1992, the overall HDI for developing countries increased from 0.260 to 0.541—more than double (UNDP 1994: 95). Countries having an HDI below 0.5 are considered to have a low level of human development, those between 0.5 and 0.8 a medium level, and those above 0.8 a high level (UNDP 1994: 92).

The HDI has been used: (*a*) to stimulate national political debate; (*b*) to give priority to human development; (*c*) to highlight disparities within countries; and (*d*) to open new avenues for analysis.

No change/modification in the method of computing HDI is contemplated in the near future. But greater emphasis will be placed on improving human development statistics. HDI is by far the most widely accepted indicator of human development (and lack of development or poverty). In 1994, India's HDI was 0.446 and its rank was 138th among 175 nations of the world. Canada had the highest HDI (0.960), and Sierra Leone the lowest (0.176). In 1993, India's HDI was 0.436, and the rank was 135th among 174 nations of the world (UNDP 1996: 136).

Measures of Distribution of Income

The level of per capita real gross national product (GNP) and its distribution are both equally important from the point of view of aggregate economic welfare. In general, higher per capita real GNP and its more equitable distribution mean a higher level of economic well-being. A country with a high per capita real GNP, but with a less equitable distribution of income, would rank lower in terms of aggregate economic welfare than the one with the same level of per capita real GNP, but with a more equitable distribution of income.

There are a wide variety of measures which are used by economists to measure income distribution. They include, among others, the Pareto index, the shares of the bottom 20 per cent and the top 20 per cent of households in the aggregate income, standard deviation of logarithms of incomes, the Lorenz Curve and the Gini Concentration Ratio. A good measure of income distribution should possess two characteristics. First, it should be unaffected by equal proportional increases in all incomes, so that if the distribution of income for the year X is simply a scaled-up version of that for the year Y, then we should regard them as characterised by the same degree of inequality. Second, it should be sensitive to disproportionate changes at all levels of income, so that if from year X to year Y, the incomes of lower-income households increase proportionately more than the incomes of the higher income households, this ought to lead to a strictly positive reduction in the index of inequality, and not merely leave it unchanged (Atkinson 1970: 253–4).

The following is a brief description of the procedure for computing some of the commonly used measures of income inequality.

The Lorenz Curve

This is a graphical measure of income distribution and income inequality. The information required to draw a Lorenz Curve consists of a frequency table showing the distribution of income by decile groups of households. In simpler words, the table should show for each of the decile groups, its share in the aggregate income, as is done in Table 3.3. To draw a Lorenz Curve, the cumulative percentage of income-receiving households is represented on the horizontal axis, the cumulative percentage of aggregate income on the vertical axis, and the curve represents the locus of all the combinations of the two cumulative percentages. The Lorenz Curves shown in Figure 3.1 are drawn on the basis of the figures presented in Table 3.3. The diagonal line represents a perfectly equal distribution of

Table 3.3

Relative Shares of Aggregate Income Received by Various Decile Groups of Households in Aligarh District in 1963–64 and 1968–69

Decile group	Percentage of aggregate income			
	1963–64		1968–69	
	Simple	Cumulative	Simple	Cumulative
Bottom 10 per cent	− 0.42	− 0.42	0.77	0.77
Second 10 per cent	1.04	0.62	2.37	3.14
Third 10 per cent	2.29	2.91	3.57	6.71
Fourth 10 per cent	4.06	6.97	5.12	11.83
Fifth 10 per cent	6.10	13.07	6.71	18.54
Sixth 10 per cent	8.00	21.07	8.89	27.43
Seventh 10 per cent	10.31	31.38	11.55	38.98
Eighth 10 per cent	13.94	45.32	13.86	52.84
Ninth 10 per cent	18.39	63.71	17.56	70.40
Top 10 per cent	36.29	100.00	29.60	100.00

Source: Singh, Katar. 1973. 'The Impact of New Agricultural Technology on Farm Income Distribution in the Aligarh District of Uttar Pradesh', in the *Indian Journal of Agricultural Economics*. 28(2): 4.

income, and hence is known as the line of equality. In general, the farther the Lorenz Curve is from the line of equality, the higher the degree of income inequality is.

The Lorenz Curve is a simple and commonly used measure of income inequality. It could be used to compare income distribution over time and across space. Its limitation is that, whereas it can show the difference in income inequality, it cannot quantify it. For instance, in Figure 3.1, since the Lorenz Curve for the year 1963–64 lies above that for the year 1968–69, we could say that the income inequality was higher in 1963–64 than in 1968–69, but we cannot quantify the difference.

The Gini Concentration Ratio

This ratio was invented by Corrado Gini in 1913. It is the most commonly used measure of income inequality these days. The ratio can be approximated either from the Lorenz Curve, or the mean difference.

When approximated from the Lorenz Curve, it represents the proportion of the area lying between the diagonal and the Lorenz Curve, to the total area under the diagonal. If we denote the area inside the Lorenz Curve as A and outside the Lorenz Curve as B, the ratio would

Figure 3.1
Distribution of Farm Family Income in Aligarh District in 1963–64 and 1968–69

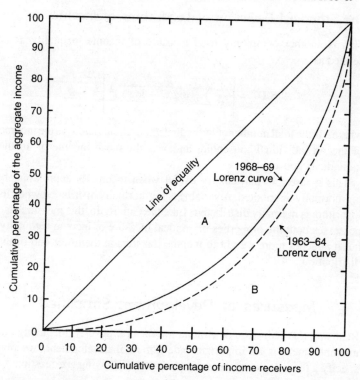

be $A/A + B$ (see Figure 3.1). Hence, the range of this ratio is from zero to one; zero being perfect equality, and one perfect inequality.

When computed from the mean difference, the Gini Concentration Ratio may be defined as

$$GCR = \sum_{i=1}^{n} \sum_{j=1}^{n} \frac{f_i f_j / x_i - x_j /}{2\bar{x}N}$$

where n is the number of income classes, f_i and f_j are the frequencies in the ith and jth classes, x_i and x_j the mean incomes of the ith and jth classes, N is the total number of income receivers, and $\bar{x}$ the overall mean income. Hence, the ratio is one-half of the weighted average of all absolute differences, between all possible pairs of incomes.

The Gini Ratio possesses both the properties of an ideal measure of income inequality described earlier.

The Standard Deviation of Logarithms of Incomes

This is another commonly used measure of income inequality. It is defined as

$$\text{S.D.} = \left[\frac{1}{N} \sum_{i=1}^{n} (\log x_i - \overline{\log x})^2 \right]^{1/2}$$

where n is the total number of individuals/households and x_i is the income of the ith individual/household, and $\bar{x}$ is the mean income of all the individuals/households.

This measure is particularly useful when income is approximately log-normally distributed. A variable is log-normally distributed when its logarithm is normally distributed. Like the Gini Ratio, this measure also possesses both the properties of an ideal measure of income inequality, but it attaches more weight to income transfers at the lower end of the distribution.

Measures of Development Simplified

Realising that reduction or elimination of rural poverty, inequality and unemployment is an important index of rural development, we may specify a few simple measures by posing the following six questions:

1. Has the number of rural people below the absolute poverty line been declining over time?
2. Has the degree of income inequality in rural areas been declining over time?
3. Has the level of rural unemployment been declining over time?
4. Have the nature and quality of public educational, health and other social and cultural services in rural areas been improving over time?
5. Has economic progress enhanced individual and group esteem of rural people, both internally vis-à-vis one another, and externally vis-à-vis other nations and regions?
6. Finally, has economic progress expanded the range of choice available to rural people, and freed them from external dependence and internal servitude to other men and institutions?

If the answer to each of these questions is yes, then clearly these phenomena constitute real rural development, and a nation in which they are manifested can unquestionably be called 'developed'.

Some Measures of Rural Poverty

The term rural poverty is the opposite of the term rural development. It implies lack of development, or underdevelopment, and therefore the knowledge of its measures also is as important for a student of rural development as that of measures of rural development. In this section, we present some commonly used measures of rural poverty.

Rural poverty is a worldwide problem; it exists in both developing and developed countries of the world. Over one billion people in the world are estimated to be living in poverty. The incidence of poverty is highly uneven among the regions of the world, among countries within those regions, and among localities within those countries. Nearly half of the world's poor live in South Asia, a region that accounts for roughly 30 per cent of the world's population. Alleviation of poverty has been an important objective of development policies and programmes all over the world, including India.

Measurement of poverty is beset with numerous conceptual, methodological and empirical problems. Conceptually, it is difficult to define poverty in operational terms that are universally acceptable. Methodologically, there is no consensus among scholars about the best indicator or measure of poverty, and empirically, given the choice of a particular measure of poverty, it is very difficult to collect reliable data necessary for computing the value of the indicator/measure chosen. These problems notwithstanding, policy makers, planners and scholars have attempted to measure poverty, and have used poverty measures to monitor changes in the level/incidence of poverty, and for other purposes.

Connotations and Definitions of Poverty

There is no universally acceptable definition of poverty, although there are several connotations and definitions in vogue. Poverty implies a condition of life characterised by deprivation of some sort or the other, and perceived as undesirable by the person(s) concerned or others. It is a multidimensional concept and phenomenon. Generally, there is a consensus among scholars about poverty being conceived and defined as absolute or relative. Absolute poverty implies a person's lack of access to objectively determined, reasonably adequate quantities of goods and services, to satisfy his/her material and non-material basic needs.

Relative poverty, on the other hand, means that a person's access to the basic needs of life is relatively lower, as compared to some reference group of people. Between two households or two persons, one may be considered as poor, while the other in comparison may not be so, even though both may be in a position to fulfil their basic material needs.

Criteria of Measuring Poverty

The magnitude of poverty at any given point in time depends on the criteria or norms used to define poverty and determine the poverty line. There are two criteria or norms usually employed to define the poverty line: (*a*) the norm based on the concept of a nutritionally adequate diet; and (*b*) the norm based on the concept of a minimum level of living. A number of research scholars have attempted to estimate the cost of providing a nutritionally adequate diet. For example, Dandekar and Rath (1971: 8–9), on the basis of an average calorie intake of 2,250 per capita per day, estimated the poverty line to correspond to a consumer expenditure of Rs 15 per capita per month for rural households, and Rs 22.50 for urban households, at 1960–61 prices.

As far as the second norm based on the concept of a minimum level of living is concerned, a distinguished Study Group[1] set up by the Government of India in July 1962 deliberated on the question of what should be regarded the nationally desirable minimum level of consumer expenditure. The study group recommended that a per capita monthly consumer expenditure of Rs 20 at 1960–61 prices should be deemed the national minimum. This does not include expenditure on health and education, which are expected to be provided by the state.

Some Common Measures and Indicators of Poverty

We now briefly present some commonly used measures/indicators of poverty.

Poverty Ratio or Head Count

This is the most commonly used single variate measure of poverty in India. This measure estimates the percentage of population below a

---

[1] The group comprised Prof. D. R. Gadgil, Dr B. N. Ganguli, Dr P. S. Lokanathan, Mr M. R. Masani, Mr Asoka Mehta, Mr Shriman Narayan, Mr Pitambar Pant, Dr V. K. R. V. Rao and Mr Anna Saheb Sahasrabuddhe.

specified poverty line. To compute this measure, it is necessary to define and determine a poverty line. Given the diversity of the basic necessities of life and intra-regional and inter-regional variations in the mix of a 'basket of basic necessities', the poverty line must of necessity be expressed in monetary terms, as it is not possible to have any meaningful physical common denominator to aggregate different elements of the basic necessities of life.

There has been a lot of debate on how the poverty line should be determined and updated. For quite some time, the Planning Commission followed a method recommended by a Task Force on Projection of Minimum Needs and Effective Consumption Demand in 1979. Following this method, the Planning Commission estimated the poverty line on the basis of the all-India consumption basket for 1973–74 at Rs 49.09 and Rs 56.64 per capita per month for rural and urban areas respectively, at 1973–74 prices. This method required an upward adjustment of the data of household consumption obtained through the National Sample Survey (NSS). The adjustment was recommended in order to close the gap between the 'Sum Total of Household Consumption' (STHC) as estimated from the NSS data, and the estimates of 'National Private Consumption Expenditure' (NPCE) as per the National Accounts Statistics (NAS). But after a careful examination of both the sets of data—NSS and NAS—it was found that the two sets were not comparable, and that there was need to look afresh into the various methodological issues involved. Consequently, in 1989 the Planning Commission constituted an Expert Group on Estimation of Proportion and Number of Poor. The Expert Group, in its report submitted in 1993, accepted the definition of the poverty line used by the Task Force, but recommended changes in the methodology of estimation of the proportion and number of the poor. The Expert Group made estimates of poverty at national and state levels using the state-specific poverty lines, and based on the data from the quinquennial rounds of NSS for the years 1973–74, 1977–78, 1983, 1987–88 and 1993–94 (Table 3.1). The Expert Group recommended that the adjustment of the NSS data on the basis of NAS data was uncalled for, and that state-specific poverty lines should be used, as against the all-India poverty line for rural and urban India. The Expert Group also recommended that for updating the poverty lines for rural and urban areas, state-specific cost of living indices for rural and urban areas should be used, instead of only the all-India index for both rural and urban areas, as used by the Task Force. The Expert Group suggested that for updating the rural poverty line, the consumer price index for

Table 3.4

*Number and Percentage of Population Below Poverty Line in India
Estimated by Using the Expert Group Methodology*

Year	No. of poor (millions)			Percentage of poor		
	Rural	Urban	Total	Rural	Urban	Total
1973–74	261.29	60.05	321.34	56.44	49.01	54.88
1977–78	264.25	64.65	328.90	53.07	45.24	51.32
1983	251.96	70.94	322.90	45.65	40.79	44.48
1987–88	231.88	75.17	307.05	39.09	38.20	38.86
1993–94	244.03	76.34	320.37	37.27	32.36	35.97

Source: Press Release dated 11 March 1997 by the Planning Commission, Government of India, New Delhi.

agricultural labourers be used, and a simple average of weighted commodity indices of the consumer price index for industrial workers and the consumer price index for urban non-manual employees be used for updating the urban poverty line. Table 3.4 presents the estimates of the number and percentage of rural and urban population below the poverty line in India, as estimated by using the Expert Group Methodology. In March 1997 the Planning Commission accepted the methodology recommended by the Expert Group, with a slight modification that only the consumer price index for industrial workers be used for estimating and updating the urban poverty line. So with effect from April 1997, a modified Expert Group Methodology is being used for estimating and updating poverty lines for rural and urban areas.

Besides per capita income/consumption expenditure, there are quite a few other commonly used single variate measures of poverty or human development. They include (a) Life expectancy at birth; (b) Literacy rate; (c) Birth rate; (d) Death rate; and (e) Infant mortality rate (Table 3.5). They are self-explanatory and hence we do not discuss them here.

The Seventh Finance Commission (GOI 1978a) used a broader concept of the poverty line—the Augmented Poverty Line (APL), which included, besides household consumer expenditure, an estimate of the benefit of public expenditure. The APL was computed first for every state, by adding to the per capita monthly private consumer expenditure in the state, the per capita monthly public expenditure by the state government in 1970–71 under the following heads: (a) health and family planning; (b) water supply and sanitation; (c) education; (d) administration of police, jails, and courts; (e) roads; and (f) social welfare. Then, to this

Table 3.5
Basic Indicators of Human Development in India, 1951–95

Year	Basic indicators of human development					
	Life expectancy at birth (years)[1]	Literacy rate (per cent)	Birth rate[2]	Death rate[2]	Infant Mortality rate[2]	Per Capita NNP at 1980–81 price[3] (Rs)
			(per thousand)			
1951	32.1	18.3	39.9	27.4	146	1,127
1961	41.3	28.3	41.7	22.8	146	1,350
1971	45.6	34.5	36.9	14.9	129	1,520
1981	50.4	43.6	33.9	12.5	110	1,630
1991	59.4	52.2	29.5	9.8	80	2,222
1995(P)	NA	NA	28.3	9.0	74	2,449

(P): Provisional.
Source: Economic Survey 1996–97, Ministry of Finance, Government of India, New Delhi.
Notes:

1. Data for 1951, 1961, 1971 and 1981 relate to the decades 1941–50, 1951–60, 1961–70 and 1971–80, respectively centred at the mid-points of the decades. The estimate centred at 1991 refers to the period 1988–92.
2. Data for 1951 and 1961 relate to the decades 1941–50 and 1951–60 respectively, and the estimates for 1971 and 1981 onwards are based on the Sample Registration System.
3. Relate to the financial years 1950–51, 1960–61, and so on.

state-specific norm, the highest per capita monthly public expenditure among the states in India in 1970–71 was added to arrive at the APL. The Commission then estimated the number of people below the APL for 15 states and found that 27.7 crore people lived below the APL in 1970–71. These poor people accounted for about 52 per cent of the total population of the 15 states.

Housing Index

Gibbons (1997) proposed this index as a cost-effective measure/tool for identifying the poor. He asserts that this index has been found to be valid and useful in a number of countries, such as China, Vietnam, the Philippines, Indonesia, India and Bangladesh, and that the index can help identify about 80 per cent of the poor very quickly; it takes about five minutes for an experienced field assistant to use the index properly.

The Housing Index has three components, namely, (a) the size of the house; (b) the physical condition of the house, as reflected in the materials used in its construction; and (c) the type of materials used for making the roof of the house. All the three dimensions of the index can be looked at and assessed through going up and down the lanes/streets in a village. One does not have to conduct any interviews using questionnaires or schedules. According to Gibbons, the material of the roof is a simple but powerful indicator of poverty in most countries of Asia. The poor in those countries live in houses having thatched roofs, or roofs made out of woven bamboo or twigs, or plastic sheets that have holes, with the roofs leaking and creating health problems. Nobody wants to live in such houses unless one has to. So the people living in such houses are really very poor. If we combine this with the small size of the houses and the very simple building materials, such as mud, jute sticks, and such other things, then we are very close to identifying most of the very poor. Gibbons admits two limitations of this index. First, some poor people live in bigger and better houses because they inherited those houses, but now they no longer have any income. Second, in many countries (including India), the government provides reasonably good houses to the poor free of cost. So, in those areas, this index cannot identify the poor. To overcome these and other similar limitations, there is an appeal procedure. The poor people living in good houses could appeal to the field assistant and convince him/her that they were not rich. A senior officer could later interview such people and take a final decision in the matter. In such cases, use of the Participatory Rural Appraisal (PRA) method of wealth ranking has been found to be useful. In the PRA method, all the villagers are brought together to find out who are the very poor, poor, not-so-poor and not poor at all. The two methods, Housing Index and PRA, were found to be comparable in terms of cost-effectiveness and the time taken. They could both be used by governmental and non-governmental organisations engaged in rural development, for identifying the poor for targeting their projects.

The Housing Index has a serious limitation, in the sense that it cannot be used for making international and even intra-national comparisons when the type of houses varies widely from country to country, or from state to state within the countries. But the primary purpose of this index is to identify the poor in a particular area, for giving some benefits or services to them. For this purpose, the index seems alright. Another limitation is that there is no way to combine the three components into a single index. Hence, the name Housing Index is misleading.

Human Poverty Index (HPI)

The *Human Development Report 1997* (UNDP 1997) presents a Human Poverty Index (HPI), and ranks 78 poor countries using it. The report asserts that poverty is multidimensional, and poverty measures based on the income criterion do not capture deprivation of many kinds.

The HPI is based on the following three different types of deprivation (UNDP 1997: 17–23).

1. Survival deprivation, as measured by the percentage of people (in a given country) not expected to survive to age 40 years (P_1).
2. Deprivation in education and knowledge, as measured by the adult literacy rate (P_2).
3. Deprivation in economic provisioning (P_3), which is computed as the mean of three variables: population without access to safe water (P_{31}), population without access to health services (P_{32}), and underweight children under the age of 5 years (P_{33})—all three expressed in percentages.

HPI is then obtained as the cube root of the average of the cubes of the three components of deprivation. This is a 'power mean' of order three. The power mean of order one is the simple mean, the average of the values.

Out of 78 developing countries, Trinidad and Tobago had the lowest HPI at 4.1, and Niger had the highest at 66.0. India's HPI was 36.7, and its rank was 47.

The report says that the HPI can be used in at least three ways: as a tool of advocacy; as a planning tool for identifying areas of concentrated poverty within a country; and as a research tool. For example, the HPI can help summarise the extent of poverty along several dimensions, the distance to go, and the progress made.

This index has some drawbacks and therefore is not yet acceptable to scholars and policy makers (Krishnaji 1997: 2202–205). HPI does not include certain critical dimensions of human poverty, such as low incomes, lack of political freedom, inability to participate in decision making, lack of personal security, and threats to sustainability and inter-generational equity. In addition, the quality and reliability of data used for computing HPI are also questionable in many cases.

Concluding Remarks

There is no universally acceptable measure of rural development that captures its multifaceted nature. The choice of measure depends upon the purpose of measurement, and the availability of requisite data/information.

Commonly used measures of rural development can be categorised into two classes, namely, measures of the *level* of rural development, and measures of the *distribution* of rural development. Of all the measures of level, the Human Development Index, when computed separately for the rural population, could be the most appropriate indicator of rural development. The Lorenz Curve and the Gini Concentration Ratio, the two most popular measures of income distribution, could also be used for measuring the distribution of benefits from rural development programmes. The percentage of the rural population below the poverty line, and the Poverty Index are two commonly used indicators of rural poverty, or lack of rural development.

4
Some Paradigms of Rural Development

Introduction

A theory is expected to perform two major functions, namely, explanation, and prediction of a phenomenon. There is no universally acceptable theory of rural development which can explain the existing phenomenon of rural development and predict its future course. What we have is a set of hypotheses and propositions that constitute higher-level generalisations in the field of development. To the extent that rural development is a subset of development, hypotheses of development apply to rural development as well. Many such hypotheses emphasise both economic and non-economic determinants of development, i.e., they are quite comprehensive. Another characteristic of some of the hypotheses propounded by development theorists is that they are not fully operational, in the sense that it is very difficult to test them, i.e., they are refractory. This chapter is devoted to a critical review of some comprehensive paradigms of development, and examines their relevance to rural development in the Indian context.

We begin with an examination of what the great thinkers of the past, particularly the classical economists, contributed to the subject. We can then, in the light of subsequent experience, determine in what respects they were right or wrong. In this manner, we can free ourselves (at least partially), from the confines of our own times, and can better equip ourselves for an objective analysis of the complex process of development.

The economists of the late eighteenth and early nineteenth centuries were primarily concerned with the conditions for economic growth. This was the period of the 'Industrial Revolution' in Europe. The Classical economists—including Adam Smith, David Ricardo, Thomas Robert Malthus, John Stuart Mill and Karl Marx—lived through the period of take-off into sustained growth. The observations of these economists regarding the nature and causes of economic growth are, therefore, of considerable interest. We shall now present some basic ideas of the Classical school of thought, which may still be relevant. An interesting element of the arguments of the Classical economists was the concept of circularity that characterised the interrelationship between technology, investment and profit. The circularity was inherent in their assertion that the level of technology depends on the level of investment, investment depends on profits, and profits depend partly on the level of technology. This circularity was no accident or oversight: it was precisely what the Classicists wished to stress, i.e., in economic development, nothing succeeds like success, and nothing fails like failure. In the circular argument, we already have a clue to the difference in the performance of developed and developing countries.

The classical economists did not focus their attention on development or rural development per se; they perhaps assumed that economic growth would naturally lead to development. It was towards the end of World War II around 1945, that development became an important field of study and attracted several scholars. Most of the initial writings on the subject dwelt on explaining the meaning of development, identifying factors affecting development, and exploring interrelationships among the factors. Two distinct schools of thought emerged in the fifties, namely, (a) Capitalist; and (b) Marxist, and two distinct theories corresponding to them, namely, the 'Modernisation Theory' of the Capitalist School, and the 'Dependency Theory' of the Marxist School.

The Modernisation Theory

The dominant arguments of the capitalist school are embodied in what is known as the Modernisation Theory, or the 'Free World' model of development. The Modernisation Theory was the justification for US hegemony in the context of the Cold War. Scholars who contributed to the growth and development of this theory comprised economists, sociologists, historians and anthropologists, and the determinants of development identified by them included both economic and non-economic factors. The essence of the theory was the transfer of Western technology and rationality, without changing class structure as a means of development, and removal of all social and ideological obstacles to such a process (Alavi and Shanin 1982: 2).

The Modernisation Theory was based on several assumptions, some of which are briefly stated here (Barnett 1988: 26; McKay 1990: 55):

1. Application of Western science and technology in order to increase production is essential for achieving development.
2. The process of development can be delineated into a series of stages, and all societies pass through those stages.
3. In the process of development, traditional social and political institutions are replaced by modern ones.
4. Traditional feudal forms of political power will be replaced by democratic forms of governance.

In a nutshell, the Modernisation Theory presented the 'American way of life' as the epitome of modernity. It envisages that development can be achieved only through industrialisation and urbanisation, along with technological transformation of agriculture—an insight validated by the experience of newly industrialised countries of East Asia and South East Asia.

In the context of rural development, the Modernisation Theory offers quite a few useful insights, such as the inevitability of the use of modern technology for increasing agricultural production, and the need for replacing traditional feudal institutions by new democratic ones, for a shift towards greater scientific temper, and secular values and norms. However, the theory has lost much of its appeal due to its failure to predict and explain many economic phenomena, such as the faltering of the post-World War II boom in the 1960s, worldwide depression in the 1970s, and the shift in the terms of international trade in favour of developed countries. The theory also did not foresee the adverse environmental impacts of the capitalist/free market model of development, and its unsustainability. In the face of these weaknesses and criticisms, the theory has taken a few new directions, such as International Keynesianism, with its emphasis on the establishment of a New International Economic Order and the Guarantee of Basic Needs and Structural Adjustments Programmes. However, these new initiatives do not directly address the problems of rural development, and to that extent are not relevant.

The recent financial (currency and stock market) turmoil in East Asian countries has proved that the free market economy model, or the capitalist path, cannot guarantee stable and sustainable economic development characterised by fast-improving living standards. From Japan and South

Korea to Malaysia and Indonesia, mounting bankruptcies, growing unemployment and rising inflation have engendered not only the loss of economic self-confidence, but also threatened the region's political and military stability.

There is yet another reason for the failure of the Modernisation Theory to be relevant in the context of developing countries like India, and that is the non-existence or ineffective implementation of rules and controls aimed at preventing private companies or groups from dominating their domestic markets. In the free market-oriented Western democracies, such rules and controls are effectively implemented, and hence they tend to even out the distribution of income and wealth. In the absence of strict control and regulation of the activities of private enterprises in developing countries, including India, not all the intended benefits from free markets accrue to society.

The Dependency Theory of the Marxist School

The growing disenchantment with the Modernisation Theory, owing to its failure to explain growing inequalities, poverty, violence and military coups in the newly independent nations in Africa and Asia, forced development scholars to ask new questions and seek new answers, using an alternative paradigm. The intellectual foundation of the new paradigm was rooted in the ideas of Karl Marx, Friedrich Engels and other Marxist thinkers. Marx (1818–83) and Engels (1820–1995) were the contemporaries of the proponents of the Modernisation Theory, notably Durkheim (1858–1917) and Weber (1864–1924). Marx and Engels believed that the process of social change was not gradual and evolutionary, as assumed by the Modernisation Theory. Instead, it was characterised by conflict of interests between classes in society, or class struggle. The Marxists saw class struggle as the engine of social change and development.

The Marxists argued that imperialism, rather than being a benign political outgrowth of European civilisation (as argued by the Modernisation Theorists), was an exploitative system of economic, social and political relations. The system changed the colonised nations into sources of cheap inputs to production in the capitalist nations, as well as markets for their products. This arrangement always worked to the advantage of the imperial power. Such a view of the dynamics at work in the capitalist system meant a complete reversal of the logic of modernisation from the promise of development to impoverishment. This was the fundamental argument of the Marxist School of thought, which came to be known as the Dependency Theory.

The initial support for the Dependency Theory came from Latin America, particularly from the work of Raul Prebisch and his associates at the Economic Commission for Latin America (ECLA). However, the chief spokesman for the theory was Andre Gunder Frank, who dismissed the Modernisation Theory as useless from a policy perspective. Frank asserted that the relation between rich and poor nations was not only *not* beneficial to the latter, but positively destructive, hindering and distorting their development. In his view, development and underdevelopment were both results of interactions between societies. He drew up detailed historical case studies of Chile and Brazil to support his assertions. The following are the main arguments of the Dependency Theory (McKay 1990: 55–56):

1. The developed countries (the First World) could not have achieved the level of development that they have, without the systematic exploitation of the developing countries (the Third World).
2. That the process of development passes through a series of stages is an illusion. Developing countries cannot attain development following the path adopted by developed countries, so long as the exploitative world system exists.
3. Countries that are now poor were not so to begin with: rather they have been *forced* into the stage of underdevelopment by a global system of capitalist exploitation.
4. Developing countries can develop only by snapping their links with the developed countries.

The Dependency Theory was very popular in the 1970s, as it provided a plausible explanation to the perpetuation of the problems of poverty and stagnation in developing countries, despite concerted efforts at solving them. Development scholars realised the need for critically examining the existing relations between rich and poor countries, to find out whether they were benign and beneficial to the poor nations, or harmful. However, in the 1980s, the theory lost much of its initial popularity, and was criticised as being 'too deterministic' and 'too simplistic'. The basic argument of the theory that 'underdevelopment' in developing countries (the periphery) is the result of 'development' in developed countries (the core/centre), was falsified by the experience of the East Asian tigers. These tigers were initially dependent on the developing countries, (i.e., they were on the periphery), but in course of time they became highly developed and competitive, i.e., they moved from the periphery to the core. Besides, the theory did not consider the role of several internal factors, such as excessive population growth, underdeveloped human resources, shortage of natural resources and class struggle, in explaining the existence of 'underdevelopment'.

In the context of rural development, we could say that the theory provides a useful caveat that, while identifying the determinants of rural development, we should critically examine various intersectoral linkages (both backward and forward) and interactions, and determine whether they are beneficial to rural people or not. If not, necessary policy measures should be suggested to make the linkages and interactions beneficial to rural people. A similar exercise needs to be done at the national level, to find out which international economic and political relationships are beneficial, and which are harmful to economic development in general, and rural development in particular.

Rosenstein-Rodan's Theory of the 'Big Push'

According to this theory, there is a minimum level of resources that must be devoted to a development programme, if it is to have any chance of success. Launching a country into self-sustaining growth is a little like getting an airplane off the ground. There is a critical ground speed which must be passed before the craft can become airborne (MIT 1957: 70). The essence of this theory is: Proceeding 'bit by bit' will not add up in its effects to the sum total of the single bits. A minimum quantum of investment is a necessary, though not sufficient, condition of success.

Rosenstein-Rodan identifies three different kinds of indivisibilities, which may be considered the main obstacles to the development of developing countries. These are the indivisibility in the supply of social overhead capital (lumpiness of capital), the indivisibility of demand (complementarity of demand), and the indivisibility (kink) in the supply of savings. He argues that a big push in terms of a high quantum of investment is required to scale the economic obstacles to development created by these three kinds of indivisibilities, and the external economies to which they give rise. This implies that the development process is a series of discontinuous 'jumps', and each jump requires a 'big push'. Besides, there may finally be a phenomenon of indivisibility in the vigour and drive required for successful development policy. Isolated and small efforts may not add up to a sufficient impact on growth. An atmosphere of development may only arise after a critical minimum level of investment has been reached.

Rosenstein-Rodan does not offer any specific and practicable suggestions to overcome the adverse effects of the indivisibilities, but he suggests that international trade may reduce the size of the minimum push required to obviate the effect of indivisibility (complementarity) of demand. Mobilisation of sufficient resources to provide the required 'big push' continues to be the biggest hurdle, which developing countries cannot overcome on their own. Rosenstein-Rodan recommends that a trust, with capital from outside, be established to plan and finance investment for the entire area simultaneously. A major criticism of this theory is that the resources required to give the 'big push' are of such a high order, that a developing country like India cannot afford them. In fact, a country capable of mobilising the requisite quantum of resources would not be a poor country. However, conceptually, this paradigm continues to be appealing to planners and scholars.

Leibenstein's 'Critical Minimum Effort Thesis'

The central idea of Harvey Leibenstein's thesis is that in order to attain sustained secular growth, it is essential that the initial stimulant to development be of a certain critical minimum size. According to Leibenstein, economic backwardness is characterised by a set of interrelated factors, which have a certain degree of stability at their small equilibrium values. The actual values are different from the equilibrium values, because the economy is always being subjected to stimulants or shocks. The stimulants have a tendency to raise per capita incomes above the equilibrium level. But in backward economies, long-term economic development does not take place because the magnitude of stimulants is too small. In other words, efforts to escape from economic backwardness, be they spontaneous or forced, are below the critical minimum needed for sustained growth.

For small values of the stimulant, the generated income-depressing factors are, in the long run, more significant than the induced income-raising forces, but the reverse is the case with high values of the stimulant. Population growth may be cited as an example of this phenomenon. A small increase in capital through raising incomes will stimulate more than an equivalent increase in population, and a proportional decline in per capita income. There is, of course, a biologically determined maximum rate of population growth between 3 and 4 per cent. As such, persistent capital accumulation above a certain minimum rate would eventually permit development. The need for a minimum effort arises to overcome internal and external diseconomies of scale, to overcome income-depressing obstacles which may be generated by the stimulants to growth, and to generate sufficient momentum in the system, so that the factors that stimulate growth continue to play their part.

Leibenstein's thesis is more realistic than Rosenstein-Rodan's big push theory. Giving a big push to the programme of industrialisation all at once is not practicable in underdeveloped countries, while the critical minimum effort can be properly timed and broken up into a series of smaller efforts to put the economy on the path of sustained development. This theory is also consistent with the concept of decentralised democratic planning, to which India, and most developing countries, are wedded. Therefore, this paradigm provides good clues as to the quantum of investment that is absolutely essential to make a programme take off.

Lewis' Model of Economic Development with Unlimited Supplies of Labour

W. Arthur Lewis' (1954: 139–92) model is based on the fact that in many developing countries, there exist large reservoirs of labour whose marginal productivity is negligible, zero, or even negative. This labour is available in unlimited quantities, at a wage equal to the subsistence level of living, plus a margin sufficient to overcome the friction of moving from the 'subsistence sector' to the 'capitalist sector', which may be called 'subsistence-plus' wage. As the supply of labour is unlimited, new industries can be set up and the existing ones can be expanded without limit, at the ruling wage rate. The capitalist sector also needs skilled workers. But Lewis maintains that skilled labour is only a temporary bottleneck, and can be removed by providing training facilities to unskilled workers.

Since the marginal productivity of labour in the capitalist sector is higher than the ruling wage rate, there results a capitalist surplus. This surplus is used for capital formation, which makes possible employment of more people from the subsistence sector. The increase in investment by the capitalists raises the marginal productivity of labour, which induces capitalist employers to increase their labour force till the marginal productivity of labour falls to a level equivalent to the ruling wage rate. This process goes on till the capital-labour ratio rises to the point where the supply of labour becomes inelastic. Some critics have pointed out that Lewis' optimism concerning development by absorption of disguised unemployment from agriculture is unfounded, because it is not possible to transfer a large number of workers permanently and on a full-time basis from agriculture to industry, without a drop in agricultural output, i.e., the marginal productivity of labour in agriculture is not zero.

Technical progress in the capitalist sector may also increase the share of profits in national income as long as there is surplus labour. The share of profits increases, both because the profit ratio within a capitalist sector of a given size may increase through innovation, and because the capitalist sector itself grows. According to Lewis, this is the major way in which the rise in capital formation from 4 or 5 per cent to about 12–15 per cent of national income takes place.

Capital is created not only out of profits, but also out of bank credit. In a developing country characterised by unemployed resources and scarcity of capital, credit creation will expand output and employment in the same way as profits do. Credit-financed capital formation, however, results in a temporary rise in prices. The inflationary process comes to an end when voluntary savings from increased profits are large enough to finance new investment, without resort to bank credit.

According to Lewis, the process of growth cannot continue indefinitely, and must come to an end on account of a number of factors. When this happens, the process of capital formation can still be kept going by stimulating immigration, or by encouraging export of capital to countries which possess abundant supplies of labour at the subsistence wage rate. Since the former measure is strongly opposed by trade unions, the latter seems more practicable.

Lewis' model seems to provide a good framework to understand the process of economic development in labour-surplus developing countries like India. Its basic premise is that labour productivity in agriculture must increase substantially in order to generate surplus in the form of food to be used for development of the non-farm sector, and to release the surplus labour from agriculture for meeting the growing needs of the non-farm sector. However, the relevance of the model is constrained by a number of factors. First, labour unions may push the wage rate up as labour productivity increases, and keep the rate of profit and rate of capital formation lower than expected. Second, the capitalist employers may use the surplus for speculative or non-productive purposes, instead of ploughing it back for development purposes. This is, in fact, what has been happening these days in India and other developing countries. Third, to meet their rising expectations, rural people may consume more and save less than predicted by the model, and thereby dampen the pace of development.

The Lewis model does not present a satisfactory analysis of the agricultural sector, in the sense that it fails to consider the possibility of a change of productivity in agriculture. Building upon the Lewis model, Gustav Ranis and John C. H. Fei construct a theory of economic growth, by first analysing the role of the 'neglected' agricultural sector in a static sense, and then generalising the 'static' analysis by introducing the possibility of an increase in agricultural productivity (Higgins 1966: Ch. 5).

Cochrane (1969: Ch. 11) critically reviews the models of Lewis and of Ranis and Fei, and concludes that the creation of investment capital needed to employ the surplus workers released from agriculture is the critical missing element in these models. He then suggests that the resources to finance the expensive process of agricultural modernisation can be obtained in any one or in a combination of three basic ways: (*a*) by squeezing more agricultural surplus; (*b*) by slowing down the rate of investment in the non-farm sector and in basic infrastructure; and (*c*) by obtaining foreign loans and grants. Of these three sources, foreign loans and grants are, he asserts, the most advantageous, or least expensive. He further states that the growth rate of agricultural production in a developing country in the early stages must be raised high enough to meet its expanding food requirements. For this to happen, he argues, the pull exerted on agriculture through higher market prices will not be enough: agriculture must be pushed, and pushed hard, by a strategy emphasising the use of modern technology and supporting infrastructure and services.

In our opinion, Cochrane's model is a good exposition of the process of agricultural development, and of the possibilities and limitations of agricultural development as a catalyst for overall national development. I would like to add two elements to Cochrane's model, and these are: (*a*) population control measures; and (*b*) the international economic and political environment. No strategy of agricultural and national development would ever succeed in the absence of appropriate population control measures, and a congenial international economic and political environment. Whereas a developing country can always do something to control its exploding population, the creation of a suitable international environment is the responsibility of the world community and its organisations.

Gunnar Myrdal's Thesis of 'Spread and Backwash' Effects

Gunnar Myrdal (1957) highlights low levels of income in most of the non-Soviet countries in the world, and international disparities in income, wealth and investment. Myrdal finds the theoretical approach (automatic self-stabilisation) inadequate to grapple with the problems of inequality. In his opinion, in the normal case, a change does not call forth countervailing changes, but, instead, supporting changes which move the system in the same direction as the first change, but much faster—the principle of circular and cumulative causation. As a result of such circular causation, a social process tends to move faster. A social process can be stopped by introducing new exogenous changes in the system. He elaborates this with an example of the African-American problem in the USA. Two factors, namely, White prejudices causing discrimination against the African-Americans, and their 'low plane of living' are mutually interrelated. Their low standard of living is kept suppressed by discrimination by the Whites. On the other hand, the African-Americans' poverty, ignorance, superstition, slum dwellings, health deficiencies and their supposedly unclean appearance, bad odour, disorderly conduct, unstable family relations and criminality, stimulate and feed the antipathy of the Whites for them. Both these factors mutually 'cause' each other.

He also emphasises the role of non-economic factors in development, and highlights the backwash effects of growth brought out by the free play of market forces. The clustering of labour, capital, goods and services in certain localities and regions leave the remaining areas, mostly rural, more or less in the backwaters and accentuate regional inequality. Concentration of firms, capital, and talented individuals in certain localities (growth points) at the expense of surrounding areas (the backwash) lowers the level of economic development below what it would have been, if growth points had never emerged.

Against the backwash effects there are, however, certain centrifugal 'spread effects' of expansionary momentum from the centres of economic expansion to other regions. Empirical evidence shows that 'backwash effects' are neutralised by 'spread effects' only at a high level of development. This is one of the reasons why rapid sustained progress becomes an almost automatic process, once a country has reached a high level of development. At low levels of development, the 'spread effects' are either very weak, or are just strong enough to cancel the 'backwash effects', and the result in both cases is poverty and stagnation.

Similarly, at the international level, trade, capital movement and migration have strong backwash effects on the developing countries. Examples can easily be cited of developing countries whose cultures have been impoverished as a result of the establishment of trading contacts with the outside world.

The Human Capital Model of Development

This model emphasises the importance of human capital investment in the process of economic and social development. By human capital, we mean acquired mental and physical ability through education, training, health care, and pursuit of some spiritual methods like *yoga* or meditation. The acquisition of human capital is largely through the investment of human effort and money. The simplest and most important of this type of model is a schooling model, which relates economic development to schooling. The classical and neoclassical economists did not explicitly include the quality of human resources in their theoretical frameworks; labour was taken to include both physical and mental effort (Alex 1983: 3–12). It was Theodore Schultz (1964) who elaborated the concept of human capital, and explicitly considered the investment in human capital as an important determinant of economic development. Subsequently, quite a few other scholars got interested in the economics of human capital, especially the economics of education, and a large number of studies were conducted on the subject. The model considers the totality of human potential, and emphasises the need to harness it for the good of the people. It respects people's culture and religion, and social values and structures.

The human capital approach to rural development is based on the following two assumptions, which have been ignored in the classical theory of development:

1. Human physical and mental capabilities are partly inherited and partly acquired, and they vary from individual to individual, i.e., the classical assumption of homogeneous labour force does not hold.

2. Human capital directly contributes to development through its positive effect on productivity, and through reduction in resistance to the diffusion of new technologies in the economy, especially in the rural sector.

Thus, this model shifts the emphasis from physical capital formation to human capital formation, and from industrial development to rural development, as a basis for overall development. This model seems most appropriate for labour-surplus developing countries like India, where a lot of underdeveloped human resources having high potential for development exist. Besides, human resources are renewable, and hence inexhaustible. Therefore, human capital can be substituted for exhaustible non-renewable physical capital in the process of development, and thus relax the constraint on development imposed by inadequacy of physical capital to a large extent. As a matter of fact, strategies for development of the tertiary (service) sector, which is the fastest growing sector all over the world, requires skilled, experienced and innovative human resources for their success. And this is the path that India should choose to bring about overall sustainable development. Human resource development through nutrition, health care, appropriate education, training and empowerment deserves the highest priority now.

Gandhian Model of Rural Development

Mohandas Karamchand Gandhi, popularly known as Mahatma Gandhi, played the leading role in securing for India political independence from the British Raj, through organising and mobilising Indian people from all walks of life in a peaceful and non-violent manner. He is therefore rightly called the 'Father of the Nation'. Gandhiji's approach to India's rural development was holistic and people-centred. It was rooted in his conviction in the tenets of truth, non-violence and the goodness of human-beings. Influenced as he was by Tolstoy, Ruskin and the teachings of the Gita, he placed more emphasis on moral and spiritual values than economic motives as a means of overall development.

Values Underlying the Model

The Gandhian Model of rural development is based on the following values and premises:

1. Real India is found not in its cities, but in its villages.
2. The revival of villages is possible only when the villagers are exploited no more. Exploitation of villagers by city dwellers was 'violence', in Gandhiji's opinion.
3. Simple living and high thinking, implying voluntary reduction of materialistic wants, and pursuit of moral and spiritual principles of life.
4. Dignity of labour: everyone must earn his bread by physical labour, and one who labours must necessarily get his subsistence.
5. Preference to the use of indigenous (*swadeshi*) products, services and institutions.
6. Balance between the ends and the means: Gandhiji believed that non-violence and truth could not be sustained unless a balance between the ends and the means was maintained.

Principal Components of the Model

The principal components of the Gandhian Model are as follows:

Self-sufficient Village Economy

Gandhiji's concept of self-sufficiency was not a narrow one, nor was it that of selfishness or arrogance. He realised the need for villagers to get those things from outside the village, which they could not produce in the village.

Decentralisation

Gandhiji believed that human happiness with mental and moral development should be the supreme goal of society, and that this goal should be achieved through decentralisation of political and economic powers.

Khadi and Village Industries

For Gandhiji, *khadi* was an instrument of decentralisation of production and distribution of the basic necessities of life, and of ensuring 'work to all'. He also favoured the promotion of other village industries, such as hand grinding, hand pounding, soap making, paper making, metal making, oilseed crushing, tanning, etc. He advocated the use of manual labour and opposed the introduction of machines, fearing that they would displace human labour. But he appreciated the role of new technologies if they were appropriate, indigenous, and did not affect the level of employment and standard of living.

Implementing Strategy

Gandhiji prescribed the following institutional structure and instruments for implementing his strategy, namely, panchayati raj, cooperatives, trusteeship, and *Nai Taleem* (New Education). A brief description of each of these instruments follows.

Panchayati Raj

Gandhiji envisaged that each village in India would be a republic, where the village panchayat would have the full power of managing its affairs, including defence. He expected the panchayat to perform the legislative, executive and judicial functions necessary for smooth functioning of the village economy. Various developmental activities such as education, health and sanitation would also be taken up by the village panchayat. It is good, and in conformity with Gandhiji's views, that India now has made panchayati raj institutions statutory bodies by passing the 73rd (Constitution) Amendment Act, 1992. It is hoped that Gandhiji's dream of local self-governance through village panchayats would now be fulfilled.

Cooperatives

Gandhiji saw a great virtue in cooperation as an instrument of rural development. He assigned specific roles to cooperatives in the field of agriculture, commending the promotion of cooperative farming and thereby preventing further fragmentation of landholdings. He also advocated the establishment of other types of cooperatives, such as credit cooperatives, weavers and spinners cooperatives and dairy cooperatives. In this matter also, we have perhaps lived up to the expectations of Gandhiji. India now has the world's largest network of cooperatives, which occupy an important place in India's rural economy. The Operation Flood programme is a living example of what cooperatives can do to promote agricultural and rural development in India. There is, therefore, need for us to adopt the cooperative path to rural development, as advocated by Gandhiji.

Trusteeship

Gandhiji considered trusteeship an instrument of transforming the capitalist order of society into an egalitarian one. In his opinion, all the land belonged to God, that is, the community, and therefore he advocated that land and other natural resources should be collectively owned by, and operated for, the welfare of the community. Landlords should merely be trustees of land and other natural resources and capital assets. He saw in the principle of trusteeship a non-violent method of persuading landowners to donate their land voluntarily for community welfare purposes, and of avoiding class conflicts.

Nai Taleem

Gandhiji had no faith in modern education, which emphasised only literacy and acquisition of information. In his opinion, modern education was 'debauchery of the mind'. Hence, he developed a new system of appropriate education and training which he called *Nai Taleem*. He believed that *Nai Taleem* would help develop the full potential of children and adults, through full development of their bodies, minds and spirits. He wanted to see *Nai Taleem* to be self-supporting and practice-oriented. It is unfortunate that India has not yet geared its education system to the needs of the country, and that is why its human resources remain underdeveloped and less productive, as compared to other countries which have given the highest priority to education and training. However, of late, universalisation of elementary education and total literacy programmes have received higher priority than in the past, with a view to achieve the national objective of 'Education for All' by the year 2000. Similarly, vocational education at the post-high school (10th class) level is now being considered as an alternative to the present traditional general education. This shows that we have now realised the relevance of Gandhiji's *Nai Taleem*.

The Gandhian model, like any other development model, has both its proponents and opponents. The proponents argue that under the prevailing sociocultural and economic conditions in India, the Gandhian model is still relevant, and is the only alternative available for bringing about equitable and sustainable rural development. They assert that panchayati raj institutions and cooperatives are still as relevant as when they were in Gandhiji's days, and that the role of appropriate education cannot be overemphasised even in the present Indian context. The critics argue that Gandhiji's ideals of swadeshi, voluntary curtailment of one's wants, trusteeship, self-sufficient villages, and use of manual labour in preference to machines sound obsolete these days, particularly in the wake of India's new economic policy characterised by privatisation, liberalisation, and globalisation. As a matter of fact, by adopting an economic growth-oriented development path and by following the Western model of industrialisation, both under the influence of Jawaharlal Nehru, India had abandoned the Gandhian model long ago, they assert further. To conclude, we could say that Gandhiji wanted India to travel east, but India decided to travel west, and we know 'the twain never meet'. Now, we have gone probably too far in the wrong direction, and turning around and travelling eastwards is perhaps not a feasible course of action. But, then, nothing is impossible, and if there is a will, there is a way.

Development Theories from Other Social Sciences

Development is a complex process which is affected by both economic and non-economic factors. The importance of non-economic factors in development was duly recognised by the Classical school. John Stuart Mill thought that non-economic factors, like beliefs, habits of thought, customs and institutions, play an important role in economic development, and he attributed the backwardness of underdeveloped countries to the despotic and anti-progressive character of their customs, institutions, and beliefs.

Boeke (1953) attempts to explain underdevelopment in terms of sociological dualism, which he defines as 'the clashing of an imported social system with an indigenous social system of another style'. On the basis of his analysis, largely based on the Indonesian experience, he concludes that the kindest thing the Western world can do for developing countries is to leave them alone; any effort to develop them along Western lines can only hasten their retrogression and decay. The acceptance of the dualism leads to two policy conclusions: (*a*) as a rule, one policy for the whole country is not possible; and (*b*) what is beneficial for one section of society may be harmful for another. An appraisal of Boeke's theory would reveal that whereas there can be no question about the existence of dualism, its explanation lies not in the nature of society as Boeke perceives it, but in economic and technological terms. This is proved by the fact that not all efforts to promote development in the developing countries through technical and capital assistance from the West have been in vain.

For example, in India, a large part of the credit for bringing about the 'Green Revolution' goes to the United States Agency for International Development (USAID) that helped India, both financially and technically, in setting up modern land-grant type state agricultural universities in the 1960s, and trained its agricultural scientists in American land-grant agricultural universities. Similarly, the Operation Flood programme that is credited with modernising India's dairy industry, also benefited a lot from food aid in the form of skimmed milk powder and butter oil, first from the World Food Programme of FAO, and then from the European Economic Community (EEC).

One may reject the theory of sociological dualism advanced by Boeke, and still consider sociological, cultural and psychological factors important in economic development. Indeed, one may say that all economists who have specialised in economic development recognise the importance of the interplay of these factors with economic factors. In the words of Meier and Baldwin (1957: 355), 'The psychological and sociological requirements for development are as important as the economic requirements. They deserve full consideration in their own right.' Relatively few economists, however, have had the courage to attempt a systematic theory of development which would incorporate strategic sociological, cultural, and psychological factors. Outstanding among these few are David McClelland and Everett Hagen (Higgins 1966: Ch. 13).

McClelland's 'Need-for-Achievement Motivation' (N-Ach) theory seeks to establish a relationship between N-Ach and economic development. His theory rests on two propositions: (*a*) that group differences in the average level of certain motives, such as N-Ach, predict differences in the rate of economic growth; and (*b*) that certain motive combinations predispose individuals to act like successful business entrepreneurs, who have played key roles in all previous economic development. On the basis of his studies and analyses, he concludes that if we are to promote economic growth, it is necessary to first change the values and motives of individuals. This, in his opinion, can be done by: (*a*) persuasion or education; (*b*) introducing changes in the social system; and (*c*) early character training. Of these three, the third is by all odds the one most likely to succeed. For in this way, values can be in-built from the very beginning. Early character training can he imparted by a corps of specially qualified nursery and primary school teachers carefully selected for the purpose.

Thus, McClelland's analysis leads to the conclusion that a take-off into economic development requires a large number of individuals with the entrepreneurial motivation complex, and particularly with high N-Ach, and for this a long period of time is required to establish psychological preconditions.

Concluding Remarks

We could, from this analysis, conclude that although there is no universally valid theory of rural development available so far, the various paradigms and hypotheses of development reviewed in this chapter furnish many valuable insights into the processes and determinants of rural development. Using an eclectic approach, we could extract relevant elements from those paradigms, and synthesise them into an operational framework of rural development suited to our times and circumstances. There is a set of elements/factors that is common to most of the paradigms of development. The common set comprises natural resources, new technology, capital accumulation and investment, educated, technically trained, enterprising and motivated human resources with values and ethos congenial to rural development, and an appropriate institutional and organisational framework. In my opinion, a people-centred strategy, akin to the Gandhian model, would be the most appropriate paradigm of sustainable rural development for India. India is rich in human resources. This has been amply demonstrated by what Indians have achieved in all fields of human endeavour, including science and technology. What is needed now is a long term policy for development of human resources through education, training, health care, and empowerment and creation of a congenial socio-economic, institutional (including legal), and political environment for the fullest possible utilisation of the vast, untapped reservoirs of human power and ingenuity. Human resources are inexhaustible and renewable, and hence the only resources which can sustain development for ever. Our axiom in the twenty-first century should be: Human beings are both the end and the means of development.

5
Determinants of Rural Development

Barriers to sustainable development.

Introduction

The factors affecting rural development favourably or adversely are so varied, and have combined over time in so many different ways, that it is very difficult to isolate a small number of crucial variables or determinants. There are many physical, technological, economic, sociocultural, institutional, organisational and political factors that affect the level and pace of rural development. These factors operate at all levels—household, village, district, state, nation, and the world as a whole. Depending upon how they are managed, these factors can have both favourable and adverse effects on development. For instance, if the human resources of a country are not properly developed by proper nutrition, health care, education and training, and are not productively utilised, these resources become liabilities and obstacles to development. But if they are properly developed and utilised, then they become great assets and major factors contributing to development. Knowledge about the nature and magnitude of the impact of various determinants on rural development is necessary for rural development managers to be able to use these factors to achieve their goals efficiently and effectively. This chapter is devoted to identifying the major determinants of rural development, and examining their role in promoting rural development.

Rural development is characterised by multiple goals, and as has been discussed in Chapter 3, there is no single index or indicator which can adequately capture the multifaceted nature of rural development. At the same time, unless we can measure the phenomenon of rural development,

Figure 5.1
Determinants of Rural Development

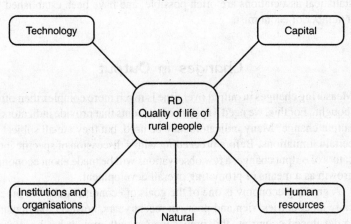

we are unlikely to know much about the quantitative impact of the factors that influence it.

In the absence of a single index of rural development, we shall use change in output as a proxy measure, and discuss the role of various factors that appear to us, on an a priori basis, as important determinants of this measure. Let us assume that change in output is a function of changes in natural resources, employment, capital, technology and institutions and organisations.

This can be expressed in notational form as follows:

$$\Delta Y = f(\Delta R, \Delta N, \Delta N \Delta K, \Delta T, \Delta O),$$

where Y = output, R = natural resources, N = employment, K = capital, T = technology, O = organisational and institutional framework and delta (Δ) means 'change in'.

This equation states that changes in output will be functions of changes in those variables appearing on the right hand side of the equation, i.e., natural resources, employment, capital, technology, and organisational and institutional framework (Figure 5.1). The variables might be called the 'instrument variables' of economic growth or change in output. Of course, it is not easy to determine the causal relationship between Y and these instrument variables. All change simultaneously, and the contribution of a single variable is difficult to isolate, but at least some statistical associations are often possible, and have been established by a number of economists.

Changes in Output

Measuring changes in output over time is much more complex than often thought. For this, we need a system of accounts that provide indicators of output change. Many indicators may be used, but they are all subject to certain limitations. Before proceeding with a discussion of specific indicators of output change, a few observations will be made about economic growth as a means of promoting overall development.

A growing economy is one of the goals of economic policy in practically all countries, rich and poor. In recent years, however, particularly in developed countries, this preoccupation with growth has been challenged. It is now pointed out that growth should not be considered as an end in itself, but only as a *means* of promoting development. In fact, it is now widely believed that economic growth produces undesirable as well as desirable consequences. It has been alleged that our preoccupation with producing bigger, better and faster objects to satisfy our insatiable appetites and whims is a kind of 'growthmania'. The implication is that we have been so concerned about increases in some indicators of income or product, that we have neglected some of the side effects of growth which are the causes of the deteriorating quality of life of people.

Before growth can be considered an end of social policy, it must be demonstrable that economic activity will enhance the level of well-being of at least some human beings. The national income accounts have been designed to provide indicators of aggregate output or, alternatively, on the other side of the accounts, aggregate income to owners of the factors of production. Some of these indicators are gross national product, net national product, national income, personal income and personal disposable income.

If we must have a single indicator which shows the growth that has occurred, that indicator must have a way of meaningfully aggregating physically unlike goods and services, such as wheat, milk, houses, clothes, steel, aeroplanes, banking and insurance. The national income indicators accomplish this by converting these physical units of output into monetary values by multiplying the physical units by market prices. The monetary values of output are thus comparable and additive.

This valuation procedure is open to one basic question. Do market prices used as weights accurately reflect the contributions of the respective units of output to aggregate income? The answer seems to be that if product and factor markets are perfectly competitive, and no externalities are present in either consumption or production of the commodities being priced, they do. If the demand for a product is less than perfectly elastic, however, the additions to income due to increase in the output of the product will be reflected by marginal revenue rather than by price, because as output expands, the price of all units sold will decline. Furthermore, if externalities are present in consumption of the product, the market demand price will not reflect the 'social' value of the product as it is consumed. By the same token, if externalities are present in production of the product, the product supply price will not reflect the complete 'social' productivity of the factors of production. Externalities may be positive or negative, and when they can be shown to exist and can be meaningfully quantified, valuation adjustments may be made to reflect their significance.

An even more serious problem relates to the statistical coverage of the traditional national income indicators. What is needed, of course, is an indicator that captures all changes in the level of output. As a rule, the income accounts provide good coverage of those goods and services which pass through the market, but do not include many of those which do not. This means that the statistical coverage becomes more comprehensive as the economy becomes more complex, and the market expands into more and more areas of the economy. If so, the consequence is that the real output of a less developed country is probably understated more by the income accounts than the real output of an advanced country.

Economists and others have recognised that a gross measure of output, such as the real gross national product, is not the best indicator of the aggregate size of the growth-producing mechanism called the economy. The reason is that part of gross output is needed to maintain the stock of capital which is part of the productive base of the economy. Some of the category called 'gross investment' constitutes net addition to the capital stock, and should thus be included in any measure of net productive capacity. But a substantial part of gross investment is simply replacement capital, called 'capital depreciation allowance' in the income account. Gross product less capital depreciation allowance is net product. We would argue that change in real net product is the best indicator of economic growth.

Although we cannot measure them in the income accounts, it is important to remember that other factors of production have precise parallels to the capital depreciation allowance. Labour sometimes depreciates as production occurs, and maintenance of the stock of human capital at a certain base requires investment in training, schooling, health, and nutrition. Resources taken from the natural environment are depleted, and to that extent should be netted out of gross productivity figures in an exactly analogous fashion as with capital. The point is equally relevant with respect to the quality as well as the quantity of the factors. If the quality of the stock of human capital and of natural resources declines over time, latent productivity of the economy declines, and these deleterious changes should be subtracted from the net product of the system. Contrarily, if the quality of the factor stock improves due to technical advances and increases in knowledge, this latent capacity to produce should be added to the net product actually produced in a given time period.

Perhaps the most devastating limitation of our productivity accounts is the manner in which we deal with negative final products. These are those final outputs of production which cause disutility to human beings, and which usually cause deterioration in the natural environment in the form of waste residues and environmental degradation. They also take the form of external diseconomies, such as crowding, congestion and crime. Before a true estimate of the effects of growth on human well-being can be assessed, therefore, these negative influences on growth should be netted out from the positive ones.

Changes in the Utilisation of Natural Resources

By a natural resource we mean any product, thing or circumstance found by man in his natural environment that he may in some way utilise for his own benefit. In this sense, the resources provided by nature include air, climate, soils, water, plants, animals, mineral ores, mineral oil, coal, natural gas, solar radiation, and certain amenities which can be used for tourism. As time goes by, the world's resource pattern changes, not because nature's basic provision alters, but because of changes in what constitutes a resource. Natural resources can be classified into two categories: non-renewable or stock resources, such as metal ores, mineral oil and coal deposits and renewable or flow resources such as solar radiation,

Figure 5.2
Role of Mother Nature/Environment in Economic Growth

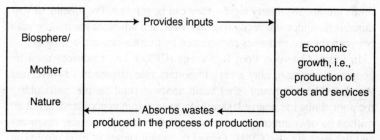

animal and plant species, and winds, among others. This distinction is very important from the point of view of policies for resource development, conservation and utilisation.

Mother Nature performs two important functions in the process of economic growth, namely, providing inputs to production processes, and assimilating the wastes generated in the process of production (Figure 5.2). Since Planet Earth is finite, closed, and non-growing, there is a natural limit to both these critical functions, i.e., the inputs provisioning and waste assimilating capacities of our planet are both limited. This means that one cannot go on increasing the production of goods and services using natural resources forever, i.e., there are ecological/natural limits to economic growth, hence it cannot be sustained forever. Sustainable development requires that in the process of economic growth, we maintain our natural resources and environment intact, and use/harvest only that quantity which is regenerated naturally, i.e., we live on the 'flows', and keep the 'stock' of natural resources and the environment intact. However, we would like to add that it is now possible to augment— through appropriate technological and management interventions—the natural flows/harvest of products of nature.

For example, fish catches can be increased sustainably through artificial feeding and breeding; crop yields can be increased through application of balanced organic and inorganic fertilisers, biopesticides and scientific soil and water management; and forests can be rejuvenated faster and their natural productivity increased through application of fertilisers and water. Thus, the carrying capacity of our biosphere in terms of the population of living beings is, to some extent, amenable to augmentation through technological and managerial intervention. Therefore, contrary to what growthmaniacs and technocrats believe, there are limits to economic growth, and also, contrary to what ecologists assert, the limits are not absolutely rigid—they can be relaxed. Proponents of sustainable development recognise this truth, and advocate the middle path between the two extremes represented by technocrats and ecologists.

In India, Common Pool Resources (CPRs), i.e., resources used by people in common, play a very important role as sources of food, fuel wood, fodder and many other basic needs of rural people, particularly the poor. India has nearly 100 million ha of common pool land, about 30 million ha of common pool forests, and the bulk of its water resources and fisheries are also CPRs. One of the major causes of rural poverty in India is the lack of access of the poor to privately-owned natural resources and natural CPRs. With the growing commercial exploitation of natural CPRs, the rural poor people find it difficult to meet their basic requirements. Depletion of CPRs of land, forests and water has increased the misery and drudgery of the rural poor, particularly women, who now have to spend a lot of their energy and time in fetching water, fuel wood and fodder from faraway places. Restoration and judicious management of natural CPRs is essential for improving the well-being of the rural poor, as also for improving the quality of the environment (Singh 1994: 16–20).

At any level of economic development, utilisation of domestically available natural resources constitutes the bedrock of an economy. The quantity and quality of available natural resources along with the intensity and efficiency of their use determine to a considerable extent, the level and pace of the economic development of a nation. Poverty of natural resources does not, however, exclude a high level of economic development, as is shown by the examples of Denmark, Switzerland, Israel, Hong Kong and Japan. These countries have compensated for the lack of natural resources by appropriate technologies, institutions and organisations and highly developed human resources. India is relatively well-endowed with natural resources, but has not been able to develop and utilise them fully and judiciously for the benefit of its people. Hence, the low level of agricultural and rural development in India.

It is almost invariably true that the poorer a country is, the greater the percentage of its income that goes to the owners of natural resources, and thus the greater the importance of natural resources to economic development. This can be easily demonstrated in the case of food production. In India, about 70 per cent of the community's income is spent on food. Of the total cost of production, approximately 30 per cent is paid out to the owners of land in the form of rent. Thus, approximately

21 per cent of the community's total income is spent on land services alone. This means that much of the capital wealth in India is held in the form of land. Who owns this land makes a tremendous difference, since economic, political and social privileges also tend to be associated with land ownership. In a developed country such as the USA, on the other hand, about 10 per cent of the total income is spent on food, and approximately 20 per cent of the cost of producing food goes towards land rent. Thus, only a little over 2 per cent of the total community income goes to the owners of land. Land ownership, then, has far less economic and political significance in the USA than in India.

The same point is relevant with respect to the production of other products that depend primarily on natural resources. If capital is scarce and labour tends to be unskilled, then land and natural resources of other kinds tend to be very significant in production, and their ownership becomes an important social issue.

Changes in Employment

The level of employment is best considered from the viewpoint of the long run and the short run. Over the long run, employment is related primarily to population growth. The correspondence between employment and population growth is especially close in societies where human beings enter the labour force at a young age, where much of the labour is utilised in agricultural pursuits, and is, therefore, likely to be utilised even if underemployed. The higher the rate of population growth, the larger will be the amount of labour used relative to the other factors of production.

The important point in this connection, however, is that it takes time and investment to get a fully productive human being. If the time is shortened by the necessity for children to work, the result tends to be less productive labour over the long run. On the other hand, if work is postponed and children go to school, the burden on public institutions such as the educational establishments becomes greater, and the net consumption embodied in per capita incomes is reduced, as resources go into institutions for training and maintenance, rather than for consumption. Thus, per capita incomes are temporarily reduced until people eventually get into the labour force, at which time per capita incomes are increased if the labour is productive enough to compensate for the time which is spent on schooling and training.

In the short run, on the other hand, employment can be increased by providing more opportunities for people to work. This may be accomplished by offering favourable wages, which attract previously unemployed workers into the labour force, and by a healthy economic environment where jobs are more plentiful.

Research undertaken in developed and developing countries of the world reveals that for an increase in output, the quality of labour is more important than the quantity. A clear picture emerges if one looks at the experience of different countries. No country with an educated, technically trained labour force is poor, and no country with a predominantly illiterate, untrained labour force is rich. In general, the quality of the labour force is much more critical in economic development than is the availability of natural resources. Japan is a country which has almost no mineral or energy resources but has high economic productivity because of a highly literate, trained and efficient working population.

It has also been seen that investment in education and training produces very high internal rates of return in economic output. Especially high are the returns to basic literacy. The rate of returns to investment in schooling is in the neighbourhood of 50 per cent per year in many rich countries, and in developing countries like India, the rate of return to primary schooling is even higher. Any poor country that wants to develop could do no better than use its scarce resources in schools, technical education, training and management.

Another point to note about people and their importance in the development process is that their values and attitudes must be conducive to development. If development is to occur, an increase of income and wealth, held either privately or publicly, must be one of the dominant goals in life. That is, people must have a desire to acquire, accumulate, or consume at increasing levels. If not, development is practically impossible. There is no denying that it was this desire that produced Western technology, money and financial intermediaries, private property, and an economic structure based on free contract and exchange. Some would argue that even political liberty, which increased social mobility, which in turn contributed to development, resulted from the dominance of pecuniary considerations in the hierarchy of privately-held goals.

India is a labour surplus country. According to the 1991 Population Census, India's labour force comprised 314 million main and marginal workers, of whom 249 million (79.3 per cent) were in the rural sector. The quality of the rural labour force is also poor in terms of skills, education, training, values and attitudes. The literacy rate for the rural population in India in 1991 was as low as 36 per cent. There is a positive correlation between the literacy rate and real per capita gross domestic product. For a sample of 43 developing countries, the simple correlation between these two variables was 0.48. The poor quality of the rural labour force, in conjunction with very low per capita availability of capital, explains to a large extent the low productivity and hence low per capita incomes in India's rural sector.

An Increase in Capital

Most development economists from developed Western countries consider capital to be the key instrument of economic development. The Harrod–Domar model represents a typical example of this school of thought. In this model, capital accumulation plays a crucial role in the process of economic growth, as the rate of economic growth is expressed as the product of the savings rate and output-capital ratio. Capital formation is, therefore, an important prerequisite of economic development. Much of new technology, such as high yielding seeds, chemical fertilisers and pesticides, tractors, combine harvesters and food processing plants, is embodied in capital. Increases in the capital stock lead to increases in the marginal productivity of labour which, in turn, generally enhances wage rates.

Capital can be classified in various ways. Long-term capital is embodied in improvements in land, machinery, equipment, basic infrastructure and other long-lived forms of capital, while operating capital exists in the form of seeds, fertilisers, fuel and other raw materials which are used up annually in the production process.

Moreover, capital may also be classified according to whether it is owned publicly or privately. Private capital is managed by the individual entrepreneur, and examples are those listed above in the examples of long-term and operating capital. Public capital, on the other hand, is society's investment in infrastructure, such as roads, schools, hospitals, national defence, and various government establishments. Private capital is, of course, acquired by individuals by their own decisions to consume less than they earn. Public capital, on the other hand, is produced by joint action through political processes, but can also come into being because society earns more than it consumes. For promoting rural development, both private and public capital investments are necessary. At present, both types of investments in India fall short of the requirement, and hence the level and pace of rural development have been affected adversely.

Looking at capital formation from the vantage point of the economy, capital resources can be acquired in one of two ways: by domestic saving, or by foreign aid. In most countries, domestic savings can be acquired from three sources. The first is from private citizens who consume less than their incomes, and make the difference available in the form of investment to the economy. In rich countries, people save as a matter of course in their attempt to provide security against various contingencies and thus, the saving takes the form of insurance premiums, retirement annuities, bank accounts, etc. Since these choices are made voluntarily, people consider their well-being enhanced in the process of saving, and therefore, no deprivation is incurred. In poor countries, on the other hand, saving is often painful, because people live so close to the edge of hunger and disease, and need all their income for consumption alone. As a result, savings are usually meagre, and if society needs more than are available by private decisions to save, then saving must be forced by inflation.

Second, savings can be acquired from corporations, which as a rule, in an effort to expand, take some of their earnings and plough them back into the firm for additional capital formation. In rich countries, where corporations are numerous, large, and powerful, this form of savings and the concomitant capital formation is extremely important.

Last, governments can acquire resources for purposes of capital formation through taxes and inflation. Income tax, property tax, excise tax, value-added tax, all have their own advantages and disadvantages. However, space will not permit an evaluation.

Inflation is also a form of taxation. The government causes inflation by increasing the money supply, which creates excess demand for goods and services. This results in price rises, and the average rise in a composite index of prices is known as inflation. With the money created by running printing presses or selling securities, the government buys goods and services. These may take the form of investment capital. Inflation is really a tax on cash balances, since those individuals and organisations in the economy who hold cash balances see their purchasing power eroded by inflation. There is, thus, a transfer of wealth from those who hold money in the form of cash balances to those (in this case the government) who obtain the resources through the creation of money. It is possible, of course, to analyse and evaluate the efficiency and equity effects of inflation vis-à-vis other forms of taxation to raise funds for government use. But this is not within the purview of this chapter.

Of course, saving is only one prong in the process of capital formation. Somehow the saving generated in the economy must be made available to the investors, those who actually produce the capital formation. If the primary reliance is given to private savings, then an organisational base must be available to make the transfer of funds to investors. In most countries, these organisations are the commercial banks, savings and loan associations, insurance companies and credit cooperatives. Likewise, if government funds are available for investment, whether they come from external aid, taxation or money creation, there must be an institutional base to transfer the resources to investors. In many countries (including India), these take the form of central banks and industrial and agricultural banks.

Foreign aid has been used extensively since World War II as a form of transfer of international capital from one country to another. It should be pointed out, however, that many of the advanced countries of today received much of their development capital from external sources. The United States and Canada were aided tremendously in the take-off phase of their development by foreign capital shipments, particularly from the UK. There is one major difference, however, between that period and the present day. The bulk of the development capital that fuelled the take-off in the US and Canada came from private foreign sources. Profit opportunities were unusually high, and this attracted capital which was seeking these profits. It goes without saying that since the capital transfer was made voluntarily, both borrowers and lenders were benefited by it.

There is also much private capital that goes abroad today. Large international firms have established branches in many countries including India. However, large quantities of financial resources are being transferred through international organisations, such as the World Bank, the Asian Development Bank, the Inter-American Development Bank, and through foreign aid from government to government. Again, as long as the transfers are mutually beneficial and voluntary, there is a lot to be gained by both the grantor and the grantee. Since a large amount of international capital is available through grants or low-cost loans, the recipients do not worry too much about the economic feasibility of projects utilising these funds. This is needless waste of scarce resources. International grants and low-cost loans should be administered just as tightly and economically as high-cost loans. The real cost to the economy of using these funds, regardless of source or terms, are the foregone opportunities of using the resources in their most productive alternative. These capital funds should be allocated to uses where they generate the greatest productivity. Planning should be just as tight and rigorous with foreign aid resources, in terms of determining their use in the economy, as would be the case if the resources were generated through domestic saving.

India's rural sector is starved of capital, and this is perhaps one of the most serious constraints on rural development. The rate of capital formation in the rural sector has been low vis-à-vis the rate required for achieving a higher level of rural development. Furthermore, much of the surplus generated in the sector is siphoned off to the urban sector for a variety of reasons, including lack of institutional arrangements for mopping up small savings and providing incentives to small savers.

Changes in Technology

In all likelihood, technological advance is the most important factor that accounts for economic development. In many ways, it is the sine qua non of development, that is, it *is* development. Studies in the advanced countries have shown that increases in natural resources, employment, and capital have accounted for less than one-half of the increases in output over time. The bulk of growth must, therefore, be accounted for by qualitative rather than quantitative increases in the factors of production. In essence, this is what technological advance is—an improvement in the processes of production, that produces increases in output per unit of input. It is improvements in knowledge and know-how; it is improved skills; it is utilising better machinery and equipment, all of which combine to increase productivity.

Many students of development, notably Hayami and Ruttan (1970), Schultz (1964) and Rostow, have constructed theories of development which have technological advance at the very centre of concern. Schultz has argued that the transition from traditional to modern agriculture is essentially one of utilising modern inputs, which are defined as those that are technologically advanced. In Rostow's scheme, once the static stage of traditional life has been disturbed, society passes through the later stages of: (*a*) establishment of the preconditions for growth; (*b*) take-off; (*c*) drive to maturity; and (*d*) mass consumption. During the period of establishment of the preconditions for growth, the insights of modern science begin to be translated into new production functions. This is just another way of saying that technological advance is occurring.

Schumpeter distinguishes between two classes of influences upon the dynamic evolution of an economy, viz., (*a*) the effects of changes in factor availability, which he calls the 'growth' component; and (*b*) the effects of technological and social changes, which he refers to as 'development' or 'evolution'. In his view, development covers five combinations.

1. The introduction of a new commodity.
2. The introduction of a new method of production.
3. The opening of a new market.
4. The conquest of a new source of supply of raw materials or half-manufactured goods.
5. The reorganisation of an industry, like the creation of a monopoly position or breaking down a monopoly situation.

In Schumpeter's model of economic development, the entrepreneur is the central figure. He revolutionises the pattern of production by exploiting inventions, by exploiting untried technological possibilities for producing new commodities, by producing old commodities in new ways, and so on. For entrepreneurial activity to flourish, the capitalist rationality and bourgeois institutions are important prerequisites. Schumpeter also assigned an important role to credit as a means of enabling entrepreneurs to obtain productive resources and to carry out innovation. He emphasises the importance of innovation in generating business cycles. In Schumpeter's opinion, there is no limit to the increase in the rate of output per head.

The critical question is, of course, how to promote a high rate of technical change. In the first place, the general economic climate must be conducive to innovation and knowledge-building. As a rule, if incentives exist for individuals to innovate, they will. A country which has a sizeable and educated middle class can rely largely on the profit motive to push inventors, scientists and entrepreneurs to undertake technological advance. In conservative traditional societies, however, public institutions must also play a very large role. Educational institutions are crucial at all levels. So are the experiment stations and the extension services. Empirical studies from both rich and poor countries clearly demonstrate that rates of return from public investment in these knowledge-building institutions and activities are very high. Over the long run, no country can afford to neglect these institutions, which act as agents of change in producing and implementing technical change.

Prior to 1965, the outlook for agriculture in India was discouraging. But the post-1965 era was characterised by a marked spurt in the use of modern inputs, like high yielding seeds, chemical fertilisers, plant protection chemicals, and improved farm machines, tools and equipment.

In his 1970 presidential address to the Indian Economic Association, M. L. Dantwala (1970: 165–92) reviewed various economic, technological, institutional and organisational factors which had been given credit for the so-called 'technical breakthrough' or 'Green Revolution' in Indian agriculture. He concluded that land tenure, credit, marketing, extension services, education, relative prices, taxes and subsidies were all of minor significance when compared with new technology. He arrived at his conclusion by a process of elimination: technology was the only causal factor which changed significantly between the pre-1965 stagnation and the post-1965 Green Revolution. What he did not appreciate was the fact that both the introduction and spread of new technology were facilitated by the efforts of various institutions and organisations, including agricultural universities, and provision of extension education services, credit, marketing and subsidies. It is, however, true that new (and appropriate) technology is a necessary condition for economic growth. But new technology unsupported by appropriate institutions and organisations cannot bring about a transformation of traditional agriculture.

In 1995 India had access to the latest available new technology in the field of crop production, but still its average paddy yield was only about 2,879 kg/ha, as compared to 6,017 kg/ha for China. What are the factors that can explain this vast yield differential? Certainly natural resources and knowledge of new technology cannot. It is the level and intensity of use of available new technology which explains these differentials, and which is a function of supporting institutions and organisations, including government policies and programmes in the fields of input and output prices, credit, marketing, subsidies and land reforms. One of the major factors responsible for low crop yields in Indian agriculture is the low level of use of fertilisers. For example, in 1994–95, the average consumption of fertiliser in terms of NPK in India was about 75 kg/ha, as compared to 352 kg/ha in Japan and 448 kg/ha in South Korea.

India has an impressive infrastructure for agricultural research, comprising 45 research institutes, 10 project directorates, 30 national research centres, four national bureaux and 86 all-India coordinated research projects, all established by the Indian Council of Agricultural Research (ICAR). Besides, there are 28 state agricultural universities (SAUs), 120 zonal research stations affiliated to SAUs, one central agricultural university, eight regional agro-economic research centres, and numerous other public and private organisations engaged in research on issues in agricultural and rural development, and finding out solutions for them. Both ICAR institutions and SAUs have played a significant role in ushering in the Green Revolution in the country. What is needed now is a change in the orientation of researchers towards demand-driven, problem-solving and action-oriented research. There is also an urgent need to step up public and private investment in agriculture research. The launching of the National Agricultural Technology Project by ICAR is a welcome move in that direction (Pal and Singh 1997).

While examining the role of new technology in rural development, we would like to caution that the adoption of technologies which are not appropriate may cause serious damage to the biosphere, albeit unintentionally. The general economic and political environments prevailing in developing countries tend to favour and promote environmentally harmful technologies. For example, indiscriminate use of chemical fertilisers, and the effluents discharged by firms producing such chemicals as napthol, disulphonic acid and its derivatives, pollute rivers, streams, land and air and cause hazards to human health and reduce the longevity. People in India, particularly the poor, suffer more from such hazards, as there are neither property rights nor liability rules to protect them. Therefore, it is necessary that environmental impacts of new technologies are carefully evaluated before they are recommended for wider use.

Changes in the Organisational and Institutional Framework

As already mentioned, rural development is influenced by a multitude of factors, such as natural resources, human resources (labour), capital, technology, and institutions and organisations. Although the classical and neoclassical economists emphasised the role of natural resources, labour, technology, and investment in economic development, they did not assign any significant role to institutions and organisations in the process of development. They assumed the institutional set-up of the economy as given (exogenous), and hence beyond scientific analysis. As a matter of fact, they even argued for minimising the role of the government in the process of development, and advocated a policy of laissez-faire. It was the institutional economists and Karl Marx who recognised the significant role that institutions and organisations play in the process of economic development.

The terms 'organisation' and 'institution' are often used interchangeably. We consider organisations as a subset of the broader set of institutional structures or arrangements. An organisation connotes coordinated acts or endeavours of two or more individuals. It is created to give effect to a certain institutional arrangement. The main function of an economic organisation is to provide signals that will guide self-interested economic agents/entities to act in the interest of the larger community. The main task of any nation-state is to create institutional arrangements that provide the needed signals to individual economic entities. Markets provide such signals efficiently, so long as they operate with low transaction costs. Non-market mechanisms, such as government agencies and non-governmental organisations, including cooperatives, can also provide such signals.

Institutions and organisations are important aids to development. They may affect agricultural and rural development in many different ways, including provision of production inputs and services, reduction of transaction costs, enhancement of bargaining power of rural producers vis-à-vis those to whom they sell their produce and from whom they buy production inputs and services, influencing investments and savings and bringing the two together, and so on. The economic life of any community takes place in a milieu of organisations and institutions. They largely determine the economic structure of the community, and set the rules in which the economic game is played. Changes in these organisations and institutions over time will probably have a pronounced effect on economic output and development. Often these effects are difficult to isolate and measure because of the interdependence between changes in organisations and institutions and between other instrument variables of agricultural development.

There are many forms of organisations, such as public (government), sole proprietorship, partnership, company, cooperative and charitable trust, that can and are in fact serving the needs of farmers in India. The form of organisation suitable for promoting agricultural development should fully identify with the interests of farmers, and both organisationally and operationally should be fully oriented to meeting their needs.

The government has been, still is, and will continue in the near future to be an important organisation in the field of agricultural and rural development in India. Development is seen as the specific responsibility of the government. This has far-reaching implications for the role of public bureaucracy, which is the arm of the state responsible for carrying out the wishes of political leaders. Efforts to bring about improvement in the quality of life of rural people depend heavily on government administration and bureaucrats.

At the institutional level, laws of property and contract have a profound impact on economic growth. The essential questions here are: (*a*) What may a man do with his property? (*b*) What may others do to his property? and (*c*) In what kinds of economic activity may he engage? Some societies, like Japan, are fairly liberal in permitting private firms and individuals to operate without restrictions, while others impose many restrictions that curtail private profits, in the name of protecting the broad public interest. Other questions relate to what kinds of agreements private individuals may make; what kinds of claims and contracts can be enforced and to what extent, and so on.

All these questions relate to the influence of government regulation of business activity and its impact on economic growth. How tightly are specific kinds of business activities regulated by the government? How are taxes, tariffs, subsidies, and other fees utilised to discourage certain activities and encourage others? How are taxes and laws of inheritance used to control the distribution of income at the expense of economic growth? All these forces and factors determine the incentives for economic production, and must not be neglected in the search for a favourable institutional and organisational climate for economic development.

The only organisation that conceptually satisfies all the criteria of a good rural organisation is a cooperative. The cooperative form of organisation is solely designed for promoting the mutual interests of user patrons on the basis of equality and equity. It is controlled by them on a democratic basis. It also resolves the conflict of interests between the lender and borrower, or between seller and buyer, for in it the lender and the borrower or the seller and buyer are the same person. The objective is not to do business for the sake of profits only, but for meeting the members' needs. It is a local organisation, and provides for local participation. It is responsive to local needs, as its policy is decided democratically by the local member-users. It serves as a training ground for rural people in business and in democracy.

In India, the Anar.d pattern dairy cooperatives have demonstrated what appropriate institutions and organisations can do to initiate and foster agricultural and rural development. (See Chapter 11 for details.)

Besides cooperatives, there are many other forms of formal and non-formal associations which could do a good job of promoting agricultural and rural development. For example, PRADAN, a Delhi-based NGO, and The Aga Khan Rural Support Programme (India), an Ahmedabad-based NGO, both promote people's organisations at the grassroots level to take up agricultural and rural development projects.

The role of NGOs is to organise people and help them with technical information, training, and, to some extent, with funds. Besides, they also help grassroots organisations to secure financial assistance from various governmental and non-governmental sources. In most cases, the performance of the programmes taken up under the auspices of NGOs has been better than that of government programmes. However, this statement cannot be generalised, as there are many NGOs which do not have the necessary technical and managerial expertise and financial discipline to initiate and support agricultural and rural development programmes.

Indian corporations and companies could play a pivotal role in promoting agricultural development. In fact, many blue chip companies such as the Tatas, Mafatlals, Larsen and Toubro and Hindustan Lever, and associations of industrialists such the Confederation of Indian Industry (CII) and the Federation of Indian Chambers of Commerce and Industry (FICCI), have already won laurels for their exemplary work in the field of agricultural and rural development, not only from Indian NGOs, and Government Organisations (GOs), but also from international donors and development agencies. Corporates can bring the benefits of modern science and technology, management and world markets to the agricultural sector, and thereby promote agricultural development, particularly now in the era of liberalisation, deregulation, privatisation and globalisation.

Relation between Rural Development and its Determinants

It is not easy to quantify the relationship between rural development and the various determinants discussed in the preceding section. For one thing, there are no time series data available on any acceptable measure of rural development, nor on these determinants, some of which cannot be quantified at all. Second, all these determinants keep changing simultaneously, and it is not possible to isolate and measure the contribution of any single determinant, without resorting to some sophisticated econometric tehniques.

A few attempts have been made in the past to measure the impact of some of these determinants on rural development. For instance, Hayami and Ruttan (1970: 895–911) attempted to explain differences in agricultural output per worker (a proxy for agricultural development) between a representative group of developed and developing countries, and found that (*a*) resource endowment (land and livestock), (*b*) technology (fertilisers and machinery); and (*c*) human capital (general and technical education), accounted for 95 per cent of the differences. The implications of their analysis for an agricultural development strategy for developing countries are clear. An attempt must be made to close the gap in the levels of modern industrial inputs, education and research between developed and developing countries. Agricultural surpluses generated by closing the gap, over and above the amount necessary to maintain the growth of agricultural productivity, must be used to finance industrial development. In India as well, a number of studies have been conducted, mostly at the farm level, to determine the effect of land, water (irrigation), fertilisers, labour and power on farm production and income. These studies furnish valuable information about the nature and magnitude of the impact of various determinants on farm income. However, no macro-level studies aimed at determining the relationship between some acceptable measure of rural development and various factors affecting it are available.

Concluding Remarks

In whatever way we define and measure it, rural development is affected by a multitude of physical, technological, economic, sociocultural and institutional factors. All these factors operate within the limits imposed by the finite, non-growing and closed Planet Earth. This means that there is a natural (ecological) limit to economic growth and development. Of all the determinants of rural development, technological advance is the most important; in fact, it is a sine qua non of development. However, to produce a constant flow of technological innovations, a large reservoir of technically trained, skilled and motivated manpower and a congenial domestic environment are necessary. Although it is not possible to produce anything without using any natural resources and environmental amenities, inadequacy or poverty of natural resources does not exclude a high level of rural development; human resources and technologies can be substituted, to a limited extent, for natural resources, as has been amply demonstrated in Japan and Israel. In countries like India, quite a big chunk of natural resources is used in common by people. It is necessary for sustainable and equitable development that such resources be judiciously developed and utilised for the benefit of common people, most of whom depend on them for their livelihood.

Generation of domestic surpluses (savings), and their mobilisation and proper utilisation through a network of well-developed financial institutions, is necessary for sustaining the process of development: foreign aid can help only in initiating the process of development. In view of the fact that all other factors can be created and/or augmented using human resources, developing countries like India would do well to accord the highest priority to human resource development as an engine of sustainable rural development; returns to investment in human resource development are the highest. Being renewable and inexhaustible, human resources are the only means available in plenty to developing countries like India for attaining sustainable development, with no adverse effects on the environment.

6
Rural Development Policies and Strategies

Introduction

Webster's dictionary defines 'policy' as a definite course of action selected (as by government, an institution, a group, or an individual) from among alternatives, and in light of given conditions to guide and usually to determine present and future decisions. The most common social and political usage of the term policy refers to a course of action or intended course of action conceived of as deliberately adopted after a review of possible alternatives and pursued, or oriented to be pursued. The policy process is the formulation, promulgation and application of these courses of action. Here we will concern ourselves with public rural development policy, by which we mean actions taken by the *government* in pursuit of certain objectives of rural development. Rural development, as usual, includes agricultural development as well.

It is important to distinguish at the outset between a (*a*) policy; (*b*) programme; and (*c*) project. Policy is a comprehensive term and connotes, as mentioned earlier, a set of intended actions. It subsumes programmes which are narrower in scope than policy, but more specific with regard to what is to be done, how, by whom, and where. A policy has to be translated into a number of programmes before it can be implemented. A project is highly specific and detailed in terms of its objectives, location, duration, funds, and executing agency, and lends itself to planning, financing, and implementation as a unit. A programme may consist of several projects. A rural development project may be defined as an investment activity, where resources are expended to create a producing asset from which we can expect to realise benefits over an extended period of time.

Freedom, Control and Public Policy

Public policy is a form of social control. A farmer accepting a production loan from a nationalised bank and a subsidy from the government is restricted in the manner in which he can spend the borrowed money and subsidy, but his freedom to expand his output, improve his income and standard of living and develop his individual talents is enhanced. The farmer is struggling with the dilemma of freedom and control. As an individual, he cherishes his dignity and independence, as a social being, he has to realise the necessity for discipline and control. However, like so many other dilemmas, this one too is sophistry, based upon two alternatives that are made to appear exhaustive and mutually exclusive. Freedom and control are not mutually exclusive alternatives: they are two principles which can be compatible. In fact, the basic purpose of restraining certain actions through social controls is to safeguard the freedom for certain other actions.

A distinction between licence and freedom is useful here. If licence is defined as self-gratification harmful to others, and freedom as self-expression not harmful to others, then social controls can promote freedom by restricting licence. Seen from this perspective, there is no necessary conflict between freedom and control; in fact, social control can serve to expand individual freedom. So the real problem is not how we can avoid social control, it is rather, how we can make social controls so selective that they will restrain licence and promote freedom in the larger interest of society.

Need for a Rural Development Policy

The farther away we move from simple, small scale handicraft industry and self-contained and subsistence agriculture, a greater need develops for public policy in the economic field. The individual, as a producer and as a consumer, depends more and more upon the general conditions of the market, of employment, output and production efficiency of the nation as a whole, and upon the way income is distributed among the people. In short, upon the economic welfare of the country. Some specific reasons favouring government intervention in the rural sector are as follows:

India's Commitment to Set Up a 'Socialist Pattern of Society'

India has chosen to establish a 'socialist pattern of society'. This means that the basic criterion for determining the lines of development must not be private profit, but social gain, and that the pattern of development and the structure of socio-economic relations should be so planned that they result not only in appreciable increases in national income and employment, but also in greater equality in incomes and wealth (GOI 1961: 30).

But the experience in India so far has been that the benefits of development have not been equitably shared by all. This has aggravated the problem of poverty, which has manifested itself in various forms, including rising unemployment, malnutrition, growth of slums, fall in real wages, and impoverishment of marginal and small farmers. The growing poverty in rural and urban areas undermines the principal objective of planned development, which is improvement in the standard of living of the masses. It has been acknowledged that a high rate of growth is not a substitute for deliberate policies to ensure equitable distribution of the gains of development. Therefore, there is need for a public policy to ensure growth with social equity or social justice.

Violent Fluctuations in Agricultural Production, Prices and Incomes

Agricultural production, being biological in nature, is more vulnerable to the vagaries of nature than non-farm production, and hence fluctuates more violently than does industrial production in response to erratic rainfall or other natural phenomena. Fluctuations in agricultural output lead to still higher fluctuations in agricultural prices and hence agricultural incomes. This is because the demand for most agricultural products is inelastic, or because of higher price flexibility of agricultural produce with respect to changes in the supply. Most farmers, being small scale operators and poor, cannot bear the consequences of fluctuations in farm output prices and incomes. They need some protection from the adverse effects of the free market and niggardly nature. Such protection can be provided only by the government in the form of price support, insurance, and credit policies.

Rural Poverty and Income Inequality

The average per capita income in rural areas is not only lower than in urban areas, but is also more unevenly distributed. In 1993–94, about

37 per cent of the rural population was below the poverty line, as compared to 32 per cent in urban areas (Table 3.4). The material blessings of development in India have been more bountiful for urban people than for the rural masses. This is true for other countries as well. The injustice of the plight of rural people is reason enough for government intervention to support rural income and improve its distribution through anti-poverty programmes.

Small, Scattered and Unorganised Rural Enterprises

Most rural enterprises are small, scattered and unorganised. Due to these characteristics, their owners have very low or practically no bargaining power vis-à-vis those to whom they sell their produce, and from whom they buy their supplies. This results in exploitation on both fronts—selling as well as buying. This heightens the need for government policies aimed at equalising opportunities, at strengthening the bargaining power of individuals and groups in rural areas, and restraining the powerful from exploiting the weak.

Inadequate and Poor Basic Infrastructure in Rural Areas

Rural areas are at a great disadvantage in relation to urban areas, as far as provision of basic infrastructural facilities and services such as roads, drinking water, electricity, schools, hospitals, police protection, transport and communications is concerned. Not only are these public facilities and amenities in rural areas inadequate, but they are also very poorly organised and undependable. As a result, poor villagers are damned, generation after generation, to poor education, poor health, unemployment and poverty. Improvement of their plight requires intensive government intervention. In fact, the government has intervened by launching programmes like the Minimum Needs Programme and the Applied Nutrition Programme.

Predominant Place of Agriculture in India's Economy

Agriculture is the single largest sector of India's economy, contributing about 29 per cent of the national income and providing the main source of livelihood for about two-thirds of India's population. Agricultural and rural development is, in fact, the sine qua non of national development. Therefore, a meaningful strategy of national development must have agricultural and rural development as one of its major planks.

Goals of Rural Development Policy

Rural development policies are designed to improve the conditions under which rural people work and live. The goals of policies are governed by what people desire, and the measures of policies by what people think the government can and ought to do to bring about the desired change. This is the theory of public policy. Changes are desired only when people do not like the way things are going. Pressure for public action arises when people feel that they, individually, cannot bring about the desired adjustments. They have in mind some 'norm', some image of an ideal situation towards which they strive. These norms become the goals of policy towards which objectives of specific programmes are directed.

From the Directive Principles of State Policy enshrined in India's Constitution, it is possible to derive two dominant goals of economic policy: first, increasing the national income; and second, improving the distribution of national income among the members of society. These goals are reflected in India's economic policies that are enunciated in its five year plans. In the Approach Paper to the Ninth Five Year Plan, the following objectives are listed (CMIE 1997: 12):

1. Priority to agriculture and rural development, with a view to generating adequate productive employment and eradication of poverty.
2. Accelerating the growth rate of the economy with stable prices.
3. Ensuring food and nutritional security for all, particularly the vulnerable sections of society.
4. Providing the basic minimum services of safe drinking water, primary health care facilities, universal primary education, shelter, and connectivity to all in a time-bound manner.
5. Containing the growth rate of the population.
6. Ensuring environmental sustainability of the development process through social mobilisation and participation of people at all levels.
7. Empowerment of women and socially disadvantaged groups such as Scheduled Castes, Scheduled Tribes and Other Backward Classes and Minorities as agents of socio-economic change and development.
8. Promoting and developing people's participatory institutions like panchayati raj institutions, cooperatives and self-help groups.
9. Strengthening efforts to build self-reliance.

The above objectives, which seek to achieve 'growth with equity', need to be seen in the context of the following four important dimensions of state policy. These are as follows:

- Quality of life of the citizens.
- Generation of productive employment.
- Regional balance.
- Self-reliance.

All these objectives seem to be worthwhile, and therefore deserve serious pursuit by policy makers. However, to be of any use to society, these objectives should be translated into specific programmes and projects that are manageable under the existing conditions. Many rural development policies are complex combinations of various goals, different sets of means or instruments, and are limited by various conditions. To understand such policies, we must break them down into several programmes or projects. For each programme, a clearly defined objective may be designated, which a particular government agency should pursue. The programme measures can then be identified and appraised as to whether they are appropriate and efficient in serving the objective, and adapted to the conditions outside the influence of that particular programme. These conditions are often the decisive factor determining whether or not a certain programme is 'administratively' feasible.

Hierarchy of Policy Goals

Given the multiplicity of policy goals, it is necessary to study the relationships among them and see that they converge towards public interest, or at least do not militate against it. This can be done if various policy goals and programme objectives are arranged in the form of a pyramid, as shown in Figure 6.1. Descending the steps of the pyramid of policy goals from the lofty top of generality to the practical base of concrete issues would reveal the following hierarchy:

1. The master goal of economic policy is to promote general welfare, which comprises economic welfare and cultural, social, and political welfare. This master goal is served by two superior goals, namely, maximum national income, and equalisation of opportunities. The master goal and the superior goals together constitute the top level of the hierarchy.

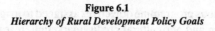

Figure 6.1
Hierarchy of Rural Development Policy Goals

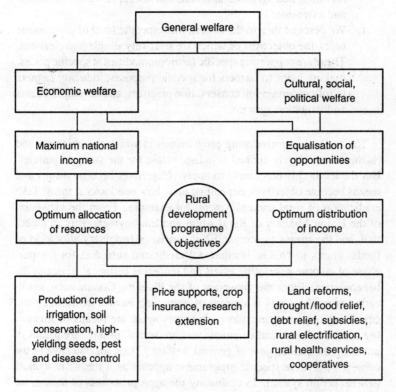

2. Descending from the top level of the hierarchy, a series of goals is developed at a lower plane of generality. These goals deal with specific maladjustments in the various sectors of the economy, and may be called the central goals of major national policies. Each of these central goals is still quite general in scope and complex in nature; for practical application, these goals have to be broken down further into more specific programme objectives directed at a great variety of situations, and concerning various groups of people, regions, and commodities.

3. At the next level, we find the objectives of specific government programmes designed to correct maladjustments, or to remove the source of dissatisfaction suffered by certain groups of people. The central goal of agricultural policy, for instance, is broken down

into various programme objectives assigned to irrigation, soil conservation and agricultural credit, marketing, research, education and extension.

4. We descend then to the lowest, most specific level of programme units, the objectives of which are relatively simple and clear-cut. These are supporting specific farm commodities at specific prices, making loans to farmers for specific purposes, inducing farmers to follow certain soil conservation practices, and developing dams and irrigation systems.

The method of formulating programmes in which the objective and its means are clearly defined is indispensable for the study of policies. But the method is not simple to apply. Objectives become means and means become objectives, depending upon how one looks at them. Take eradication of rural unemployment, for example. From the viewpoint of the Union Ministry of Rural Areas and Employment, it is an objective, and the means to accomplish it consist of budgetary allocation of funds, grants to NGOs, institutional credit and subsidies for the purchase of income-generating assets and rendering technical advice to the beneficiaries. From the viewpoint of the Planning Commission, eradication of rural poverty is a means of improving income distribution and equalising opportunities; those objectives again are means of improving social, cultural, and economic welfare which, in turn, are means of attaining the master goal of general welfare. Thus, an objective in the context of a more specific programme appears as a means in a more general action system. In evaluating the appropriateness of means, we take the objective for granted; in order to evaluate the appropriateness of an objective, we must place it in the position of a means serving a superior end.

Rural Development Policy in India

Tinbergen (1952: 2) distinguishes between a qualitative policy and a quantitative policy. A qualitative policy seeks to change the economic structure through the creation of new institutions, modification of existing institutions and nationalisation of private firms. A quantitative policy seeks to change the magnitude of certain parameters; for example, change in the tax rate. An example which represents both qualitative and quantitative policy is the introduction of an education system free of charge, if previously tuition fees were charged. It is qualitative because it represents a change in the economic structure, and is quantitative because it represents a change in the fee, from something to zero.

Heady (1965: 15) classifies agricultural policies into development policies and compensation policies. A development policy seeks to increase the supply of commodities and resources, and to improve the quality of products and inputs. A compensation policy is aimed at compensating its target group in various manners—through subsidies, price support, etc.

India has a long history of government intervention in the rural sector of its economy. In the pre-Independence era, British government intervention was aimed at promoting the export of food and raw materials to Great Britain. There was no state policy for the development of resources of India for the welfare of its people. Introduction of a land tenure system, opening up of road and rail communications, and promotion of export trade in certain agricultural commodities were the important measures taken by the British government. The other landmarks of that era were the creation of the Forest Department in 1864, and the Department of Agriculture in 1871, the appointment of the Royal Commission on Agriculture (RCA) in 1926, and the establishment of the Imperial (now Indian) Council of Agricultural Research in 1929. The report of the RCA was accepted as the basis for future development of agriculture in a conference convened by the Government of India (GOI) at Shimla in October 1928. The report emphasised, *inter alia*, the importance of providing a minimum standard of life in villages and modernisation of agriculture through research, extension and greater coordination of various departments dealing with agriculture, and development of cooperative institutions. However, due to lack of financial resources and the Great Economic Depression (1929–30), many of the recommendations of the RCA could not be implemented.

In January 1946, the GOI issued a 'Statement of Agriculture and Food Policy in India', which spelt out the objectives to be achieved, the measures to be taken, and the respective roles of the centre and the provinces. According to the statement, the all-India policy was to promote the welfare of the people and to secure a progressive improvement of their standard of living (GOI 1976: 127–36).

Sadly, even after 50 years of Independence, India does not have a unified national policy for agricultural and rural development. A Draft National Agricultural Policy Resolution was prepared by the Ministry of Agriculture, Government of India in 1992, but it was not adopted. What exists now is a National Forest Policy, a National Water Policy, some semblance of a land reforms policy, and an assortment of agricultural and rural development programmes not integrated with one another or coordinated properly. Now we briefly discuss the major national-level public policies in the field of agriculture and rural development.

National Forest Policy

India is one of the few countries in the world that has had a forest policy since 1894. After Independence, in recognition of the importance of forests in the national economy and to ensure the best possible use of land, a new Forest Policy was enunciated in May 1952. The new policy provided, *inter alia*, that the area under forests should be at least one-third of the total geographical area, and that the forest areas should not be brought under cultivation of crops indiscriminately. The National Commission on Agriculture (1976) recommended a further revision of the 1952 Forest Policy. The forest policy was revised in 1988. The main plank of the revised Forest Policy of 1988 is protection, conservation and development of forests. The salient features of the revised policy are as follows:

- A minimum of one-third of the total land area of the country has to be brought under forest or tree cover.
- Total protection of tropical rain/moist forests.
- The extent of forest use for grazing and extraction will be determined on the basis of the carrying capacity of the forests.
- Involvement of tribals/forest dwellers in protection, regeneration and development of forests to be encouraged.
- Forest-based industries would have to raise their own plantations to meet their requirements, and the practice of supplying forest produce to industries at concessional rates would cease.

These principles are necessary to ensure that the forest area can increase from its present level of 75 mha to 110 mha (33 per cent of the total land area). The revised Forest Policy has several implications for various sectors of the economy like energy, industry and agriculture. Development projects now are carefully examined to ensure that the ecological balance is not destroyed. This is done through assessment of their impacts on ecosystems.

In view of the rising demand for forest-based products, there is need to pay far greater attention to increasing the productivity of forests and to their scientific management on modern lines. The national forest policy should rest on two pivotal points, namely, meeting the requirement of raw materials for forest-based industry, and of small timber, fuel wood, and fodder for the rural community, and satisfying present and future demands for protective and recreative functions of forests and for environmental amenities. Social forestry and afforestation of wastelands should receive a very high priority.

In June 1990 the Union Ministry of Environment and Forests issued guidelines to the forest departments of all states and union territories, directing them to involve village communities and voluntary agencies for regeneration of degraded forest lands on usufruct sharing basis. Most of the state governments responded positively to the Ministry's directive, and launched what have come to be known as Joint Forest Management Programmes. The Ministry has also recently launched an eco-development project in seven selected Protected Areas (PAs) in India, namely, Buxa (West Bengal), Gir (Gujarat), Nagarhole (Karnataka), Palamau (Bihar), Pench (Madhya Pradesh), Periyar (Kerala) and Ranthambhore (Rajasthan). The project is financially supported by the Global Environment Facility (GEF) and the International Development Association. The project employs the Protected Area Approach to bio-diversity conservation and participatory eco-development in and around protected areas.

Land Reforms Policy

To lay the foundation for a progressive rural society, it is necessary to reorder the agrarian structure. A sound land reforms policy can contribute significantly to agricultural and rural development, and therefore deserves high priority. The land policy should be such that it ensures the scientific and intensive use of land, creates productive employment, reduces disparities in the distribution of land, provides incentives to increase productivity of land, and induces changes in property relations and social structure, with a view to enabling the wider participation of landowners and tenants in the process of rural development. The agrarian structure should be based on peasant proprietorship, strengthened and supplemented by cooperative and joint farming systems, and backed by necessary supplies and services for optimum utilisation of land.

After Independence, the Government of India formulated a comprehensive national land reforms policy for the first time in the First Five Year Plan. The main objectives of the policy were to remove such impediments to the modernisation of agriculture as were innate in the agrarian structure inherited from the past, and reduction of gross inequalities in the agrarian economy and rural society. It accorded a high priority to programmes that increased agricultural production, promoted diversification, reduced disparities in distribution of income and wealth, eliminated exploitation, and provided security to tenants and workers. This policy has been followed in all the subsequent five year plans with marginal reshuffling of the priorities of its components. Necessary land reform legislation has already been enacted by the state governments, and is now in force. The policy and the programmes have been periodically reviewed and evaluated. One of the common findings of the reviews is that the implementation of the programmes has been lax. Many glaring gaps have occurred between the objectives of the policy and the legislation enacted to achieve them, and between the laws and their enforcement (Singh 1997: 152–55). The programmes, therefore, need to be implemented more rigorously than in the past. For optimum results, the programmes of land reforms, consolidation of fragmented landholdings, land development, irrigation and drainage and acquisition of surplus land and its distribution should be integrated and executed properly. Special attention must be directed at the restoration of degraded common property land resources, and their proper utilisation for the larger benefit of the rural masses. With the establishment of the National Wastelands Development Board, it is hoped that some 100 million ha of India's wastelands would be properly developed and utilised.

National Water Policy

Water is the most critical natural resource affecting the level and pace of agricultural and rural development. Optimum development and efficient utilisation of water resources, therefore, assumes great significance. Nearly 36 per cent of the total gross cropped area in the country is irrigated, and the irrigated area contributes over 55 per cent of the total agricultural output. Since Independence, India has invested close to Rs 53,000 crores in irrigation development. As a result, the irrigation potential has increased from 22.6 mha in 1951 to 91.79 mha by the end of the Eighth Plan (1992–97).

The Union Ministry of Water Resources is responsible for laying down policies and programmes for development and regulation of the country's water resources. The National Water Policy adopted in September 1987 stresses that 'Water is a prime natural resource, a basic human need and a precious national asset. Planning and development of water resources need to be governed by national perspectives.' It recommends an integrated and multi-disciplinary approach to planning, formulation and implementation of projects in such a way as to be able to meet the demands of water from various sectors and to free the country, as far as possible, from the scourge of recurring floods and droughts. The Water Policy highlights the following points:

- Need for efficient use of water.
- Need for a well-designed information system.
- Need for preservation of the quality of the environment and the ecological balance.
- Periodic reassessment on a scientific basis of the ground water potential taking into account the quality of water available, and the economic viability of its exploitation.
- Integrated and coordinated development of surface water and ground water and their conjunctive use.
- Equity and social justice considerations in water allocation.
- Involvement of farmers in various aspects of water management, particularly water distribution and collection of water charges through water users' associations.

The NWP does not specify its goals clearly. In our opinion, the main goals of the NWP should be to restore, develop, conserve and utilise the surface water and ground water resources of the country in the socially optimum and ecologically sound and sustainable way. It is also necessary to specify various policy instruments to be used to achieve the goals of the policy. Professional/public policy and management experts can do the tasks of setting goals and identifying appropriate policy instruments to achieve them better than technocrats and bureaucrats. At present, requisite management expertise is lacking at all levels of the hierarchy of the irrigation administration in India, and this constitutes a severe constraint on improving the performance in the irrigation subsector (Singh and Shishodia 1992: 39–41).

Agricultural Price Policy

Before Independence, there was no semblance of an agricultural price policy in India. After Independence, the government introduced a price policy mainly to protect the interests of consumers, by making available to them food at reasonable prices, i.e., the policy was consumer-oriented. A broad framework for a price policy was specified for the first time in the Terms of Reference of the Agricultural Prices Commission (later renamed as the Commission for Agricultural Costs and Prices), which was set up in 1965 for evolving a balanced and integrated price structure. The Commission was required to keep in view the interests of both the producer and the consumer while formulating a price policy. The framework of the policy was reviewed and modified in 1980, and again in 1986. The latest review was done in 1991, after India became a signatory to the new world trade arrangement, which, for the first time, included agriculture also. The new price policy for the agricultural sector aims at setting the prices right and withdrawing the subsidies on inputs, targeting the public distribution system (PDS) to only the poor, abolition of the food management system, and liberalisation of trade in agricultural commodities.

At present, 24 agricultural commodities are covered under the Minimum Price Support programme. Besides, some other commodities like onions, potatoes, ginger, etc., are included under the Market Intervention Scheme. The Food Corporation of India, which has been the nodal agency for implementing the price support policy for rice and wheat, was entrusted with the work of price support for coarse cereals also. As regards targeting the poorer sections, a revamped PDS was launched in 1992 with a view to extending the coverage of distribution of specially subsidised foodgrains to the population living in hilly and arid areas also.

Food and input subsidies have been used as complementary instruments of the agricultural price policy, which seeks to: (*a*) assure a remunerative and relatively stable price environment for farmers for inducing them to increase their production, and thereby augmenting the availability of foodgrains; (*b*) improve the physical and economic access of the people to food; and (*c*) evolve a production pattern which is in line with the overall needs of the economy. Contrary to the general impression that the price support programme and input and food subsidies have benefited only a few crops and farmers in only some regions, it is now well established that these instruments have played an important role in achieving the objectives of food security and accelerated growth of the economy, and have benefited all the sections of society (Acharya 1997: 26).

It is important for rural development that the overall relationship between input and output prices within agriculture, and the terms of trade between agriculture and other sectors of the economy be such that growth is stimulated in the rural areas. The major aim of an agricultural price policy should be to correct market distortions, which are generally socially harmful. Being parts of the same policy, the interests of the producer should be safeguarded through price support (above the market price) operations when there is a sharp fall in market prices, and the interests of the consumers, particularly the vulnerable sections of the population, should be protected through distribution of foodgrains and other basic necessities at a fair price (below the market price) when there is a sharp rise in market prices. Since the minimum support price is expected to take into account changes in input prices, widespread use of input subsidy as incentive to increase production should, by and large, be avoided except in the case of small and marginal farmers and difficult areas. In the latter case, a transport subsidy will be more appropriate.

Rural Credit Policy

India has a long history of government intervention in the rural credit market. Duly recognising the need for providing institutional credit to cultivators to protect them from the exploitation of private moneylenders and traders, the Government of India started granting loans to the cultivators under (a) the Improvements Loans Act of 1883, and (b) the Agriculturists' Loans Act of 1884. Such loans are called *taccavi* loans. The act of 1883 authorises the grant of long-term loans for effecting permanent improvements on land. Under the act of 1884, short- and medium-term loans are granted to meet the current agricultural needs, such as purchase of seeds, fertilisers and small tools and implements. The record of taccavi loans has been rather poor. Some of the drawbacks are inadequate amount, inordinate delays in sanctioning the loans, lack of supervision, poor recovery and lack of coordination.

The Reserve Bank of India and the National Bank for Agriculture and Rural Development have both played a very important role in shaping the rural credit policies of India, and in building its rural economy through institutional credit. The rural credit policy has been reviewed by a number of committees from time to time. The following are the major landmarks in the history of the evolution of India's rural credit policy:

- The Cooperative Credit Societies Act of 1904.
- All-India Rural Credit Survey Committee (1954): Introduction of three-tier cooperative credit structure and state participation in the equity of cooperatives.
- All-India Credit Review Committee (1969): Multi-agency approach with the entry of commercial banks in the field of rural credit.
- Nationalisation of 14 commercial banks, 1969.
- Nariman Committee 1971: Priority sector lending and Lead Bank Scheme.
- Introduction of Differential Rate of Interest (DRI) Scheme 1972.
- Narasimham Committee 1975: Regional Rural Banks were set up.
- Committee to Review Arrangements for Institutional Credit for

Agricultural and Rural Development, 1981 (CRAFICARD): NABARD was set up in 1982.

- Agriculture Credit Review Committee 1989: A new credit policy was formulated.
- Agricultural and Rural Debt Relief Scheme 1990.
- Narasimham Committee 1991: Financial Sector reforms were introduced.

Cooperative credit societies were the first of all types of cooperatives established in India, with the objective of liberating the poor cultivator from the clutches of the moneylender through providing adequate credit on easy terms. The credit cooperatives have played an important role in purveying credit to farmers and occupy a significant place in India's rural credit system, accounting for about 62 per cent of the total credit supply in the rural sector. But, sadly, their main objective remains, by and large, unfulfilled even after 94 years of their existence in India. They suffer from many financial, organisational, managerial and legal constraints. Their limited ability to mobilise resources, low levels of recovery, high transaction costs, frequent suspension of recovery, low administered interest rates, government controls, and political interference in their business and management affairs have all taken a heavy toll on their viability and sustainability. There is need to liberate them from these constraints, and revamp the cooperative credit structure to make it viable, vibrant, and robust enough to face the challenges posed by the new economic policy of liberalisation and privatisation. Otherwise, most of the credit cooperatives will have to die sooner or later.

The present credit policy needs to be reoriented, so that a package of all essential financial services is provided to the needy rural people to enable them to adopt new technologies, and thereby enhance their income and socio-economic condition. Greater flexibility in timing the repayment of loans is also needed. In a nutshell, rural credit institutions should try to copy those of the practices of private moneylenders that make them so popular even now, after 50 years of independence.

In India, agricultural and rural development, being a state subject, the major responsibility for development is that of the state governments. However, the role of the central government is, and will continue to be, important in certain areas which are of concern to the whole of India, like provision of food for the country, enacting model legislation, formulating national policies and programmes, and so on. Central initiative is necessary to forge a national consensus and a broad pattern of rural development. Centre-state relations in the matter of agricultural development should be based on consultations, consensus, cooperation and complementarity, to foster the discipline of national rural development, expand the area of mutual commitment and collaboration, and ensure harmonious growth through both national and local initiative. The centre would have to take a number of developmental measures and create institutions which support state initiative, and help in the effective execution of programmes by the states. Similarly, the centre may have to legislate for the country as a whole with the consent of the states, where a uniform policy has to be pursued throughout the country. Alternatively, it may have to make skeletal legislation to set the pattern for the country and guide the states.

There are several aspects of agricultural and rural development which may need a certain amount of enforcement in the interest of the common good. For example, consolidation of landholdings, soil conservation, land development, drainage and plant protection programmes have to be organised on an area basis. If a majority of the beneficiaries agree, there should be a provision to make the participation of others obligatory, and to undertake the operations and realise the cost from all the beneficiaries. Further, in regard to fertilisers and pesticides, quality control is important. Improved seeds need certification, guaranteeing purity and germination. Food products need to be certified as hygienic by health standards. For these as well, appropriate legislation will be necessary. Generally, the regulation of crop acreages through legislation may not be practicable under Indian conditions. In some cases, however, certain areas can be delineated to grow certain specific varieties of the crop, as in the case of cotton. In areas prone to disease, the cultivation of certain crops like tobacco or potato can be prohibited. In these cases, regulation may become necessary in the interests of agricultural production. Land reforms, minimum wages, restrictions on movement, etc., are other spheres in which legislation is necessary. In all these cases, it is desirable to have a certain amount of uniformity, subject to local adaptation and modification.

Liberalisation and Rural Development

After the launching of the New Economic Policy (NEP) in India in August 1991, a process of privatisation, deregulation, and globalisation has been set in motion. The statist model of rural development characterised by the predominant role of the state in initiating, fostering, and directing rural development is likely to be abandoned, giving way to a market-driven and guided model. It has become fashionable once again these days to believe that a greater reliance on market forces and the integration of national economies within a global economy, i.e., globalisation, would reduce the problems of poverty and unemployment through speeding up the pace and level of economic growth. Furthermore, this new faith in market forces has also led to a reorientation of international development policies more in favour of liberal trade than aid as an instrument of development. But despite all this, there is a nagging doubt among the majority of development scholars and practitioners about the relevance of the new model for developing countries like India, where a very large section of population is below the poverty line, and hence outside the influence zone of market forces.

Indian agriculture has been protected from the influence of international market forces, mainly through a system of quantitative restrictions on the import of some 800 agricultural commodities. Now that India is a member of the World Trade Organisation (WTO) and a signatory to the Uruguay Round of General Agreement on Trade and Tariffs (GATT), we are under an obligation to replace non-tariff measures (quantitative restrictions/quotas) by reasonable levels of tariffs. There are apprehensions that the liberalisation of agricultural imports would hit our farmers and impair the growth prospects of the agricultural sector. According to a study conducted by Chand (1997: 1–6), liberalisation of international trade in agricultural commodities may have the following major impacts on producers and consumers:

- Removal of quantitative restrictions on international trade is expected to promote both imports and exports of agricultural commodities and production inputs. This would speed up the pace of commercialisation and specialisation on the basis of higher comparative advantage in the agricultural sector. Export orientation of agricultural production could necessitate the use of increased quantities of chemical fertilisers, pesticides and irrigation water, which would adversely affect the quality of the environment, unless adequate safeguards such as the use of biofertilisers and biopesticides, provision of recharging of ground water aquifers in water scarce areas, and of drainage in water-surplus waterlogged areas are taken.
- Liberalisation of international trade in agricultural commodities would pave the way for the entry of private companies and

corporations in the import business, which at present is monopo-
lised by government organisations, which are the sole canalising
agencies for imports of many commodities. Agricultural producers and consumers would be affected through changes in prices—
producers from higher prices, and consumers from lower and/or
better quality—due to increased competition and consequent increased efficiency.

- Importers would have an advantage over domestic producers if the
  agricultural sector is not liberated from internal restrictions. Furthermore, government controls and intervention in the sector need
  to be reduced, to encourage greater participation of the private
  sector in processing, marketing and distribution.

Like any other economic phenomenon, globalisation is based on a set
of values, such as competitiveness, efficiency, wealth accumulation and
the free play of market forces. Globalisation of business and trade without a global view of the society as a global family would lead to social
tensions and economic strife, and this is what is happening today in many
developing countries which have adopted the structural adjustment programmes. In the paradigm of globalisation, there is no place for such
values as sympathy, kindness, compassion, world-brotherhood, cooperation and so on. Because of relatively easy flow of capital internationally
as compared to labour, capitalists/portfolio investors would benefit the
most from globalisation. This would aggravate the problem of disparities
in income and wealth between the rich and the poor. Further, globalisation would also engender corruption, black money and other social evils,
as portfolio investors would like to keep the bureaucrats and politicians
on their side by bribing them. Besides, the powerful and rich countries
define and redefine the rules of the game of globalisation to suit their own
national interests or the vested interest of their capitalist investors. This
leads to clashes of interest and financial instability, as has been recently
experienced in several East Asian countries.

It is clear that globalisation is good for only a fraction of Indian
society—maybe the top 10 per cent of the people. The number of people
who are likely to lose, or are already losing from globalisation, has been
increasing, particularly in those poor countries which are outside North
America, Europe and the Pacific Rim. But the issue is not whether globalisation is good or bad or whether it is inevitable. We should understand
that globalisation is here and that we are unavoidably part of the process
of globalisation, which demands a new focus and a restructuring and

re-engineering of our polity and economy. The questions to be asked are: What can we do about it? How could we benefit from it?

The current opposition of farmers, workers, women and environmentalists to globalisation in both developed and developing countries is increasing, as more and more people are questioning the drive for globalisation and profit-seeking competition. In a nutshell, the current state of affairs suggests that we are in the process of redefining/remapping global economic and political relations to reflect a diversity of positions, as well as shared concerns and tensions. If the process is pursued to its logical conclusion, it could expose the hypocrisy of the old order, and create a new political environment where the powerful hegemony of transnational, commercial and financial institutions can be challenged through cooperative action by the losers. Acting individually, developing countries are unable to protect their people and natural resources from the havocs of globalisation and transnational companies, which are taking over life-supporting industries. But acting collectively/cooperatively, they could face the challenges posed by globalisation, and benefit from the opportunities that it opens up. Similarly, within a country, rural producers' cooperatives could protect the small and marginal farmers from the adverse effects of globalisation, and also enable them to benefit from it. What is needed most in the rural sector now is to liberate the rural producers and their organisations from the shackles of unnecessary government controls and archaic laws.

Strategies of Rural Development

Agricultural and rural development have been accorded a high priority in India's five year plans. The First Plan was dominated by the Community Development Programme (CDP), which reflected India's overriding concern with nation building and equity. The Second Plan accorded a high priority to the development of heavy industries, and consequently, under the constraint of limited resources, food production suffered. By the middle of the Second Plan, it became increasingly evident that whatever the success of the CDP, a new approach would be required if agricultural production was to stay ahead of the demands of India's mounting population. In 1957–58, India faced its first post-Independence food crisis. In response to this crisis, and on the basis of the recommendations of the Ford Foundation-sponsored Team of American Agricultural Production Specialists, a new programme called the Intensive Agriculture

District Programme (IADP), or Package Programme, was formulated and launched in seven selected districts in the country in 1960–61, and was later extended to eight more districts.

The IADP represented a significant departure from the CDP, in that it employed the concentration principle in deploying resources, as opposed to the equity criterion of the CDP. Its main objective was to achieve rapid increases in agricultural production through the use of complementary inputs and services (package approach) at the farm level. Farm planning formed the core of IADP. By 1966, the basic concept of concentration and effective use and better management of resources had gained national acceptance, and a number of new agricultural development programmes, such as the Intensive Agricultural Area Programme (IAAP), the High Yielding Varieties Programme (HYVP), and the Intensive Cattle Development Programme (ICDP) had been patterned like the IADP. All these programmes were growth oriented; they did not address themselves to equity issues. They demonstrated, on one hand, the effectiveness of the concentration principle in achieving rapid increases in food production, and on the other, the failure of the growth oriented strategy to solve the basic problems of rural poverty and income inequality. The most important lesson learned from the experience with these programmes was that a rising economic growth rate was no guarantee against worsening poverty, and that a direct frontal attack on the basic problems of poverty and unemployment was called for.

The failure of the growth oriented strategies of the sixties to make any marked impact on the problem of poverty led to a re-examination of these strategies. As a consequence, special programmes like the Small Farmer Development Agency, Marginal Farmers and Agricultural Labourers Scheme, Drought Prone Area Programme, and Tribal Area Development Programme for the 'weaker sections' and 'economically depressed areas' were introduced in the seventies. These programmes were aimed at tackling the problems of poverty and backwardness directly, by helping the weaker sections to increase their incomes through self-employment and wage-paid employment. To supplement the income-increasing effect of these programmes, a programme to provide civic amenities and community facilities was launched in the Fifth Plan. This programme was known as the Minimum Needs Programme (MNP). In 1978–79, the Integrated Rural Development Programme (IRDP) was launched in 2,300 selected community development blocks in the country, and from 2 October 1980 it was extended to all the blocks in the country. It is the single largest anti-poverty programme currently under way in the country. The major premise of the special programmes launched in the seventies was that their benefits would flow to the weaker sections and backward areas, because of the specificity of the target groups and target areas. The details of some of the important agricultural and rural development programmes launched in India after Independence are presented in Chapters 8–12.

A review of various rural development programmes and policies followed in India after Independence reveal four strategies of development.[1]

Growth Oriented Strategy

This is based on the philosophy that rural people, like any other people, are rational decision makers, who, when given adequate opportunity and a proper environment, will try to maximise their incomes. The role of the state in this strategy is to build infrastructure, and maintain a favourable climate to stimulate the growth of rural enterprises. The critical assumption of this strategy is that the benefits of increased production will gradually 'trickle down' to the poor. The regulation and coordination of the activities of private and public agencies is primarily through market mechanisms. This paradigm formed the basis of the predominant agricultural development strategy of the 1960s, when programmes like the Intensive Agriculture District Programme (IADP), the Intensive Cattle Development Programme (ICDP), the High Yielding Varieties Programme (HYVP), were launched. But this paradigm failed to make any dent on the basic problems of poverty, unemployment and inequality, and had to be abandoned.

Welfare Oriented Strategy

This seeks to promote the well-being of the rural population in general, and the rural poor in particular, through large-scale social programmes like the Minimum Needs Programme, Applied Nutrition Programme, Mid-Day Meals Programme, etc. The primary means used in this strategy are free provision/distribution of goods, services and civic amenities in rural areas.

The critical assumptions of this strategy are that people are not competent to identify and resolve their problems, and that government specialists can identify their needs and meet them with the financial and

---

[1] On the basis of a general survey of recent strategies of rural development followed in five Central American governments, John C. Ickis has identified three basic approaches, namely, growth, welfare, and responsive strategies. For details see John C. Ickis (1983).

administrative resources available with the government. The role of villagers is that of passive receptors of services. This strategy has a paternalistic orientation. The performance of the programmes is judged by the quantity of goods, services, and civic amenities delivered. The welfare oriented programmes present a mixed picture; the rural poor have benefited significantly through some programmes in a few areas, but not in others. There are two major criticisms of this strategy, namely, (*a*) it has created dependence; and (*b*) it requires resources that are beyond the means of governments.

Responsive Strategy

This is aimed at helping rural people help themselves through their own organisations and other support systems. Its concern is with responding to the felt needs of the rural people, as defined by *them*. The role of the government is to facilitate the self-help efforts of villagers by providing technologies and resources that are not locally available. The critical assumption of this strategy is that the rural poor will identify and resolve their problems if provided with minimal support, and otherwise left to their own devices and initiatives. Community participation in, and control of, project activities is the primary performance indicator of this strategy. India's Operation Flood, which was launched in 1970 in 18 milksheds in 10 states, is a good example of this strategy. Operation Flood aimed at modernising and developing India's dairy industry through a three-tier structure of Anand pattern dairy cooperatives. (For details see Ch. 11.) Many voluntary agencies are also following this paradigm of development.

Integrated or Holistic Strategy

This combines all the positive features of the earlier three strategies, and is designed to simultaneously achieve the goals of growth, welfare, equity and community participation. This paradigm takes a very comprehensive but integrated view of the basic problems of poverty, unemployment and inequality, and seeks to address the physical, economic, technological, social, motivational, organisational and political bases of these problems.

The multiple goals of this strategy are sought to be achieved by building the capacity of the community to involve itself in development in partnership with the government. The critical assumption underlying this approach is that the government can restructure societal power relationships, and centralised bureaucracies can learn to share power with community groups. Successful implementation of this strategy requires complex decentralised matrix structures, with permanent mechanisms for vertical and lateral integration, a combination of specialist and generalist skills, institutional leadership, social intervention capability and systems management (Ickis 1983: Ch. 1). The anti-poverty programmes launched in India in the 1970s, particularly the Integrated Rural Development Programme, National Rural Employment Programme, and Training of Rural Youth for Self-Employment, were intended to follow this paradigm. But given the existing organisational structure, which does not have many of the prerequisites discussed earlier for the successful implementation of this strategy, there is very little hope that this paradigm would yield the desired results.

Concluding Remarks

India has a very long history of government intervention in the rural sector, with a view to improve the socio-economic condition of rural people, especially the poor. However, there is no comprehensive integrated national policy for agricultural and rural development yet declared and adopted by the government. What exists now is an assortment of a few subsectoral policies, such as a land reforms policy, a national water policy, a national forest policy, and a host of agricultural and rural development programmes. In many cases, the objectives of one programme conflict with those of others, and there is no institutional mechanism for reconciling them. Consequently, many programmes not only fail to produce the intended benefits, but also cause, albeit unintentionally, harm to other programmes. What is, therefore, needed is a long term comprehensive integrated national policy which clearly charts the future course of agricultural and rural development in the country in the twenty-first century. This is all the more necessary in the wake of the new economic policy characterised by the liberalisation, privatisation and globalisation of India's economy. To do this successfully, we need to build up and strengthen the expertise in the area of public policy at the national level. Besides, some national centres of excellence in public policy may also be established in reputed institutes/universities.

7

Policy Instruments of Rural Development

Introduction

An instrument is defined as something which the manager or actor can change or manipulate in order to produce a desired effect. It may be an economic quantity such as interest rate, or it may be a part of the institutional framework such as nationalisation of banks. An instrument, therefore, is the means by which an objective is pursued. A measure is the use of a particular instrument at a particular time in order to promote one or more objectives; for instance, the decision to raise the bank rate on a certain day, or to reduce income tax in a particular budget year. The removal of a measure, for instance, the removal of price control, is also a measure. Knowledge about what instruments can be used to achieve the objectives of various rural development programmes is essential for rural development policy makers and managers in order for these programmes to be effective and successful. This chapter is devoted to a discussion of some instruments which can be used by rural development policy makers, administrators and managers to achieve their objectives.

A Conceptual Framework

Perhaps the most useful framework to illustrate the relationship among policy instruments, target variables and social welfare, and for policy analysis, has been provided by Nobel Laureate Jan Tinbergen (1952: Ch. 2). This is illustrated in Figure 7.1.

Figure 7.1
A Conceptual Framework for Policy Analysis

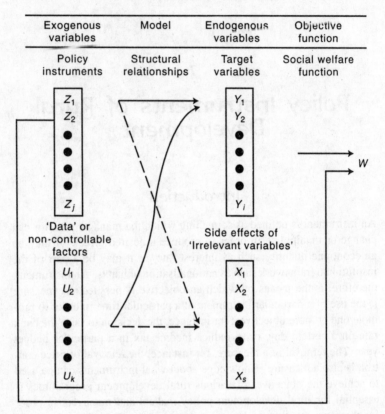

Exogenous variables	Model	Endogenous variables	Objective function
Policy instruments	Structural relationships	Target variables	Social welfare function

The important elements of the framework for policy analysis are W, the Y_i, the Z_j, and the structural relationships that link the Z_j to the Y_i. Each of these elements needs elaboration.

Social Welfare Function (W)

Economists call W the social welfare function. It reflects the level of well-being achieved by the society. As such, it represents the aggregate of the satisfaction reached by the individuals comprising society. 'Utility' is 'consumed' ultimately only by individuals, and no social or community welfare function exists independent of the well-being achieved by individuals. Because no method has been found to measure utility or well-being, W is entirely psychological and subjective. It is nevertheless a useful concept, since it suggests that the end of all policy and planning is the well-being of people. It is well to emphasise that W consists of much more than purely economic factors. In fact, even the size and distribution of incomes extant in society are really only the means to superior human ends. W is composed of such final ends as freedom, equality, justice, opportunity and security. Thus, social, political, and cultural factors as well as economic ones must be included in any conceptualisation of welfare, and must be evaluated in any policy analysis.

In a democratic society, W is best regarded as given to the policy makers. That is, W is the welfare function of society, and not that of the policy maker. He must look outside himself for society's ultimate values: to statutes enacted by representatives of the people, to the constitution under which the people are governed, to rulings of the judicial system, etc. Of course, the determination of precisely what society's values are, is often a difficult problem, the solution of which the policy maker may participate in, or give articulation to. But he should not assume the responsibility of deciding what social values should be.

Policy Goals (Y_i)

The Y_i are the articulated goals of policy. They are deduced from the values of W. An example will illustrate this. An element of W may be an improvement in the range of opportunities for members of the society—the target goal may be a rise of per capita incomes of 5 per cent per annum, a rise in the literacy level to 70 per cent, or the complete eradication of poliomyelitis. It should be obvious that W and the Y_i are related, and the precise nature of the relationship between the two should be as clear as possible.

The policy maker may well decide the Y_i. In a democratic system, the people at the ballot box will judge the reasonableness of the Y_i chosen by the policy maker, as well as whether or not the targets are achieved. A great deal of thought and care should be given to the matter of selecting appropriate target variables.

It is especially important that the Y_i be framed in such a way that they are capable of being evaluated. Vaguely stated goals often cannot be. Contrast the following goals: (*a*) incomes should be increased; and (*b*) average annual per capita real incomes should be increased by 5 per cent. The first statement is general and vague, and cannot be easily appraised. The second is specific and quantitative, and can be readily evaluated.

Policy Instruments (Z_j)

The policy instruments available to achieve the target goals are the Z_j. For example, to reduce unemployment to 5 per cent of the workforce (a target to be sought), various policies (Z_j) may be utilised. The government may increase the quantity of money in the economic system, believing that more demand for goods will ultimately reduce unemployment. Or, a tax reduction may be given to businesses which invest in new capital equipment, under the theory that capital growth will produce more jobs. A great number of policies may be alleged to contribute to the accomplishment of the target. Policy analysis is largely composed of looking for and evaluating alternative ways to achieve the target goals. The great bulk of science, and most of economics, is concerned with these tasks.

Like any other scientific study, policy analysis should utilise scientific methods. Hypotheses that postulate how a given policy is expected to theoretically influence a given target should be formulated. Experimentation is the process of determining whether or not in fact the policy works in the way expected. Scientists call the set of theoretical hypotheses a model, and this is the analytical bridge between policy instruments and target variables. Models must be tested, however, both for logical consistency and for empirical validity. A set of statistical relationships must be established that reveal the processes of getting from the Z_j to the Y_i, and how efficient the processes are.

It should be remembered that just as the Y_i are prescribed by the ultimate values of society, so are the Z_j. That is, the Z_j must be evaluated in terms of political and moral acceptability, as well as efficiency in reaching the target. Certain kinds of policies, accepted and even encouraged in one class of society, are anathema to another class. Most democratic or non-totalitarian societies would never permit policies which seriously compromise the rights of individuals.

Non-controllable Factors and Irrelevant Variables (U_k) and (X_s)

There are some factors that affect the targets, and which cannot be manipulated or affected by policy. In the framework above, these are the U_k. An example might be the weather. Any target of agricultural production would be affected by rainfall or by frost, but till now, man has been largely ineffective in controlling these factors. They must be treated simply as 'non-controllable' in any policy analysis, but nonetheless must always be recognised and accounted for.

Finally, some effects of policy do not apply to the targets, or do not directly enter the community's welfare function, but should nevertheless be monitored because they are potentially significant. These are the X_s in the above framework, and are called the 'side effects' of policy. A policy to shift the production of energy from steam engines to internal combustion engines will have side effects that will not be significant for most situations. Internal combustion engines produce a variety of invisible pollutants in the air that are not a problem, until they reach certain dangerous threshold levels. These types of side effects must be watched, but may not affect the evaluation of policy until they reach problem proportions, in which case they may be shifted into the category of Y_i.

So much for the policy framework. It is primarily a taxonomic device, and should be of value in elucidating what is being sought, the available means of reaching what is being sought, and at what cost. It helps the policy maker to keep things straight.

An Action System

In the context of development management, an action system may be conceived of as consisting of four elements: the manager/actor, the objectives, the conditions (physical, technological, economic, social and political), and the means or instruments. Their relationships can be indicated by a simple diagram, as shown in Figure 7.2 (Schickele 1954: 60).

The manager or actor may be an employee of a public, private, cooperative, corporate or any other entity. The manager in any given system makes the decisions as to what means should be employed towards a given objective or set of objectives.

The objectives are what the manager wants to accomplish. They need to be clearly defined in operational terms.

The conditions of an action system are all those technical and institutional circumstances beyond the control of the manager, at least with respect to the particular programme under consideration. The instruments must be adapted to, or compatible with, the conditions under which the programme must operate.

The instruments are the policy measures or programme provisions employed to achieve the objectives. There are often many different

Figure 7.2
Diagram of an Action System

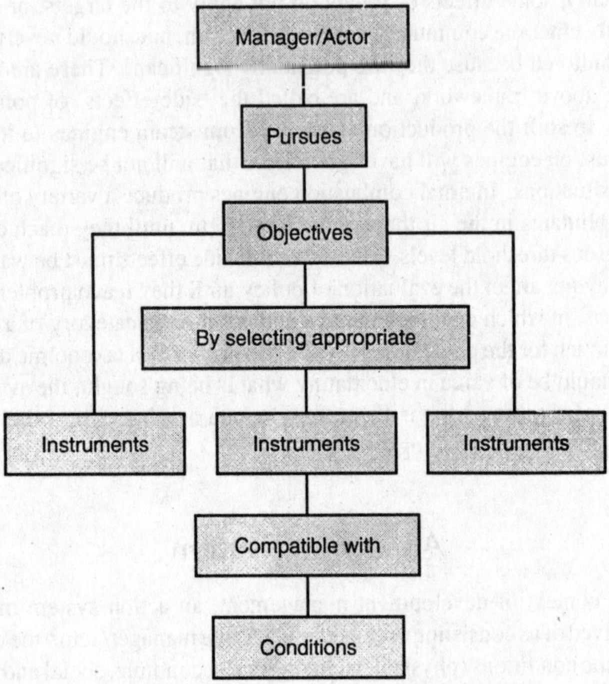

```
          ┌─────────────────────┐
          │    Manager/Actor     │
          └─────────────────────┘
                     │
          ┌─────────────────────┐
          │      Pursues         │
          └─────────────────────┘
                     │
          ┌─────────────────────┐
          │     Objectives       │
          └─────────────────────┘
                     │
          ┌─────────────────────┐
          │ By selecting appropriate │
          └─────────────────────┘
                     │
  ┌───────────┐ ┌───────────┐ ┌───────────┐
  │Instruments│ │Instruments│ │Instruments│
  └───────────┘ └───────────┘ └───────────┘
                     │
          ┌─────────────────────┐
          │   Compatible with    │
          └─────────────────────┘
                     │
          ┌─────────────────────┐
          │    Conditions        │
          └─────────────────────┘
```

instruments that could possibly serve a certain objective. Knowledge of economics is especially useful in making a wise choice in the selection of instruments.

The instruments can be grouped in the following five categories (Kirschen et al. 1964: Ch. 13):

1. Public finance.
2. Money and credit.
3. Exchange rate.
4. Direct controls.
5. Changes in the institutional framework.

A brief description of some of the major instruments follows.

The Instruments of Public Finance

Main Characteristics

This set of instruments covers most income and expenditure of the central, state and local governments. Government expenditure is largely devoted to the objective of the satisfaction of collective needs.

The main occasion for the use of the instruments of public finance is the annual budget; consequently many (but not all) of these instruments can be employed at annual intervals only. Because these instruments involve sums of money paid in or out of government accounts, the statistical documentation is accurate. *Not all items of government expenditure* and income can be regarded as instruments of economic policy. There are some flows which enter the public accounts, but which the government cannot, or does not, seek to change in order to achieve economic objectives. This is true, for instance, of interest paid on the public debt, imputed rent of government buildings, sales of government goods and services, its income from property, and its depreciation allowance.

The financial transactions of public enterprises are excluded from public finance because, in general, public enterprises behave in the same way as private ones.

Classification

There are 17 instruments in this category, and they can be further classified as follows:

Two Balances

1. The Current Balance, or Government Net Saving.
2. The Overall Balance, or the Change in the Government's Net Claims on Other Sectors.

Governments use both the current and overall balances as instruments of economic policy. They frequently decide to first increase or reduce the size of the current or overall deficit or surplus, and subsequently decide which items of income or expenditure to adjust. In this sense, the use of the current and overall balances is a separate instrument from the use of items of income and expenditure.

The extent to which governments can use the current and overall balances is limited by the fact that it is not easy to cut back government expenditure. People have opposed the idea both of a budget current surplus, and a budget current deficit.

Seven Expenditure Instruments

1. **Government Investment.** This is the most powerful of the expenditure instruments. But, in the short run, it is not always easy to change government investment. In the short run, the main form of government intervention is to advance or postpone the starting dates for public investment. Government investment is good for serving long-term objectives, and it is a major instrument of rural development in India. Although the central and state governments in India have invested thousands of crores of rupees in agricultural and rural development programmes since the commencement of the five year plans, the real investment (in terms of the rate of fixed capital formation) in the rural sector has been declining over the last many years. There is need to reverse the declining trend, and raise it to at least 12 per cent of the agricultural gross domestic product. Given the complementarity between public investment and private investment in the rural sector, any increase in the former will induce an increase in the latter also, and thus the total investment in the sector will increase at a higher rate. Increased investment is needed in basic infrastructure, such as rural roads, transport and communications, irrigation, watershed development, agro-processing and marketing facilities, and agricultural research and extension. The establishment by the central government of a Rural Infrastructure Development Fund under NABARD in 1995–96 is a welcome step in the right direction.

2. **Subsidies and Capital Transfers to Enterprises.** Subsidies are, in principle, fairly flexible, and they can be used selectively and given to any particular inputs, or type of activity, or a particular region. The main objective which this instrument can serve is protection and priorities, either to particular regions or to particular inputs or activities. The instrument can take several forms, such as the promotion of use of new inputs by subsidising their prices, promotion of investment (by subsidising interest rates) or exports, keeping down the prices of the products of rural industries, and thus helping to keep up their sales. When subsidies on investments or exports are given for long periods of time, they serve the objective of expansion.

In India, subsidies constitute an important means of promoting agricultural and rural development. Subsidies are provided on food, canal irrigation water, electricity for agricultural uses, fertilisers, institutional credit to certain categories of borrowers, and purchase of certain income-generating assets by the poor under poverty alleviation and employment programmes, such as the Integrated Rural Development Programme, Million Wells Scheme, and the *Ganga Kalyan Yojana*. In the wake of the new economic policy, there is a strong pressure on the government from the World Bank and the International Monetary Fund, as also from certain sections of Indian society, to phase out all kinds of subsidies. However, the government has so far withstood all the pressures, as it is a politically hazardous decision for any government to withdraw subsidies to the rural sector, which constitutes the biggest vote bank and hence determines the fate of political parties. Besides, there is also a strong economic rationale for subsidies to the rural sector. First, the rural sector produces and supplies the basic necessities of life to people, and thus provides food security, for which no amount of cost (subsidies) is high enough. Second, it has been established through empirical studies that Indian agriculture is net-taxed, i.e., considering the producer prices of agricultural produce and the input prices paid by the farmer vis-à-vis the corresponding world prices, the agricultural sector gives more to our society than it receives from it in terms of subsidies and grants (Gulati 1989: A57-A65; Gulati and Sharma 1992: A106-A116). Third, the extent of subsidies in Indian agriculture is much less than in many developed countries, such as the USA, Canada, Denmark, Japan, and so on.

3. **Transfers to Households.** Governments in many developed countries pay pensions to old people, sickness allowances to invalids, unemployment benefits, and so on. Such expenditure is financed partly by contributions paid to the social security agencies, and partly by transfers from the central government. Although this expenditure is large, it is not of great value as an instrument of economic policy—certainly not for a short-term policy. Its influence is mainly limited to its effects on income distribution-transfer from taxpayers to lower income groups. In India, this instrument so far has been of relatively minor importance. However, a significant step in this direction was taken by the central government by launching, on 15 August 1995, a National Social

Welfare Programme. The programme comprises three components, namely, the National Old Age Pension Scheme, the National Family Benefit Scheme, and the National Maternity Benefit Scheme (GOI 1997a: 53–54).

4. **Government Stock Changes.** Governments sometimes build up stocks themselves by direct controls or subsidies for the satisfaction of collective needs and security of supply, e.g., stockpiling of foodgrains, minerals, metals, coal, etc. Stockpiling of wheat, rice and sugar represents the use of this measure in India. Stocks of foodgrains consist of buffer stocks, and of operational stocks. Buffer stocks include the base level stocks which cannot be pulled out of the system, and operational stocks are those which are used to reduce fluctuations in availability and prices of foodgrains, and to reaching the foodgrains to the poor at reasonable prices through fair price shops under the revamped Public Distribution System (PDS).

5. **Current Purchases of Goods and Services.** This instrument can be selective, for example, purchases in a particular region or from a particular subsector. Purchases can be delayed or advanced, with the objective of price stability or full employment. Some governments try to concentrate their orders, particularly their military orders, in periods of slackening economic activity. There are many examples of current purchases of goods by the central and state governments in India.

6. **Wages and Salaries.** Governments do not often attempt to manipulate their wage and salary bill for purposes of economic policy. Some expenditure on in-service education or training can serve to increase the mobility of labour, or to improve income distribution. In India, wages and salaries in the public and organised sectors are linked to the cost of living index, and hence are revised from time to time to neutralise the effect of inflation on incomes.

7. **Transfers to the Rest of the World.** This is not a very important instrument in India. Transfers are usually made to poor countries and international institutions, like the United Nations Development Programme, and the International Labour Organisation.

Eight Revenue Instruments

1. **Direct Taxes on Incomes of Households.** There are fairly strict limits on the extent to which governments, in times of peace,

can increase their revenue from personal income tax. First, this tax is very unpopular with the middle and upper income groups. Second, it is a tax which is often avoided or evaded, and the higher it is, the greater is the temptation to evade it.

However, direct taxes are very important in economic policy because they are progressive, they redistribute income and they act as built-in stabilisers: their yield varies more than incomes, and therefore stimulates demand in periods of depression and reduces it in boom periods, thus serving the objectives of full employment and price stability. With a 'pay as you earn' system, there is not much time-lag before the stabilising action comes into play.

In India, income from agriculture is exempt from tax mainly because (a) most of the 91 per cent of farms having landholdings of four hectares or less are not financially viable, and their income is well below the level of income exempted from income tax under the Income Tax Act 1961; (b) it is very difficult and costly to assess farm incomes correctly; and (c) the cost of collection of tax is very high vis-à-vis the revenue collected.

2. **Direct Taxes on Enterprises' Incomes.** Company profits are taxed as a whole, i.e., with no distinction between distributed and undistributed profits. They also have an automatic anticyclical effect, as in economic fluctuations profits tend to vary more than national income as a whole. Investment can be encouraged by special depreciation allowances.

3. **Indirect Taxes on Internal Transactions.** They are the largest of the income instruments, and have two great advantages. First, they are politically convenient because their incidence is less obviously painful than those of income taxes. Second, they can be made highly selective. One minor disadvantage of these taxes is that there may be awkward economic effects if people expect a change—there may be a rush of anticipatory buying if they think the tax will go up, or demand may fall sharply, if they think the tax will fall.

4. **Customs Duties.** Export duties are rarely used, but import duties are used universally. They can be both flexible and selective, but their use is limited by international agreements and the fear of reprisals by foreign governments. The main purpose of the imposition of these duties is protection—usually of particular industries and particular commodities. In India, until the end of the 1980s, both imports and exports of agricultural commodities, excepting

tea, coffee, tobacco and spices, were restricted through tariff (customs duties) and non-tariff barriers. But now, under the new trade policy, import duties on most of the agricultural commodities have been drastically reduced, or completely waived.

5. **Social Security Contributions.** They have been rarely used as instruments of economic policy. They have a regressive effect on income distribution.

6. **Taxes on Property.** They include both taxes on wealth, and separate taxes on land and buildings, and serve as instruments for the distribution of incomes.

7. **Succession Duties and Inheritance Tax.** They have some effect on income distribution.

8. **Transfers from the Rest of the World.** Donations from the rich to the poor countries are important aids to development.

Constraints on the Use of the Instruments of Public Finance

The main purpose of public expenditure is to satisfy collective needs, and this limits the extent to which it can be manipulated for other objectives. Political pressures and pressure groups can have a very strong influence on policies in the field of public finance.

The Instruments of Money and Credit

Main Characteristics

This set of instruments includes those which serve to make it either more difficult, or easier, for persons, companies or governments to borrow money. In contrast to budgetary measures, which can be described as open decisions openly arrived at, a great deal of mystery and mystique surrounds monetary and credit policy. It is not always possible to find out exactly what is being done.

Institutions

The government and the Reserve Bank of India are responsible for promulgating these instruments.

Classification

The list of instruments may be classified as follows:

1. *Government's New Borrowing and Lending.*

    a) Lending abroad.
    b) Lending to households and enterprises.
    c) Borrowing from abroad.
    d) Borrowing from households and enterprises.

2. *Government Operation in Existing Debt.*

    a) Open-market operations in short-term securities.
    b) Other open-market operations.

3. *Interest Rate Instruments.*

    a) Bank rate.
    b) Legal imposition of maximum rates.
    c) Government guarantees of loans.

4. *Instruments Acting on Credit Creation by Banks.*

    a) Reserve ratios (Statutory Liquidity Ratio and Cash Reserve Ratio).
    b) Quantitative stops on advances.
    c) Approval of individual loans.
    d) Other directives, recommendations and persuasion.

5. *Instruments Acting on Lending or Borrowing by Other Agents.*

    a) Control of borrowings of local authorities and nationalised enterprises.
    b) Control of borrowings of private companies by new issues.
    c) Control of hire purchase transactions.
    d) Control of other financial institutions.

The Instrument of Exchange Rate

Main Characteristics

This instrument has the following three main features:

1. It is extremely powerful, can have considerable effects on the economy of the country concerned, and also on the countries from which it imports and exports.
2. It has a strong emotional content. The exchange rate of a country's currency gives its price in terms of gold and foreign currencies. Any reduction in this price is considered a kind of national defeat.

3. Further, any reduction brings with it the risk that it will lead to a loss of confidence in the national currency. Moreover, it leads to price rises and changes in the distribution of incomes, which seem particularly perilous.

The Way in Which Exchange Rates can be Changed

The exchange rate is a single instrument, not a family of instruments. But there are different types of exchange rates, and consequently different types of changes in them. The exchange rate can be single or multiple, fixed or floating.

The Policy Makers

Decisions to alter the exchange rate are, of course, national decisions. But foreign and international influences can often be very important. In most countries, it is the decision of the cabinet, and it is the prime minister and minister of finance who together take the responsibility of changing the exchange rate. Parliament is virtually never concerned with the decision to devalue or revalue. The rules of the International Monetary Fund (IMF) require that all member countries should consult the Fund and obtain its prior approval to all changes of 10 per cent or more.

The Objectives

Changes in exchange rate must either be revaluations or devaluations. The objectives of revaluation are price stability, and to a lesser extent, the international division of labour. Devaluations are always meant to improve the balance of payments, sometimes to expand production, and also for the international division of labour.

If there is some unutilised capacity in the country which devalues (whereas the countries which buy its exports are fully employed), then its elasticity of supply will be high enough for it to be able to meet the increased demand for its exports. If the country which devalues is fully employed, devaluation might *worsen* the balance of payments. Devaluation can be used as a method of increasing employment in an underemployed country, since it stimulates exports and holds back imports.

Constraints on the Use of the Exchange Rate

There is a tendency for it to be used as an instrument of last resort, when all other weapons which serve the same objectives have failed. There is a strong hostility to the use of this instrument, among politicians, among certain pressure groups, and among the public in general.

The Instruments of Direct Controls

Main Characteristics

Direct controls are powerful instruments of economic policy. They can take effect very quickly, and they can be selective. Because of their quick effect, these instruments are particularly used in crises, emergency and periods of war and to deal with short-term economic problems. The results are graduated and fairly precisely calculable. In general, direct controls are less effective in dealing with long-term problems than with short-term ones.

Classification

Three main categories of this set of instruments can be identified:

1. *Control of Foreign Trade, Foreign Exchange and Immigration.*

   a) Control of private imports.
   b) State import trading.
   c) Control of private exports.
   d) Exchange control.
   e) Control of immigration.

2. *Control of Prices.*

   a) Price control of goods and services.
   b) Rent control.
   c) Dividend control.
   d) Control of wages.

3. *Other Controls on the Internal Economy.*

   a) Control of investment.
   b) Raw material allocations.
   c) Control of operations.
   d) Regulation of conditions of work.
   e) Control of exploitation of natural resources.
   f) Rationing of consumer goods.
   g) Quality controls and standards.

Institutions

Direct controls are normally administered by the ordinary civil service departments. Sometimes special institutions are set up for this purpose. In the field of international trade, decisions are taken in the framework of international institutions and agreements.

Constraints

Direct controls are very effective in the short term in holding back economic activity, but they are much less effective in stimulating it. Businessmen and consumers can be prevented by controls from doing certain things, but it is often virtually impossible to compel them to take positive action.

Direct controls have also been used much more to deal with short-term than with long-term or structural problems. Controls do not, as a general rule, modify the underlying market forces which brought about the situation which needed control. Consequently, two things may happen in the long run. First, the market forces which are held back by controls in one sector may break out in another. Second, if it is in the interests of both consumers and producers to evade the controls, then as time goes on, evasion is likely to become more widespread: black markets will spring up and administration will become more expensive.

With this instrument, as with others, there are psychological complications to be taken into account. Any prior warning that controls may be imposed will cause consumers to stock up.

Changes in the Institutional Framework

Main Characteristics

The instruments described so far have all been instruments which are used within the existing institutional framework, and the changes made in these instruments can be quantified.

Changes in the institutional framework do not lend themselves easily to quantification, and usually require a change in the laws. Since it takes time to change the institutional framework, these changes are usually made with long-term rather than short-term objectives in mind. But there are occasions on which the institutional framework has been changed in order to facilitate the use of the instruments for short-term policy. The nationalisation of 14 major commercial banks in India in 1969 is a good example of the use of this instrument.

Classification

There are three categories in this set of instruments.

1. *Institutional Changes Involving Other Instruments.*

a) Changes in the system of transfers to households (Public Finance).
b) Changes in the system of subsidies to enterprises (Public Finance).
c) Changes in the tax system (Public Finance).
d) Changes in the credit system (Money and Credit).
e) Changes in the system of direct controls (Direct Control).

2. *Institutional Changes Directly Affecting Production.*

a) Agricultural land reforms.
b) Changing the conditions of competition (restriction on monopolies).
c) Changes increasing labour's influence in management.
d) Changes in the extent of public ownership in industry.
e) Creation of national institutions.

3. *Institutional Changes in the International Framework.*

a) Creation of international institutions.

Constraints on the Use of Changes in the Institutional Framework

1. The establishment of a new institution, or a major change in the institutional framework, is usually a fairly major policy step which often meets with more opposition than does the use of an existing instrument.
2. Since changes of this kind usually involve new laws, they have to go through a lengthy procedure of parliamentary approval.

In a developing country like India, institutional changes constitute the most important instrument of promoting rural development. Institutional changes, particularly land reforms, contributed significantly to agricultural development in China and Taiwan. In India, although the process of institutional reforms was initiated in the early fifties, it is not yet complete, and rural development still continues to be stifled by the lack of appropriate institutions and organisations.

Concluding Remarks

To achieve the objectives of a rural development policy efficiently, it is necessary that a set of appropriate instruments be identified for each of the objectives of the policy, and that the chosen instruments are set at their optimal levels. Identification of appropriate instruments, and determination of their optimal levels, are both better done by public policy analysts than anyone else, using a quantitative framework that relates the instruments to the objectives of the policy. For rural development policies, instruments belonging to all the five categories, namely, public finance, money and credit, exchange rate, direct controls, and changes in the institutional framework, are relevant. Out of some 62 instruments in these five categories, the following are more potent and are more commonly used than the others:

- Public investment.
- Subsidies.
- Direct income transfers to households.
- Buffer stocks of foodgrains.
- Direct taxes and tax relief measures.
- Customs duties.
- Institutional credit.
- Bank rate.
- Control of imports and exports.
- Minimum support prices.
- Control of wages.
- Control of exploitation of natural resources.
- Allocation of raw materials.
- Quality control and standards.
- Agrarian reforms, including land reforms.
- Creation of new institutions.

Choice of appropriate instruments needs to be made carefully, keeping in view the prevailing socio-economic and political environment. In many cases, instruments are not properly selected, and their levels are not consistent with the objectives they seek to achieve. This results in the wastage of valuable public resources, and unnecessary delays in achieving the objectives.

●

8

Community Development Programme

Introduction

India has a very long history of experimenting with various approaches to rural development. Even in the pre-Independence era, a number of rural reconstruction experiments were initiated by nationalist thinkers and social reformers. Well-known among them were the Gurgaon Experiment of F. L. Brayne (1920), the Marthandam Experiment of Spencer Hatch (1921), the Sriniketan Experiment of poet Rabindra Nath Tagore (in the 1920s), the Sewagram Experiment of Mahatma Gandhi (1933), the Firka Development Scheme (1946), and the Etawah Pilot Project of Albert Mayer (1948). Besides these experiments by social reformers and missionaries, various departments of the government—agriculture, cooperation, irrigation, health, education—also tried in their own way to resolve rural problems falling within their respective jurisdictions.

The Grow More Food Campaign (GMFC) was India's first organised effort to increase food production. Although the campaign was launched in 1943 in the wake of the Bengal famine, it did not make much headway until 1947. The campaign had a two-pronged approach. First, to bring idle but potentially productive land under the plough, and second, to stimulate cultivator interest in increasing crop yield per hectare. In 1948, the GMFC was reviewed by the Thakurdass Committee, and following its recommendations, the campaign was reoriented in 1950–51. In the following year, the GMFC became a part of the First Plan. In 1952, the Government of India appointed the Grow More Food Inquiry Committee under the chairmanship of Sir V.T. Krishnamachari to evaluate the campaign. The Committee found, *inter alia*, that (*a*) all aspects of village life are interrelated, and no lasting results can be achieved if individual aspects of it are dealt with in isolation; and (*b*) the movement touched only a fringe of the population, and did not arouse widespread enthusiasm, or become in any sense a national programme. The committee also made a number of recommendations regarding the future policy of the GMFC. One of the recommendations was that an extension agency should be set up for rural work, which would reach every farmer and assist in the coordinated development of rural life. It was out of this background and experience that India's Community Development Programme (CDP) was born.

The following basic premises were fundamental in India's decision to create the National Community Development Programme in 1952 (Ensminger 1968: 3):

1. The overall development of the rural community can be brought about only with effective participation of the people, backed by the coordination of technical and other services necessary for securing the best from such initiative and self-help. It was to provide the necessary institutional structure and services that early attention was given to the development of basic democratic village institutions especially panchayati raj, cooperatives and village schools.
2. The problems of rural development have to be viewed from a holistic perspective, and the efforts to solve them have to be multifaceted.

One of the important initial moving forces in community development was Prime Minister Jawaharlal Nehru's interest in the programme. Nehru felt that one of India's most important undeveloped resources was the people, living in its some six hundred thousand villages. Nehru saw in community development the way to involve the village people in building a new India. He visualised that through their involvement in self-help oriented programmes, would come the development of the people and people's institutions—both essential ingredients in moving India towards one of its most clearly stated objectives, that of developing into a viable democracy.

Meaning and Objectives

Community development may be defined as a process by which the efforts of the people themselves are combined with those of governmental authorities, to improve the economic, social and cultural conditions of communities, to integrate these communities into the life of the nation, and to enable them to contribute fully to national progress.

The central objective of the CDP was to secure the total development of the material and human resources of rural areas, and to develop local leadership and self-governing institutions. The basic idea was to raise the levels of living of rural people through a number of programmes. This objective was to be attained by bringing about a rapid increase in food and agricultural production by strengthening programmes of resource development, such as minor irrigation and soil conservation, by improving the effectiveness of farm inputs supply systems, and by providing agricultural extension services to farmers.

The draft outline of the programme, which received the sanction of the Government of India, stated at the beginning that:

> The purpose of the Community Projects shall be to serve as a pilot in the establishment, for men, women and children covered by the project areas, of the 'Right to Live'; food—the principal item in the wherewithals for this purpose—receiving the primary emphasis in the initial stages of the programme (quoted in Ensminger 1972: 4).

Coverage

The CDP was formally inaugurated on 2 October 1952. It was intended to be the first step in a programme of intensive development, which was expected over a period of time to cover the entire country. Initially, the CDP was launched in 55 project areas located in different parts of the country. Another 110 areas had necessarily to be added to the original 55 in the course of six months. Demands for the expansion of the CDP from members in the state legislatures and from members of parliament continued skyrocketing. It was difficult to resist the mounting political pressure to expand the programme.

A new, somewhat less ambitious scheme, called the National Extension Service (NES) was evolved and launched in 1953. Whereas in the CDP, intensive development was taken up in all fields, the NES scheme was designed to provide the essential basic staff and a small amount of funds, with which the people could start the development work, essentially on the basis of self-help. The NES blocks were subsequently converted into CDP blocks. The pattern of the CDP was further revised with effect from 1 April 1958. According to this pattern, the CDP blocks had a life of 10 years, consisting of Stages I and II of equal duration, the budget provision in Stage I being higher. Besides, a one-year pre-extension phase preceding Stage I, with attention exclusively devoted to agricultural development, was introduced from 1 April 1959. From 1 April 1969, the CDP was transferred to the state sector.

Originally, each of the 55 project areas was to embrace approximately 300 villages, with a population of about 200,000 people, and cover a cultivated area of approximately 150,000 acres. A project area was to be divided into three development blocks, each comprising about 100 villages and a population of about 65,000 people. In areas where a full project was not considered feasible, one or two development blocks were started to begin with. The 55 projects were to include approximately 16,500 villages, and over a crore of people.

However, as mentioned earlier, the CDP had to be expanded phenomenally under political pressure, and soon it became a national programme encompassing 400 million rural people across the four corners of the country. Indeed, while America took 50 years, despite its enormous resources, to establish a rural extension programme covering 7 per cent of its rural population, India was obliged under political pressure to set a target to cover the whole country with the NES programme in eight years, and the more extensive CDP in 12 years. Both the programme as well as the inputs had necessarily to be diluted under this abnormal rate of expansion. The CDP now covers all the rural areas in the country.

Activities

The following rural community development activities are undertaken in such varying degrees (within the limits of the available funds), as are advisable under the circumstances peculiar to each block (Ensminger 1972: 105–07):

Agricultural and Related Matters

1. Reclamation of available virgin and waste land.
2. Provision of water for agriculture through irrigation canals, tube-wells, surface wells, tanks, lift irrigation from rivers, lakes and pools, etc.
3. Development of rural electrification.
4. Provision of commercial fertilisers.

5. Provision of quality seeds.
6. Promotion of improved agricultural techniques and land utilisation.
7. Provision of veterinary aid.
8. Provision of technical information, materials and bulletins on agriculture.
9. Provision for the dissemination of information through slides, films, radio broadcasts and lectures.
10. Provision of improved agricultural implements.
11. Promotion of marketing and credit facilities.
12. Provision of breeding centres for animal husbandry.
13. Development of inland fisheries.
14. Promotion of home economics.
15. Development of fruit and vegetable cultivation.
16. Provision of soil surveys and information.
17. Encouragement of the use of natural and compost manures.
18. Provision of arboriculture, including plantation of forests.

Communications

1. Provision of roads.
2. Encouragement of mechanical road transport services.
3. Development of animal transport facilities.

Education

1. Provision of compulsory and free education, preferably basic education, at the elementary stage.
2. Provision of high and middle schools.
3. Provision of adult education and library services.

Health

1. Provision of sanitation (including drainage and disposal of wastes) and public health measures.
2. Provision for the control of malaria and other diseases.
3. Provision of improved drinking water supplies.
4. Provision of medical aid for the ailing.
5. Antenatal care of expectant mothers and midwifery services.
6. Provision of generalised public health service and education.

Training

1. Refresher courses to improve the existing standard of artisans.
2. Training of agriculturists.
3. Training of extension assistants.
4. Training of artisans.
5. Training of supervisors, managerial personnel, health workers and executive officers for projects.

Social Welfare

1. Organisation of community entertainment.
2. Provision of audio-visual aids for instruction and recreation.
3. Organisation of sports activities.
4. Organisation of *melas* (village fairs).
5. Organisation of the cooperative and self-help movement.

Supplementary Employment

1. Encouragement of cottage industries and crafts as the main or subsidiary occupation.
2. Encouragement of medium and small-scale industries to employ surplus hands for local needs, or for export outside project areas.
3. Encouragement of employment through trade, auxiliary and welfare services.
4. Construction of brick kilns and sawmills to provide building materials for local needs.

Housing

1. Demonstration and training in improved techniques and designs for rural housing.
2. Encouragement of improved rural housing on a self-help basis.

Organisation

The CDP was undertaken and implemented by the Government of India and the various state governments in cooperation with one another. For this purpose, an organisational structure was contemplated under the Technical Cooperation Programme Agreement of 5 January 1952 between the GOI and the Government of USA. Some salient features of the organisational structure are briefly presented in the following paragraphs.

Central Organisation

The GOI formed a Central Committee at the national level with the Prime Minister as the Chairperson, the Members of the Planning Commission, and the Minister of Food and Agriculture as members to lay down the broad policies, and provide the general supervision for the agreed projects. An Administrator was appointed to plan, direct, and coordinate the programme throughout India, under the general supervision of the Central Committee, and in consultation with appropriate authorities in the various states. All nation-building ministries were directed to collaborate with the programme through the Community Projects Administration (CPA) which was specially created for the purpose. The Administrator was assisted by a team of highly qualified executive staff, in areas such as administration, finance, personnel (training), community planning and other matters, and by operating divisions in the fields of (a) agriculture; (b) irrigation; (c) health; (d) education; (e) industries; (f) housing; and (g) community facilities. This staff worked with the state, district and project level workers to implement the CDP.

The CDP organisation at the national level has undergone a number of changes. In September 1956, a new Ministry of Community Development was created. Thereafter, for many years, the Department of Rural Development under the Ministry of Agriculture and Rural Development was in overall charge of the programme in the country. Now (1998–99), there is a separate Ministry of Rural Areas and Employment in charge of all centrally sponsored rural development programmes.

State Organisation

Each state government established a state development committee or similar body consisting of the Chief Minister as the chairperson, ministers representing the nation-building departments as members, and a highly competent officer as Development Commissioner, who acted as the secretary to the Committee. He was responsible for directing the programme within the state, and coordinated the activities of the heads of various departments concerned with the programme. He was assisted by suitable operating staff.

Many states constituted state planning commissions or state planning boards for this purpose, and the Development Commissioner in many states was redesignated as the Agricultural Production Commissioner, or the Principal Secretary, Agriculture.

District Organisation

This was established at the district level. Where necessary, a District Development Officer (DDO) was responsible for the CDP in his district. This officer has the status of an additional collector, and is responsible for the execution of the community projects as well as the general development in the district. He operates under the direction of the state Development Commissioner, and is advised by a district development board consisting of the officers of the various departments concerned with community development, with the collector as chairperson, and the district development officer as the executive secretary.

Now, after the 73rd Constitution Amendment, statutory zila parishads are responsible for the implementation of the programme in the districts. The zila parishad is chaired by an elected non-official, and the DDO is the chief executive officer of the zila parishad. There are state-to-state variations in the organisational structure of the CDP at the district level.

Block Organisation

At the block level, a Block Development Committee (BDC) was established with the sub-divisional officer acting as its chairperson, and a Block Development Officer (BDO) acting as its executive secretary. The BDO is responsible for the implementation of the programme within the block. He is assisted by a number of Extension Officers (EOs) in the fields of agriculture, animal husbandry, rural engineering, public health, cooperation, social education, women's and children's programmes, and rural industries.

After the introduction of panchayati raj, the BDC has been replaced by the statutory block parishad or *samiti* or block panchayati samiti, which is chaired by an elected non-official. The BDO is the secretary of the block samiti.

Village Organisation

Initially, at the village level, 10 Village Level Workers (VLWs) or *gram sevaks* and two *gram sevikas* were responsible for implementing the programme within a cluster of villages. VLWs work under the advice and control of the BDO. With the establishment of panchayati raj in all states now, the village or gram panchayat, which is headed by an elected non-official, is responsible for implementing the programme within its jurisdiction. The VLW assigned to the panchayat is its secretary.

The Community Development Programme and Panchayati Raj

Soon after the creation of the new Ministry of Community Development in January 1957, the Government of India appointed a committee under the chairmanship of Balwantray Mehta to study the working of the CDP, and suggest how best it could be maintained and implemented. The committee recommended a three-tier system of local government, christened 'Panchayati Raj' by Jawaharlal Nehru. At the grassroots or village level were to be formed village panchayats, at the middle or block level were to be panchayat samitis, and at the apex or district level, zila parishads were to be formed. These new bodies were to have wide powers and adequate finance. The committee offered two broad directional thrusts: first, it argued that there should be administrative decentralisation for the effective implementation of development programmes; and second; that the decentralised administrative system should be under the control of elected bodies.

The three-tier structure of panchayati raj institutions was brought into existence after the Mehta Committee Scheme was approved by the National Development Council (NDC) in January 1958. The NDC affirmed the objectives behind the introduction of democratic institutions at the district and block levels, and suggested that each state should work out the structure which suited its conditions best.

The new system of panchayati raj institutions was first adopted in Rajasthan and Andhra Pradesh in 1959, followed by Assam, Tamil Nadu and Karnataka in 1960, Maharashtra in 1962, and Gujarat and West Bengal in 1963 and 1964 respectively. The new system was implemented without any reservations whatsoever in Gujarat and Maharashtra, and with some reservations in Rajasthan, Andhra Pradesh, Tamil Nadu and Assam. In the rest of the states, the response varied from reluctant implementation to dilution, diarchy and ritualism in the system. With the operationalisation of the 73rd Constitution Amendment, a three-tier structure of panchayati raj institutions has been adopted all over the country.

Financing

The Community Development Programme was conceived, planned and initiated as a people's self-help programme. Parliament appropriated funds annually on the condition that the funds had to be committed within the year appropriated, or reverted to the treasury. The administrative bureaucracy—centre and state—projected targets and allocated funds for the specific projects undertaken by community development blocks.

Initially, financial and technical assistance to the CDP was made available by the US government under the Technical Cooperation Programme Agreement signed on 5 January 1952. Financial assistance worth $8.67 million was made available for payments to be made outside India in US dollars for the procurement of supplies, equipment, services and other programme materials and their transportation to India (exclusive of allotments from other operational agreements). The dollar funds provided under the agreement to finance the programme were to be treated as a loan to the states to the extent deemed feasible and advisable by the GOI, estimated at about 55 per cent of the total dollar funds, to be repaid upon such terms and conditions as would be determined. The proceeds of such repayments were to be deposited in a fund for the prosecution of further projects of economic development mutually agreeable to the Governments of India and the USA, as provided in the agreement.

The US government also made available funds necessary to pay the salaries and other expenses of the technicians employed by the United States government for the purpose of providing technical assistance in the CDP.

To meet the local expenditure on the implementation of the CDP, funds were drawn from the GOI, the state governments, as well as the people. For each project area, the programme prescribed a qualifying scale of voluntary contribution from the people in the form of money as well as labour. Where the state offered material assistance for the execution of these projects, the expenses were shared by the state and central governments in the proportion of 1 : 3 in the case of non-recurring items. However, the recurring expenditure was shared equally between them. For productive works like irrigation and reclamation of land, to mention just two, necessary funds were advanced by the central government to the state governments in the form of loans. From 1 April 1969, the CDP was transferred to the state sector. The state governments are now free to provide resources for the programme from within their state plan ceiling, according to the priority accorded to the programme by them. The central government's assistance to the states is now given as annual lump-sum grants, as block grants and block loans.

Technical Assistance and Supporting Projects

The Technical Cooperation Administration (TCA) for India provided technical assistance to the CDP at both the central and state levels. At the central level, the services of the Director of the TCA were made available to the Central Committee. The Director was assisted by a deputy director for community development, who coordinated and expedited all technical assistance to the CDP. The TCA also provided specialists in agriculture, irrigation, education, health, agricultural extension, vocational training, agricultural engineering, and extension methods and materials. These specialists served as advisers and consultants to the extent required.

The CDP was related to, and supported in part by, most of the other projects under the Indo-American Technical Cooperation Programme.

The fertilisers required by the CDP were acquired and distributed, pursuant to Operational Agreement No. 1 dated 1 May 1952. The iron and steel needed for farm implements and tools was acquired and distributed, pursuant to Operational Agreement No. 2 dated 29 May 1952.

The tubewells to be constructed in community project areas were allocated from the project for ground water irrigation, pursuant to Operational Agreement No. 6 dated 31 May 1952.

Information and services with respect to soils and fertiliser application were made available to the programme from the project, to determine soil fertility and fertiliser use, pursuant to Operational Agreement No. 4 dated 31 May 1952. Similarly, assistance in malaria control in the community project areas was forthcoming from the project for malaria control planned under the Technical Cooperation Programme between the two governments.

Training of VLWs and project supervisors for the CDP was carried out under the village workers training programme by the two governments and the Ford Foundation of America.

The necessary allocation of funds for equipment, construction, supplies, information and other support for such projects was determined by the particular ministry supervising the project, and the Administrator. Each ministry supervising the project was responsible for all necessary arrangements for the proper and effective allocation of such support to the CDP.

Evaluation

A continuing evaluation of the progress of the CDP was expected to be undertaken by the Planning Commission, in close cooperation with the Ford Foundation and the Technical Cooperation Administration. Accordingly, the CDP has been reviewed from time to time by the Programme Evaluation Organisation of the Planning Commission, the National

Institute of Rural Development (formerly known as the National Institute of Community Development), and by various other research institutes and individual research scholars. In addition, various committees and commissions were also appointed by the government to look into the functioning of the CDP, and make recommendations for the improvement of its effectiveness.

There have been a number of surveys and studies which have highlighted the tangible achievements of the CDP in terms of distribution of improved seeds, use of chemical fertilisers, plant protection chemicals, improved farm tools and equipment, construction of roads, wells, irrigation canals, establishment of primary health centres, rural dispensaries, *balwadis* (nurseries), etc. On the basis of these studies, it would be fair to say that the CDP contributed significantly towards the creation of basic socio-economic infrastructure in rural areas, and helped expand and improve the production base of the rural economy of India. The CDP has also fulfilled, to a large extent, the equity norm of rural development.

However, the CDP failed to achieve the expected increase in agricultural production. This failure could be attributed to its diffused character, as it did not put sufficient and direct emphasis on agricultural production. The financial, material and administrative resources of the CDP were spread too thinly—albeit uniformly—all over the countryside to produce any tangible impact on agricultural production and rural poverty. In other words, the resources devoted to agricultural production fell short of the 'critical minimum' required to escape from the perpetual problem of low productivity in Indian agriculture.

By the middle of the Second Plan, it became increasingly evident that whatever the success of the CDP, a new approach would be required if agricultural production was to keep ahead of the demands of India's mounting population. With foodgrain production at 64 million tonnes in 1957–58 (five million tonnes below the 1953–54 level), India faced its first post-Independence food crisis, and as a result there was a substantial shift in the agricultural development strategy of the CDP.

Douglas Ensminger (1968: 12), however, does not subscribe to this criticism of the CDP. In his opinion, the failure on the agricultural front was due partly to the fact that the agricultural prices had, prior to 1964, been oriented towards cheap food for poor people, and had thus served as disincentives to the producers to produce more, and partly due to the planners' unrealistically low estimate of the time required (15 years) to attain self-sufficiency in food production in India. He asserts that a more realistic time-frame for India to achieve self-sufficiency in this area must be thought of as closer to 25 years, starting in 1952, and not 15 years.

Some of the other criticisms of the CDP include that: (*a*) it has not been a people's programme; (*b*) it has followed a 'blueprint' approach to rural development; (*c*) it has employed a large army of untrained extension workers who, because of lack of coordination among themselves, were less a source of help to the villagers and more a source of bewilderment and confusion; (*d*) a spirit of ritualism has permeated the block programmes, and the inauguration, opening or foundation stone laying became the 'be-all and end-all' of all block activities; and (*e*) there was lack of functional responsibility at the block level that led to a good deal of confusion and interdepartmental jealousy.

Despite all this criticism, however, it would be fair to say that the CDP was instrumental in laying the foundation for further growth and development of the rural economy of India.

Major Points

One can briefly highlight some of the lessons learnt from the experience of the CDP in India as follows:

1. Agriculture should be treated second only to defence in national importance, and in its claim to development funds.
2. Agricultural price policy should be producer-oriented.
3. The scarce financial, material and administrative resources should be concentrated in the most responsive areas, if rapid increase in food production is to be attained.
4. An appropriate combination of populistic and paternalistic approaches to development has a higher chance of success than either the *populistic approach* alone, or the *paternalistic approach* alone.
5. The government alone cannot effectively tackle all the problems of agricultural and rural development. The private sector, voluntary agencies, cooperatives, corporations, multinationals, foreign governments, international agencies and organisations can all play important roles in the process of development. The role of the government should be to define the roles of other agencies, coordinate, and, if necessary, regulate their activities and provide such infrastructural facilities and services as cannot be provided by any other agency.

6. A review of the failure of a number of development programmes reveals significant lacunae in the application of requisite management skills in the planning and execution of these programmes. The lack of adequate management analysis in the planning process, insufficient management competence in 'nation-building' departments, and the short supply of professional managers for local enterprises and agencies which provide the essential services for development programmes at the final point of application, can be identified as three general lacunae.

7. Implementation of the CDP deserved much more in the form of resources and attention than it had received. Better implementation can be ensured only if those responsible for the actual implementation are paid reasonably well, trained appropriately and motivated sufficiently.

8. In replicating a pilot project on a national scale, it is better to follow what is known as the 'learning process' approach, instead of a mandated blueprint design. This would allow the programme to evolve and grow on the basis of its own experience.

●

9

Intensive Agricultural District Programme

Introduction

The Intensive Agricultural District Programme (IADP), popularly known as the Package Programme, represents a significant departure in approach from the Community Development Programme (CDP), in that it employs the concentration principle in deploying resources, as opposed to the equity criterion used in the CDP. Its basic premise was that India needed to organise its agricultural production with enough resources to make it effective. The IADP experienced rough weather and hard going during the first five years, 1960–65; its basic premise of concentration of resources in better agricultural areas continued to be challenged. By 1966, however, the basic concept of concentration, effective use and better management of resources had gained national importance, and had emerged as the foundation of India's present strategy of agricultural development. IADP clearly demonstrated that India can, in the future, produce the food required for its needs.

Given IADP's success in demonstrating how foodgrain production could be increased rapidly, a number of related questions come to mind: How was the IADP planned, organised, administered, implemented and evaluated? What are the important lessons learnt from its experience? How could the concentration principle be extended to other sectors, etc.? This chapter attempts to answer these, and other related questions.

Genesis

In response to the foodgrain crisis of 1957–58, the Government of India invited an Agricultural Production Team from the USA in January 1959 to study the country's food production problems, and to make recommendations for a coordinated effort to increase agricultural production on an emergency basis. The team was sponsored by the Ford Foundation. It submitted its report, entitled 'India's Food Crisis and Steps to Meet It', in April 1959.

The team recommended a number of measures to increase food production rapidly, and the GOI accepted them in principle in June 1959. To give precise shape to the recommendations of the team, a second team of agricultural experts, sponsored by the Ford Foundation, visited India in October 1959. This team made a rapid survey of a few selected areas in various states, and in consultation with the experts of the central and state governments, developed a programme for an intensive and coordinated approach to agricultural production. This was outlined in their 'Suggestions for a 10-Point Pilot Programme to Increase Food Production' (GOI 1963: 2–3). IADP was developed on the basis of the '10-Point Programme'. It envisaged the selection of favourable areas with maximum irrigation facilities and minimum natural hazards, simultaneously providing all the essential inputs and services (package concept) needed to increase agricultural production.

Objectives

As its immediate goal, IADP sought to achieve rapid increases in agricultural production through concentration of financial, technical, extension and administrative resources. Its aim in the long run was to achieve a self-generating breakthrough in productivity, and raise the production potential by stimulating the human and physical processes of change. The programme was also intended to provide lessons for extending such intensified agricultural production programmes to other areas.

Coverage

The state governments selected the following seven districts for implementation of IADP: Thanjavur (Tamil Nadu), West Godavari (Andhra Pradesh), Shahabad (Bihar), Raipur (Madhya Pradesh), Aligarh (Uttar Pradesh), Ludhiana (Punjab) and Pali (Rajasthan). The GOI approved the implementation of the programme in these seven districts in June 1960, and suggested that the scheme be implemented in one district in each of the 15 states of the country. The seven districts were delimited into 140 community development blocks with 14,038 villages, and a total gross cropped area of about 45 lakh ha.

Thanjavur was the first district to launch the programme in April 1960, followed by West Godavari and Shahabad, where the work was started in October 1960. The remaining four districts of Raipur, Ludhiana, Pali and Aligarh entered the operational phase of the programme from April 1961. As per the suggestion of the GOI, eight more districts were selected by the state governments for implementation of the programme: Mandya (Karnataka), Surat-Valsad (Gujarat), Sambalpur (Orissa), Alleppey and Palghat (Kerala), Burdwan (West Bengal), Bhandara (Maharashtra), Cachar (Assam) and Jammu and Anantnag (Jammu & Kashmir). In the first five of these districts, the programme was launched in the *kharif* season of 1962–63 and in the remaining three districts in the kharif season of 1963–64. Later, one more district, Karnal (in Haryana), was also brought under the programme. IADP was originally sanctioned for a period of five years, but was later extended by another five.

Activities

In the districts selected for implementation of IADP, all the elements required to increase production were provided simultaneously. They included the following:

1. Adequate and prompt supply of credit, based on production plans and made available through strengthened cooperative societies.
2. Adequate and timely supply of production requisites, such as fertilisers, pesticides and implements, channelled mainly through cooperatives.
3. Arrangements for marketing and other services through cooperatives, so as to enable the cultivators to obtain a remunerative price for their marketable surplus.
4. Adequate storage facilities for supplies, such as seeds, fertilisers, implements and pesticides, and for farm produce, so that the cultivators would not have to travel long distances to procure supplies and market their produce.
5. Intensive educational efforts, particularly through crop demonstrations, to disseminate knowledge of improved agricultural practices.
6. Strengthening transport arrangements to ensure mobility of supplies and staff.

7. Village planning for increased production, and strengthening of village organisations like cooperatives and panchayats.
8. Analysis and evaluation of the programme from its initiation to its completion.
9. Establishment of agricultural implement workshops, seed and soil testing laboratories, and implementation of local works programmes having a direct bearing on production.

The means through which production increases were sought to be achieved under the programme included many of the known methods and practices. What was new in the programme was the collective application of all the inputs and practices in optimum doses, backed by adequate technical guidance and financial resources. Farm planning was the core of the programme, and was used as a tool to educate cultivators in the use of new technology, and assist them in obtaining the requisite production supplies, such as improved seeds, fertilisers, implements, plant protection chemicals and credit facilities from the cooperative societies.

Organisation and Administration

Another important feature of IADP was that it created a machinery specifically responsible for supervising this programme at the centre, strengthened the machinery for guiding the programme at the state level and designated a district functionary as project officer to be responsible for programme administration at the district level. At the block level, the normal complement of the Community Development Programme (CDP) staff was strengthened by providing additional staff: 10 VLWs, up to four extension officers (agriculture), one extension officer (cooperation), and four to five cooperative supervisors. At the district level, the project officer was assisted by three or four Subject Matter Specialists (SMSs), and one assistant or deputy registrar of cooperative societies. Within the framework of this staffing pattern, the actual requirements of additional staff differed from district to district, depending on the existing administrative structure and the local situation.

Appropriate machinery to coordinate the activities of different departments and agencies was provided for at various levels. At the central level, an Inter-Ministerial Committee including the representatives of the Department of Agriculture, Ministry of Community Development, panchayati raj and Cooperation, Ministry of Finance, Ministry of Irrigation and Power, the Reserve Bank of India and the Planning Commission was constituted under the overall chairmanship of the Special Secretary, Department of Agriculture. Similarly, at the state and district levels, Coordination Committees comprising officials and non-officials were set up. The state level committees were presided over by the Development Commissioner or Planning Secretary, and the district level committees by the Collectors.

While the role of the centre was to provide overall direction, guidance and coordination, responsibility for the implementation of the programme rested with the state governments. Usually, the state departments of agriculture had been placed in charge of the programme. At the district level, the overall responsibility rested with the District Collector, assisted by a full-time Project Officer. As mentioned earlier, each district had a team of three to four SMSs in fields like agronomy, farm management, plant protection, and soil conservation. The assistant or deputy registrar of cooperative societies was responsible for credit supply, and marketing arrangements under the programme. The SMSs provided technical assistance and training to the block level staff.

To ensure quick and speedy action, adequate financial and administrative powers were delegated to the District Collectors and Project Officers. These powers were reviewed from time to time, and additional powers, wherever necessary, given to the officers to meet the needs of the programme:

Implementation

The implementation of IADP involved two broad stages. The first may be termed a preparatory stage, during which the following activities were undertaken:

1. Selection of areas within the district for implementing the programme.
2. Creating general awareness among the farmers and non-official agencies, such as panchayats and cooperatives, and securing their participation.
3. Strengthening the cooperative institutions in the areas selected for coverage.
4. Selection, appointment and posting of additional staff.
5. Training of staff.

6. Organisation of a resource and production benchmark survey.
7. Assessment of the supplies needed.
8. Constructing and/or hiring storage godowns to bring the supplies within easy reach of the farmers.
9. Strengthening the transport arrangements.

It was only after these preparatory measures were completed that the programme entered the second stage—that of operation and execution. The activities at this stage included the following:

1. Preparation and follow-up of farm and village production plans.
2. Adequate and prompt supply of credit, based on production plans.
3. Adequate and timely supply of production requisites, such as seeds, fertilisers, pesticides and implements, to be channelled primarily through cooperatives.
4. Intensification of information and extension education activities, such as demonstrations and use of other creative information media.
5. Arrangements for marketing and other services through cooperatives.
6. Analysis and evaluation of the programme.

Farm and Village Planning

Farm planning was the core of IADP. Planned utilisation of production resources, use of scientific knowledge and improvement of management skills formed the modus operandi to increase agricultural production and productivity.

Farm planning, to be realistic, should take into account the realities of the situation facing the Indian farmer. It would not be enough to help the farmer to prepare a farm plan which sets forth his decisions. The plan should be backed by an assurance to provide the needed production supplies, such as improved seeds, fertilisers, improved implements and plant protection materials. Farm planning without such an assurance will have no meaning. IADP sought to provide all the production supplies called for in the plan, to implement the decisions.

The process of change from traditional to scientific farming, from production mainly for home consumption to production for sale, from extensive cultivation to intensive cropping, and from low income enterprises to higher income ones, calls for a phased programme of farm planning. This process of transformation is a progressive one, and must suit the ability of the farmers, their skills and aspirations. Hence, farm planning in IADP was organised into the following three phases:

1. The first phase consisted of implementing a simple farm plan, which emphasised the use of a 'package of improved and tested agricultural practices' on key crops. For a majority of farmers who began to move towards scientific farming, this was the first logical step.
2. The second phase consisted of further refining 'the package of improved agricultural practices', and using them on all the crops and enterprises raised on a farm.
3. The third phase set out to develop full use of farming resources, by working out the optimum combination of enterprises, practices and methods. The implementation of this phase required more and more research in the area of farm management. The extension workers involved in farm planning work needed additional training in farm management. A greater knowledge and appreciation of farm management principles, especially those of costs and returns for enterprises, enterprise combination, comparative advantage and opportunity costs, in addition to responses of enterprises to different sets of practices, was required.

The first phase of farm planning, which was one of simple farm planning, was a logical beginning in the development of this transformation process. The objectives of a simple farm plan were as follows:

1. It should be simple, so that a large number of farmers will be able to understand and implement it.
2. It should be such that it would result in substantial increases in agricultural production, even on very small holdings.
3. It should be one that is easily understood by the extension workers, so that they can be of real help to the farmers.
4. It should result in increased sale of crops, and provide more net cash income.
5. It should be one that could be financed by the existing credit institutions, especially the cooperative societies.
6. It should result in a highly flexible farm organisation, which would provide avenues for further planning.

The major emphasis in the first stage of farm planning was on developing and implementing a package of improved practices on important crops. This implied the following measures:

1. The farm plan (or crop plan) must emphasise the added costs, and the added returns for each crop, due to improved practices. The cash costs and cash income need to be stressed at this stage.
2. Production factors such as improved seed, chemical fertilisers, plant protection materials and others should be made available on the basis of the estimates worked out in the farm plan.
3. The cooperative societies were expected to provide the needed short-term production credit based on the production plan.
4. The farm plan proforma, which was developed to suit the farming needs of each geographically homogeneous area, emphasised the following basic elements:

   a) An inventory of the resources.
   b) The present land use and cropping system.
   c) Improved production practices to be adopted.
   d) Production supplies that have to be purchased for cash.
   e) Production credit to be tied to the additional production due to improved practices, and not to tangible security.
   f) Expected net returns from all enterprises.
   g) A repayment plan.
   h) A credit application which links production needs to credit requirements.

The second phase in farm planning was not wholly different from the first phase in that, instead of concentrating on key crops only, all the enterprises and all the crop areas were brought under the improved farm practices. The difference between the first and the second phase was one of degree, rather than of kind.

The third phase was a detailed farm plan, or a complete budgeting approach which considered the whole farm as a unit of operation. The farmer may have liked to change his cropping programme with a view to having a better crop rotation. New and more paying enterprises would possibly have to be introduced in place of low income enterprises. This would definitely lead to more specialised farming. The farmer would need to be informed of the research findings, development of new markets and the like, in order to take advantage of the external economies. Successful implementation of a detailed or complete farm plan required a great deal of training on the part of the extension workers, who assisted the farmers in taking the necessary decisions. Research data was also made available to enable the farmers to take decisions, and the extension staff to advise them properly.

Farm planning under IADP had been effective on the whole in getting a substantial number of cultivators to use simple, improved inputs such as improved seeds, fertilisers and plant protection measures. It made considerable progress in the first seven districts during the period the programme had been in operation.

The state governments had also made a beginning with the 'Farm Records' project for a few selected farmers in each block. Such farm records were useful, as they showed the actual accomplishments as compared to the anticipated benefits worked out in the farm plans. Farm records were desirable for two reasons: (*a*) to assess the actual gains made from farm planning, as input and output data of the farms would be available; and (*b*) to show the direction (in physical terms) of the whole programme.

As a general policy during the Third Five Year Plan period, it was decided that agricultural production plans should be prepared for each village, block and district. An attempt was made to prepare village production plans for each village covered under the programme, the responsibility for which rested with the village panchayats and cooperatives. The village plan represented the sum total of individual farm plans and the programmes based on self-aid, and village community efforts, such as maintenance of field channels, building and utilisation of irrigation potential, soil conservation, contour bunding and adoption of plant protection measures on an area-wise basis.

Training

National, regional and district level training conferences were organised under IADP for the district and state level programme staff. Block level training camps for the village level staff and the cultivators were also organised. Special training programmes were conducted for the office-bearers of the cooperative and marketing institutions. The staff of the central and state governments and of the Ford Foundation invariably assisted in these programmes. These training conferences were aimed at enhancing the competence of the participants in certain areas, as follows:

1. Identifying problems and deciding what was important to the cultivators.
2. Providing technical help in preparing and implementing production plans.

3. Facilitating the supply of expedient and adequate credit, production material, and marketing services.
4. Providing guidance in the use of fertilisers, high quality seeds, insecticides, water management and improved implements.
5. Implementing a variety of other related programmes.

Financing

In the first seven districts, IADP was implemented with financial assistance from the Ford Foundation. A memorandum of agreement between the Government of India and the Ford Foundation was signed on 18 June 1960, setting forth the financial obligations of the different parties involved in the programme, namely, the Government of India, the participating state governments and the Ford Foundation. As mentioned earlier, the seven districts were delimited into 140 community development blocks. According to the agreement, the Ford Foundation's financial participation in the programme was limited to 100 blocks, although the programme covered all the 140 blocks in the seven districts. For the remaining 40 blocks, as well as the selected districts in the remaining nine states, no assistance from any outside agency was available. In pursuance of the decision to treat all the districts alike with regard to governmental help, in these 40 blocks as well as in the nine districts in the remaining nine states to which the programme had been extended, the GOI, in addition to meeting its share of expenditure, assumed responsibility for the expenditure on different items of the programme, which was met from the Ford Foundation grant in the first seven districts. This implied that the financial commitment of the nine state governments was restricted to the limit accepted in respect of the first seven states.

In 100 blocks of the first seven districts, the Ford Foundation met 50 per cent of the expenditure on the additional staff, and 100 per cent of the expenditure each on transport, survey and evaluation, implements workshops, scientific demonstrations, training of staff, soil-testing laboratories and quality seed programmes. The GOI met 50 per cent of the expenditure on the additional staff in the first year, 25 per cent in the subsequent four years, and contributed 50 per cent of the outright grant to cooperatives for special bad debt reserves. The participating state governments did not meet any expenditure on the additional staff in the first year, but met 25 per cent of the expenditure in the subsequent four years. Besides, they also met 100 per cent of the expenditure each on equipment for demonstrations and local works, and contributed 50 per cent of the outright grant to cooperatives for special bad debt reserves. Storage godowns were financed under the normal plan scheme of the state departments of cooperation. This pattern of expenditure applied to non-loan expenditure.

The programme also envisaged provision of funds in the form of short- and medium-term credit, to enable the cultivators to purchase various wherewithals of production, and also to meet such requirements as purchase of bullocks, construction and repair of minor irrigation works, purchase of implements and equipment, land development measures, etc. The short-term loans were provided mainly by the cooperatives with the assistance of the Reserve Bank of India, and medium-term loans partly by the government and partly by the cooperative institutions.

For 100 blocks in the first seven districts, the total non-loan expenditure on the programme was estimated at approximately Rs 7.77 crore over a period of five years. Of this, the contributions of the Ford Foundation and the GOI worked out to Rs 4.40 crore and Rs 0.60 crore respectively, and the share of the concerned state governments to Rs 2.77 crore. In the remaining 40 blocks of the first seven districts, the total non-loan expenditure on the programme over a period of five years was estimated at about Rs 2 crore, the bulk of which was borne by the GOI. In the selected districts of the remaining states, the implementation of the programme was estimated to involve a total outlay of about Rs 8.5 crore over the five year period. Adequate financial provision was made both in the central and state Third Five Year Plans for IADP.

Apart from financial assistance, the Ford Foundation also rendered technical assistance through a team of subject matter specialists and consultants. These consultants were located in New Delhi, and they assisted the central and state governments in planning, implementation and evaluation of the programme. Besides the Ford Foundation, the Technical Cooperation Mission (TCM) of the United States Agency for International Development (USAID) also provided technical experts. These experts were assigned to the IADP districts, and they assisted the district staff in the study of field problems and in analysing and resolving those problems.

Evaluation

A large number of problem-oriented analytical studies covering various aspects of IADP have been conducted, mostly by scholars working in agricultural universities and agro-economic research centres. Besides, the performance of IADP has been analysed from time to time by the Expert Committee on Assessment and Evaluation, which was set up by the Ministry of Food and Agriculture in June 1961 for this purpose.

In its fourth assessment of IADP, covering the period from its inception in 1960 through 1967 68, the Expert Committee on Assessment and Evaluation sought to identify useful lessons from eight years of experience with IADP. The committee concluded that (GOI 1968: v):

> The programme in general has lived upto its promise in the setting in which it operated. It has shown that where effectively organised and where improved technology was available, it has been able to move agricultural production forward more rapidly than did earlier approaches and to reach a wider range of farmers—large, medium, and small.

Douglas Ensminger, the representative of the Ford Foundation in India then, made the following remarks about the contributions of IADP (Ensminger 1968: 8):

> The IADP made a significant contribution in its formative years by pointing up the inadequacies of much of the contemporary research and by documenting the problems faced by the cultivator in his decision on whether or not to accept or reject the package of practices. It also pointed up many of the problems which had their origin outside the district and for which solutions had to be found in an examination and reformulation of national policies. By 1966 the basic concept of concentration, effective use and better management of resources had gained national acceptance and had emerged as the foundation of India's present strategy of agricultural development.

One of the major drawbacks of IADP was its neglect of the equity aspect of development. It has been criticised for having aggravated the inter-district and intra-district inequalities in income distribution. However, a study conducted by Singh (1973) in IADP, Aligarh showed that the degree of inequality in farm income distribution had decreased from 1963–64 to 1968–69.

To conclude, we could say that although the IADP model per se was not extended to more than 300 blocks in 16 districts, a number of new agricultural development programmes, such as the Intensive Agricultural Area Programme, the Intensive Cattle Development Programme, the High Yielding Varieties Programme, etc., were patterned on IADP.

Important Lessons

The following lessons can be distilled from the IADP experience:

1. Rapid increases in agricultural production can be achieved by concentrating resources in the areas of the greatest production potential. In other words, if efficiency is a major consideration in a programme, the concentration principle yields the desired results.

2. Farm planning is a good instrument to educate farmers, and assist them in procuring needed production supplies and institutional credit. It is also a good basis for working out the requirements of production supplies and credit at the village, block and district levels.

3. A simple and easy-to-understand farm plan prepared with the active involvement of the farmer concerned, and backed by necessary production supplies and institutional credit, has a very high chance of being successfully implemented.

4. In assisting participating families, the 'package' approach, i.e., provision of a complete package of all necessary and complementary inputs and services, is most appropriate to enable the beneficiaries to realise full benefits from a programme.

5. Keeping the target population informed, through appropriate mass media, about the programme provisions and benefits, and training the participants in the new methods and techniques introduced under the programme, raises the level of adoption of the programme and increases its effectiveness.

6. Interdepartmental coordination through formal committees and network structures improves the chances of success of a programme more than the reliance on hierarchical controls alone.

7. Even within a given bureaucratic organisational structure, a programme could be successfully administered if the bureaucrats are properly oriented and motivated, and if there is a delegation of power downward and sideways, consistent with the requirements of the jobs.

8. Training of programme functionaries at all levels is necessary for the smooth and effective implementation of a programme.

9. Monitoring and concurrent evaluation by an independent agency are important aids to the successful implementation of a programme.

10. Concentration of programme resources in relatively progressive regions/areas increases inter-regional disparities in the distribution of programme benefits. To compensate for this adverse effect, area-based remedial programmes are necessary.

11. In general, the bigger and more heterogeneous a target group of a programme, the higher will be the degree of inter-group disparity in the distribution of programme benefits. This adverse effect may be offset by a small and homogeneous target-group oriented programme.

12. Association of a catalyst, which is independent of the government departments/agencies directly involved in the programme, helps in proper and effective implementation. The catalyst could be a non-government organisation—national or international—interested in the programme.

10

Special Group- and Area-specific Programmes

Introduction

The failure of the growth-oriented strategy of the sixties to make any significant dent on the problems of rural poverty and unemployment led to its re-examination in the late sixties. Inequitable distribution of the benefits of the growth-oriented programmes between prosperous and backward areas, and between rich and poor households within an area, was officially acknowledged, and corrective measures in the form of group-specific and area-specific programmes were initiated in the early seventies. While the growth rate of agricultural production was still not satisfactory, distribution was not to wait any longer: faith in the 'Trickle Down Theory' had been completely eroded.

The special programmes introduced in the seventies for the weaker sections of the rural population and backward areas included the Small Farmer Development Agency (SFDA), the Marginal Farmers and Agricultural Labourers (MFAL) programme, the Drought-Prone Area Programme (DPAP), the Desert Development Programme (DDP), Hill Area Development Programme (HADP), Tribal Area Development Programme (TADP), Crash Scheme for Rural Employment (CSRE) and Food For Work (FFW) programme. These programmes were aimed at attacking the problems of rural poverty and backwardness directly, by helping the weaker sections to increase their incomes. To supplement the income-increasing effect of these special programmes, a programme known as the Minimum Needs Programme (MNP), aimed at providing civic amenities and community facilities, like elementary education, drinking water, hospitals, roads and electricity, was launched in the Fifth

Plan. The MNP attempted to raise the level of social consumption of the poor people in rural areas.

The major premise of the group-specific and area-specific programmes launched in the seventies was that their benefits would flow to the weaker sections and backward areas, because of the specificity of the target groups and target areas.

This chapter critically reviews some major group-specific and area-specific programmes and distils lessons from their experience.

The Small Farmer Development Agency

The report of the All-India Rural Credit Review Committee (1969) recommended the establishment of an agency to assist the small farmer who had not benefited from the gains of the Green Revolution. Accordingly, the Fourth Plan laid special emphasis on enabling small farmers to participate in the process of development, and share in its benefits. To achieve this objective, the plan provided for the initiation of a project, namely, the Small Farmer Development Agency (SFDA) scheme, which was sanctioned during 1970–71, but whose actual implementation started only during 1971–72. The objective of SFDA was to ensure the viability of small farmers. An autonomous agency registered under the Societies Registration Act, 1860 was established at the district level to implement SFDA projects. It acted as a catalyst in identifying small farmers, investigating their problems, and helping them to obtain inputs from various developmental organisations.

During the Fourth Plan, SFDA projects were started in 87 areas in the country. Each project was expected to cover, during the five-year period, approximately 50,000 families of identified small farmers, defined as those who owned landholdings ranging from 2.5 to 5.0 acres. Programmes based on land and animal husbandry were included in the project. SFDA provided subsidy to the extent of 25 per cent to identified small farmers on capital investments and inputs. Besides, loans were also made available from cooperatives and commercial banks.

SFDA was a central sector scheme until 1978–79, with 100 per cent assistance from central funds. From the year 1979–80, it became a joint venture of the central and the state governments, each sharing the cost of the scheme in a 50 : 50 ratio.

During the Fifth Plan, based on the recommendations of the National Commission on Agriculture, SFDA and the Marginal Farmers and

Agricultural Labourers (MFAL) schemes were merged into one composite scheme, called the Small Farmers, Marginal Farmers and Agricultural Labourers Project. An assessment of the performance of the SFDA/MFAL scheme is presented in the next section, after a brief review of the MFAL scheme.

The Marginal Farmers and Agricultural Labourers Scheme

Like SFDA, the Marginal Farmers and Agricultural Labourers (MFAL) scheme was also launched in 1970–71, following the recommendations of the All-India Rural Credit Review Committee (1969). Its objective was to assist marginal farmers (with landholdings below 2.5 acres) and agricultural labourers to improve their productivity and income through a variety of activities, like crop husbandry (including multiple cropping), increased use of new inputs, water harvesting techniques, minor irrigation, livestock, poultry and fishery, among others. Each project aimed at covering, over the five-year period, 15,000 marginal farmers and 5,000 agricultural labourers—those defined as owning a homestead and deriving more than 50 per cent of their family income from agricultural wages.

During the Fourth Plan, MFAL schemes were started in 81 areas. As mentioned earlier, during the Fifth Plan, the MFAL and SFDA schemes were merged. Thereafter, they continued to operate in 168 project areas, covering 1,818 blocks all over the country. Like SFDA, each MFAL project was implemented by an autonomous agency registered under the Societies Registration Act, 1860. MFAL projects were, by and large, implemented through the existing state departments, organisations and extension staff. Resources for the projects were made available to the participants, partly in the form of subsidy (33.3 per cent of the capital cost of the project), and partly in the form of loans from cooperatives and commercial banks. The governing body of the SFDA/MFAL agencies consists of a chairman, who is normally the district head for development work, like the district collector, deputy commissioner or chief executive of the zila parishad. District officers of the concerned departments are members of the governing body. After the extension of the Integrated Rural Development Programme (IRDP) to all the community development blocks, the SFDA/MFAL agencies have been renamed the District Rural Development Agency (DRDA), and now the DRDAs are responsible for the implementation of all rural development programmes in the districts.

In a study conducted by the Planning Commission, it was found that proper care was not exercised in the selection of some of the project areas, that very little attention had been paid to the identification of agricultural labourers, and that the progress of identification of participants was, on the whole, slow in most of the project areas. As a result of improper identification and verification of beneficiaries, the benefits of the schemes accrued to undeserving persons to the extent of about 9 per cent in both the SFDA and MFAL projects. Cooperative infrastructure— a basic necessity to meet the credit needs of the target groups—was found to be very weak in most of the project areas. Agricultural labourers were found to have been totally neglected in the matter of credit; their share in total loans advanced till the end of 1973–74 was only 1 per cent (GOI 1975: Ch. 6).

In view of these findings, as well as the experience of the implementation of these projects, a number of measures were taken to improve their performance. Some of the important measures included strengthening of essential staff, cooperative structure and regulated markets, and construction of rural godowns. It was also expected that the projects would be supported with large-scale state works with respect to minor irrigation and land development programmes. It would be fair to say that SFDA/MFAL projects have helped substantially in enabling the target groups to share in the benefits of agricultural development, which had remained inaccessible to them so far.

The Drought-Prone Area Programme

A Rural Works Programme was initiated in 1970–71, with the focus on the execution of rural works and employment generation, in an attempt to mitigate the conditions of scarcity in drought-prone areas. Subsequently, it was realised that a mere rural works programme would not help in attaining these goals.

The programme was sought to be reoriented on the basis of an area development approach, and was redesignated as the Drought-Prone Area Programme (DPAP) at the time of the mid-term appraisal of the Fourth Five Year Plan. The programme was confined to those areas which were originally taken up under the Rural Works Programme.

The basic objectives of the programme are as follows:

1. Reducing the severity of the impact of drought.
2. Stabilising the income of the people, particularly weaker sections of the society.
3. Restoring the ecological balance.

Some important elements constituting the strategy are: (*a*) development and management of water resources; (*b*) soil and moisture conservation; (*c*) afforestation; (*d*) restructuring the cropping pattern and pasture development; (*e*) changes in agronomic practices; (*f*) livestock and dairy development; and (*g*) development of small farmers, marginal farmers and agricultural labourers.

During the Fourth Plan, DPAP was a central sector scheme with 100 per cent financial assistance from the centre. From the Fifth Plan onwards, this scheme has been operating with funds being shared between the centre and the states on a 50 : 50 ratio.

Under the new strategy of rural development adopted in the Sixth Plan, DPAP was merged with the Integrated Rural Development Programme (IRDP). Considering the innovativeness and utility of DPAP, the World Bank provided 35 million US dollars under an agreement for six projects in the states of Rajasthan, Maharashtra, Andhra Pradesh and Karnataka. An interdisciplinary task force was set up by the GOI in June 1980 to review the scope and coverage of the programme. The task force submitted its report in July 1982. The report stressed the importance of interlinkages between various rural development programmes, and made many useful recommendations to enhance the effectiveness of the programme. The programme continued during the Eighth Plan, and is likely to continue in the Ninth Plan also. As of 1996–97, the programme was in operation in 947 blocks of 155 districts in 13 states. An expenditure of Rs 1,742 crore had been incurred under the programme since its inception in 1973–74 to 1994–95, and 57.29 lakh ha of land had been covered under the three core activities of land development, water resources development, and afforestation over the same period of time (GOI 1997b: 41–45).

The Desert Development Programme

The Desert Development Programme (DDP) was launched in 1977–78 in the hot desert areas of Rajasthan, Gujarat and Haryana, and the cold desert areas of Jammu & Kashmir and Himachal Pradesh as a central sector scheme with 100 per cent financing by the centre. With effect from 1979–80, it has been operating as a central sector scheme, with expenditure being shared between the centre and the states in the ratio of 50 : 50.

DDP aims at mitigating the adverse effects of drought on crops and human and livestock populations, through control of further desertification of desert areas and enhancing the productivity of local resources to raise the income and employment levels of the local inhabitants. The strategy adopted to achieve the objectives of the programme involves development of the selected areas on a watershed basis. The activities taken up under DDP include afforestation, water harvesting, rural electrification and animal husbandry. In hot, sandy, desert areas, sand dune stabilisation and shelter belt protection were given a higher weightage than other activities. With a view to identifying the weaknesses of the programme, and to consider the requests of some state governments for including more areas under the programme, in 1993 the GOI, Ministry of Rural Areas and Employment, constituted a technical committee on DPAP and DDP under the chairmanship of C. H. Hanumantha Rao. The committee submitted its report in April 1994. Based on the recommendations of the committee, new districts/blocks were brought under the fold of the programme, and fresh Guidelines for Watershed Development applicable to DPAP and DDP were issued in October 1994, and made applicable from 1995–96. The committee found the performance of the programme poor. The main reasons identified by it for the poor performance included the failure of the implementing agencies to adopt the watershed approach, lack of people's participation in planning and implementation of the programme, inadequacy of funds, and non-availability of trained personnel (GOI 1997a: 42–43). DDP continued during the Eighth Plan, and is likely to continue in the Ninth Plan also. As of 1996–97, the programme was in operation in 227 blocks of 36 districts in seven states. Since the inception of the programme in 1977–78, till 1994–95, a total expenditure of Rs 595.51 crore had been incurred and an area of 5.52 lakh ha covered under the core sector activities of the programme (GOI 1997a: 41–45).

Wage Employment and Infrastructure Development Programmes

To eradicate the problems of rural unemployment and underemployment, what is required is a multi-pronged strategy which should aim, on one hand, at resource development of vulnerable sections of the population and, on the other, should provide supplementary employment opportunities to the rural poor, particularly during lean periods. And this should be done in a manner which can at the same time contribute directly to the creation of durable assets for the community. Programmes like SFDA/MFAL, DPAP and IRDP aim at resource development on an individual or area basis. To provide supplementary employment opportunities to the rural areas, special programmes are needed. The Rural Works Programme (RWP) was the first major public programme aimed at providing employment to the unemployed, particularly in the lean season. It was introduced in 1971. However, due to its limited scope and its various organisational and administrative deficiencies, it did not make any significant dent on the problem of unemployment.

A series of special employment programmes followed RWP, each of these trying to learn from the experiences of the previous one, and trying to improve upon it. The major programmes of the series were the Crash Scheme of Rural Employment (CSRE), Pilot Intensive Rural Employment Projects (PIREP), Employment Guarantee Schemes (EGS), Food For Work Programme (FFWP), National Rural Employment Programme (NREP) and Rural Landless Employment Guarantee Programme (RLEGP). In the early seventies, when the planning strategy emphasised a direct attack on poverty, the Crash Scheme for Rural Employment (CSRE) was introduced in April 1971, as a crash scheme to alleviate the prevailing conditions of unemployment and underemployment in rural areas, by generating additional employment through additional rural works. Apart from employment generation, the other objective of CSRE was to generate assets of a durable nature in the areas of minor irrigation, land development, roads, afforestation, school buildings, etc.

Evaluation studies of CSRE, however, did not rate it as a successful programme. The Programme Evaluation Organisation's (PEO) evaluation revealed that the programme neither generated sizeable employment, nor provided any important guidelines for employment planning in the future (GOI 1979). The reasons for this, according to the studies, were poor planning organisation and administration of the scheme. The use of labour contractors and unrealistic wages paid under the CSRE also created problems.

The experience of CSRE indicated the need for more concentrated efforts to tackle the problem of rural unemployment. The Bhagavati Committee on Rural Unemployment drew attention to this aspect in its report, and recommended the initiation of the Pilot Intensive Rural

Employment Project (PIREP) as an action-cum-research programme in rural areas. PIREP was introduced in 15 selected blocks in October 1972 for a period of three years. Over and above employment generation, it also aimed at studying the nature and dimensions of the problem of unemployment among wage-seeking rural workers. Though PIREP proved to be a slightly better programme—in the sense that it threw light on certain characteristics of rural unemployment—it was not rated as successful by the review committee on PIREP. The review committee pointed out that due to certain organisational problems, PIREP could not be of much use in evolving a comprehensive programme for the whole country (GOI 1977a: 11–19).

The Employment Guarantee Scheme (EGS) of Maharashtra was introduced in 1972 as a part of the 15-point programme of the state, which aimed at accelerating the pace of growth of the state economy. The main emphasis of EGS was to guarantee employment to the unemployed. EGS guaranteed employment in the field of unskilled manual work to all adults above 18 years of age (also to the 15–18 year group if there was no earner in the family), within 15 days of the demand for work. It was specified that the worker would not have any choice about the nature of work. The programme also aimed at producing durable community assets, which would increase the growth as well as employment potential of the economy. The activities to be undertaken under EGS were expected to have a 60 : 40 ratio between their labour and material components, and were expected to be implemented by the government departments, without any help from labour contractors.

EGS has been evaluated by a number of agencies. The reports show that in spite of various limitations, the programme has proved successful in terms of its impact on employment generation and the wage rate. It has been suggested, however, that the programme needs to be strengthened in the areas of planning and organisation.

The Food For Work Programme (FFWP) was introduced in April 1977 as a non-plan scheme. As some surplus food stocks were available with the government, it planned to use them in this employment programme. FFWP was implemented by the development administration directly, without any help from labour contractors. One special advantage of FFWP was its part wage payment in foodgrains at subsidised prices, which assured minimum food consumption and, therefore, minimum nutrition to the beneficiaries. FFWP was evaluated by the PEO of the Planning Commission. It pointed out that the major problems of the programme pertained to its administration and implementation. FFWP continued until 1980.

Though the public works programmes suffered from a number of drawbacks, some important lessons were learnt from them.

1. Public works should be planned systematically on the basis of the needs of the assets, and the nature and extent of unemployment and underemployment.
2. Public works should be implemented by the concerned departments, and not by labour contractors.
3. If the workers on public works are paid partly in foodgrains, it assures minimum nutrition to them.
4. Public works should be organised and implemented efficiently, so that bottlenecks are avoided.

The National Rural Employment Programme (NREP), which was introduced during the Sixth Five Year Plan, was formulated on the basis of these lessons. It was an important part of the anti-poverty programme of the Sixth Plan. In fact, it was included in the revised 20-point programme of the GOI. The basic objectives of the programme were: (*a*) generation of additional gainful employment for the unemployed and underemployed men and women in the rural areas; and (*b*) creation of durable community assets to strengthen the rural infrastructure, which would lead to a rapid growth of the rural economy, a steady rise in the income level of the rural poor, and an improvement in their nutritional status and living standards. NREP was implemented as a centrally sponsored scheme, with the expenditure shared between the centre and the states on a 50 : 50 basis.

Jawahar Rozgar Yojana

The Jawahar Rozgar Yojana (JRY) was launched in April 1989 (i.e., the last year of the Seventh Plan), after merging the two on-going wage employment programmes, i.e., NREP and the Rural Landless Employment Guarantee Programme (RLEGP). The main objective of JRY was to provide additional gainful wage employment to unemployed and underemployed persons in the rural areas during the lean agricultural season. JRY was targeted at people living below the poverty line. However, preference is given to the Scheduled Castes, the Scheduled Tribes and the freed bonded labourers, and at least 30 per cent of the employment is to be provided to women. JRY is a centrally-sponsored scheme, but is implemented by the state governments. The expenditure under the programme is shared between the centre and the states in the ratio of 80 : 20. Jawahar Rozgar Yojana funds are allocated to the states union/territories (UTs) in proportion to the percentage of India's rural poor living in the state/UT. From a state to its districts, the allocation is made on the basis of a weighted Index of Backwardness, computed by summing the proportion of the rural SC and ST population in the district, to the total rural SC and ST population in the state and the inverse of agricultural production per agricultural worker in the district, assigning equal weights to each of the two components. Based on a recommendation of the chief ministers' conference held on 4–5 July 1996, JRY funds are now distributed among district rural development agencies/zila parishads, intermediate level (block) panchayats, and village panchayats in the ratio of 20 : 15 : 65.

Any works that create durable productive assets can be taken up under JRY. Higher priority is given to those works that can be taken up by a group of eligible people, that provide infrastructure support to other poverty alleviation programmes, and to construction of primary school buildings. The wage and material ratio for JRY works is 60 : 40. The wages can be paid partly in cash and partly in foodgrains.

After three years of the implementation of JRY, it was felt that the resources were being too thinly spread to make any tangible impact, and adequate attention was not being paid to the backward areas. Accordingly, the strategy for implementation of JRY was modified in 1993 to ensure better implementation of the programme during the Eighth Plan, especially to achieve the target of providing 90–100 days of employment per person in the backward districts, where there was concentration of unemployed and underemployed persons. The implementation of JRY was done through three different streams. The first (original) stream of JRY was implemented almost all over the country. The second stream, called Intensified JRY, was implemented in 120 selected backward districts of the country, with the stipulation that the allocation to it would not be less than Rs 700 crore, or 20 per cent of the total funds earmarked for JRY. The third stream was implemented for taking up special and innovative projects. In January 1996, JRY was again restructured and strengthened and, consequently, the second stream of JRY was discontinued by merging the backward districts covered under it with the Employment Assurance Scheme. The Indira Awas Yojana and the Million Wells Scheme, which were earlier sub-schemes of JRY, were made independent and separate schemes.

The progress and performance of JRY is regularly monitored by the central and state governments. The Union Ministry of Rural Areas and Employment conducted a concurrent evaluation of JRY from June 1993 to May 1994, covering 470 districts, 933 blocks and 4,700 village panchayats. The findings revealed, *inter alia*, that nearly 82 per cent of the available funds were expended on community development projects, that construction of rural link roads received the highest priority, and that the average wages paid per manday of unskilled workers were more or less in conformity with the minimum wages prescribed under the act. The evaluation also highlighted the need for training of elected heads of panchayats, for increasing the share of women in the employment generated, and for providing adequate funds for completing the works undertaken (GOI 1997a: 7–8).

Since its inception in 1989–90, until 1995–96, JRY had generated 5823.54 million mandays of employment, which is 98 per cent of the target set for it. The share of SC and ST beneficiaries in the total employment generated was about 56 per cent, whereas that of women was 25 per cent. The total amount of funds available with the states over the same period of time for implementing JRY was Rs 21,953.65 crore, of which Rs 21,335.58 crore (98.18 per cent) were utilised (GOI 1997a: 5–6).

Employment Assurance Scheme

The Employment Assurance Scheme (EAS) was started with effect from 2 October 1993, in 1,778 blocks of 261 districts, in which the Revamped Public Distribution System was in operation. In 1994–95, it was extended to 409 blocks under DPAP/DDP and Modified Area Development Approach (MADA) blocks having a relatively larger concentration of tribals. In March 1995, it was further extended to 256 blocks out of which 233 blocks were prone to floods. From 1 January 1996, the Intensified Jawahar Rozgar Yojana (I-JRY) has been merged with the EAS. It now covers all the rural blocks of the country.

The scheme aims at providing assured employment of 100 days of unskilled manual works to the rural poor, who are in need of employment and seek it. The secondary objective is the creation of economic infrastructure and community assets for sustained production and employment generation. The assurance of 100 days of employment extends to men and women above 18 years and below 60 years of age, normally residing in the villages of the blocks covered by EAS. A maximum of two adults per family are to be provided assured employment of 100 days under the scheme, if and when they seek it during the lean agricultural season.

Persons who need and seek employment under the scheme are required to register themselves in the village panchayats where they are residing. A family card is issued to every family whose adult members are registered. Employment provided to the members of the registered family under EAS, or any other plan or non-plan scheme, is recorded in the family card. The expenditure under EAS is shared between the centre and the states on an 80 : 20 basis. Central assistance under this scheme is released directly to the District Rural Development Agencies (DRDAs)/zila parishads. The matching share of the states to the DRDAs is to be released within a fortnight of the release of the central share. The District Collector/Deputy Commissioner of the district is the overall incharge of EAS as the Implementing Authority. The implementing agencies of EAS within a district can be the heads of the development departments at the district level.

All works to be taken up under EAS have to be labour-intensive, i.e., works which have a ratio of wages of unskilled labour to equipment, materials, and other skilled works of not less than 60 : 40. Works requiring a larger component of materials are not be sanctioned under the scheme, unless the excess cost of materials is provided from other sectoral schemes.

The scheme envisages regular inspection of works by the implementing agencies and supervisory authority. For this purpose, the state governments are required to prescribe a minimum number of field visits for each supervisory level functionary, and ensure its strict adherence. The state level coordination committee constituted for rural development programmes is responsible for overall supervision, guidance and monitoring of EAS also. The states are required to constitute a district EAS committee in every district, and a block EAS committee in every block where the scheme is in operation.

Since the inception of the scheme in October 1993, until 31 May 1997, 269.92 lakh persons had registered themselves under the scheme, and 10,953.33 lakh mandays of employment had been generated, with a total resource utilisation of Rs 5,439.13 crores. The scheme will continue in the Ninth Plan also.

Million Wells Scheme

The Million Wells Scheme (MWS) was launched as a sub-scheme of the National Rural Employment Programme (NREP) and the Rural Landless Employment Guarantee Programme (RLEGP) during the year 1988–89. After the merger of NREP and RLEGP into the Jawahar Rozgar Yojana (JRY) in April 1989, the scheme continued as a sub-scheme of JRY until 31 December 1995. With effect from 1 January 1996, it is being implemented as an independent scheme. The scheme is primarily intended to provide open irrigation wells only, free of cost, to individual poor, small and marginal farmers belonging to the SC/ST and freed bonded labourers. Where wells are not feasible due to geological factors, other minor irrigation works can be undertaken, such as irrigation tanks, water harvesting structures, as also development of land belonging to small and marginal farmers. From the year 1993–94, the target group was expanded to include non-SC/ST poor, small and marginal farmers also. The beneficiaries themselves are required to undertake construction of their wells through their own labour, and local labour for which they are paid. Use of contractors is banned. A wage-to-material ratio of 60 : 40 is required to be maintained. Supplementary material cost, if any, can be met from other private/public sources. Lifting devices are not provided under the scheme. However, beneficiaries intending to install a lifting device are given preference under IRDP for obtaining assistance.

The scheme is funded by the centre and states in the ratio of 80 : 20. For union territories, 100 per cent of the funds are provided by the centre. Funds are allocated to states/UTs on the basis of the proportion of the rural poor in the State/UT to the total rural poor in the country.

The Collector, along with the Project Director of DRDA, is incharge of monitoring and supervision of the scheme in the district. They are also responsible for maintenance of accounts, and taking such steps as are necessary for speedy implementation of the projects. The state secretary of the rural development department performs the nodal functions relating to the scheme. The scheme is monitored through monthly, quarterly and annual progress reports. Million Wells Scheme funds are allocated to the districts by the state governments, with reference to the un-irrigated land with potential for well irrigation and improvement of lands held by the rural poor. During 1996–97, an amount of Rs 559.07 crores (central-state share) was allocated under MWS, and 1,08,760 wells were constructed, with an expenditure of Rs 501.69 crore.

National Social Assistance Programme

The National Social Assistance Programme (NSAP) was conceived by the central government to provide social assistance to poor households. The programme came into force from 15 August 1995 and includes, for the time being, three schemes as its components, viz., (*a*) National Old Age Pension Scheme (NOAPS)—central assistance is available at the rate of Rs 75 per month to persons who are aged 65 years or more, and are destitute; (*b*) National Family Benefit Scheme (NFBS)—central assistance is available as a lump sum family benefit for households below the poverty line, on the death of the primary bread winner in the bereaved family, the ceiling on the amount of benefit being Rs 5,000 in the case of death due to a natural cause, and Rs 10,000 in the case of death due to an accidental cause; and (*c*) National Maternity Benefit Scheme (NMBS)—central assistance is available to pregnant women belonging to households below the poverty line for the first two live births, provided the mother is 19 years of age or above, the maximum amount of benefit available under this component being Rs 300, to be disbursed in one instalment, 8–12 weeks prior to the delivery.

Indira Awas Yojana

For the first 25 years after Independence, the problem of rural housing did not receive any serious attention of the government. A housing programme for rehabilitation of refugees was taken up immediately after the partition of the country. Nearly five lakh families were provided houses under the programme, that lasted until 1960. A Village Housing Scheme was also launched as part of the Community Development Programme in 1957. However, only 67,000 houses had been built under the scheme by the end of the Fifth Plan. The genesis of the Indira Awas Yojana (IAY) can be traced to NREP and RLEGP, both of which provided for construction of rural houses. There was, however, no uniform policy followed by the states for financing the construction of houses under the programmes. In June 1985, the Union Finance Minister made an announcement in parliament earmarking a portion of the RLEGP funds for construction of houses for SC and ST people and freed bonded labour. IAY was a result of that announcement. IAY became part of JRY, when it came into being after the merger of NREP and RLEGP in April 1989. IAY is a centrally-sponsored scheme, with its funds contributed by the centre and the states in the ratio of 80 : 20. Until 1992–93, the scheme provided dwelling units free of cost to SC and ST persons and freed bonded labourers living below the poverty line in rural areas. In 1993–94, the scope of the scheme was broadened to cover non-SC/ST rural poor, subject to the condition that the benefits to non-SC/ST should not exceed 40 per cent of the total allocation. In 1995–96, families of servicemen of the armed and paramilitary forces killed in action were also brought under its fold, subject to their fulfilling certain conditions.

The cost norms under IAY have been changed from time to time. With effect from 1 August 1996, the ceiling of assistance for house construction under IAY is Rs 20,000 per unit in the plains, and Rs 22,000 per unit in hilly and other difficult areas.

Funds under the scheme allocated to the states/UTs are further distributed to the districts in proportion to the SC/ST population in the district. A minimum of 60 per cent of the funds are allocated for construction of houses for SC/ST below the poverty line in rural areas. IAY funds are operated by the DRDAs/zila parishads at the district level.

The allotment of houses under the scheme is done in the name of the female member of the beneficiary household. Alternatively, it can be allotted in the joint names of both the husband and wife. The beneficiaries are to be involved from the very beginning in construction work, and have to make their own arrangements for construction to suit their requirements. As far as possible, houses are built in clusters so as to facilitate provision of common facilities. The programme has been very well-received by all the states, and the targets set for it have been exceeded almost every year since its inception (GOI 1997b: 35–39).

By the end of 1996–97, about 37 lakh houses had been constructed under this programme since its inception, with an estimated cost of Rs 5,038.37 crore. The Union Finance Minister in his Union Budget 1998–99 speech announced that 20 lakh additional dwelling units would be constructed in the year 1998–99, of which 13 lakh would be in rural areas, and that the budget allocation for IAY was being substantially enhanced to Rs 1,600 crore from Rs 1,144 crore in 1997–98.

Minimum Needs Programme (MNP)

The availability of certain public services, facilities and amenities represents 'real income', and constitutes part of the standard of living. It is particularly with respect to community facilities and civic amenities that rural people are at a great disadvantage. Duly recognising the need for provision of such facilities and services in rural areas, the GOI developed and launched a scheme called the Minimum Needs Programme (MNP) in the Fifth Plan. The MNP initially included eight components. During the Sixth Plan, one more component, Adult Education, was added, and in the Seventh Plan, the list of items was further expanded by three more components, namely, Rural Domestic Energy, Rural Sanitation, and the Public Distribution System. So now, there are 12 components of MNP: (*a*) elementary education; (*b*) adult education; (*c*) rural health; (*d*) rural water supply; (*e*) rural roads; (*f*) rural housing; (*g*) rural electrification; (*h*) environmental improvement of urban slums; (*i*) nutrition; (*j*) rural domestic cooking energy; (*k*) rural sanitation; and (*l*) the public distribution system.

The concept of MNP emerged and crystallised out of the experience of the previous plans, which showed that neither growth nor social consumption could be sustained, much less accelerated, without being mutually supportive. The main objective of MNP was to provide the rural population, particularly the rural poor, with access to certain items of social consumption which form an integral part of basic needs. It was envisaged that certain national-level norms would be fixed with respect to each of these items, and that within the specified time frame all areas in the country would achieve these national goals. The programme emphasises the urgency for providing social services according to nationally accepted norms within a stipulated time frame. To optimise benefits, all the 12 components of MNP are taken as a package, and related to specific areas and beneficiary groups. The programme is essentially an aid to human resource development. The provision of free or subsidised services through public agencies is expected to improve the consumption levels of those living below the poverty line, and thereby improve the productive efficiency of both rural and urban workers. The integration of social consumption programmes with economic development programmes is necessary to accelerate growth, and to ensure the achievement of plan objectives.

In the absence of such a programme, the pressure for investment in the development of infrastructure and production sectors left a relatively small allocation for social services. Even such outlays as were available were the first to get reduced in any conflict of priorities created by resource constraints. Further, the benefits of social services cannot reach the poorest without conscious efforts to that end. Disparities in social consumption obtain not only between income groups, but also between areas. The level of development of the various social services and infrastructure varies widely from state to state.

A review of the programme revealed that in most cases, the physical and financial targets had been achieved satisfactorily. However, the quantitative achievements do not mean much in themselves. For example, the performance of elementary education should be judged in terms of literacy rates and retention ratios, rather than in terms of the number of children enrolled. Similarly, the performance of rural health schemes should be judged in terms of decline in the death rate, infant mortality rate and birth rate, and not in terms of the number of primary health centres and sub-centres. The review also pointed to significant inter-state variations with respect to the initial levels of each of these components, and in view of this, highlighted the need for giving higher attention to the states lagging behind, in order that they achieve the national norms. Besides, the need for integration of MNP with other on-going rural development programmes at the district level was also emphasised. Table 10.1

Table 10.1

Physical Progress and Expenditure on MNP during 1993–94

S.No.	MNP component	Unit of physical achievement	1993–94	
			Physical achievement	Anticipated expenditure (Rs crores)
1.	Elementary education	lakhs	66.94	1,493.21
2.	Adult education	lakhs	311.14	254.32
3.	Rural health			312.78
	(i) Sub-centres	Nos	147	NA
	(ii) PHCs	Nos	174	NA
	(iii) CHCs	Nos	71	NA
4.	Rural water supply	No. of villages	38,079	1,517.16
5.	Rural roads	No. of villages connected	1,355	421.40
6.	Rural electrification			160.00
	(i) Villages electrified	Nos	2,195	NA
	(ii) Pumpsets energised	Nos	9,900	NA
7.	Rural housing			251.25
	(i) House sites	lakhs	7.28	NA
	(ii) Construction assistance	lakhs	3.15	NA
8.	Environmental improvement of urban slums	lakhs	9.75	62.84
9.	Nutrition			293.88
	(i) SNP	millions	19.32	NA
	(ii) MDM	millions	20.48	NA
10.	Rural domestic cooking energy			
	(i) Improved *chulhas*	lakhs	20.60	19.80
	(ii) Rural fuelwood plantation scheme	Thousand ha.	50.00	78.84
11.	Rural sanitation	Lakh latrines	2.94	65.28
12.	Public distribution system	No. of FPS in lakhs	NA	36.26
	Total			4,966.90

Source: *Rural Development Statistics 1994–95,* National Institute of Rural Development, Rajendranagar, Hyderabad, pp. 166–67.

presents the physical progress and expenditure incurred on MNP during the year 1993–94.

Concluding Remarks

This review of the experience of various group-specific and area-specific programmes brings to light the following important points:

1. A target group-specific approach can be more effective than a diffused approach in ensuring that the benefits of development programmes reach the rural poor, who need them the most.

2. An area-specific approach can reduce the inter-regional disparities in growth and development, by promoting all-round development of economically and socially backward areas which have been left out or left behind during the process of normal development.

3. The problems of rural poverty and unemployment can be better solved if the rural poor are provided opportunities for *both* self-employment *and* supplementary wage-paid employment within the rural sector itself, rather than with self-employment alone, or wage-paid employment alone.

4. Provision of basic minimum needs and social welfare assistance in rural areas is as crucial to improve the standards of living there, as is the provision of income-earning opportunities.

5. Integration of group-specific and area-specific programmes with sectoral programmes is necessary for the beneficiaries to realise the full potential benefits from them.

6. Implementation of group-specific and area-specific programmes deserves far more resources—financial, manpower and managerial—than devoted to them so far. Better implementation can be ensured only if those responsible for actual implementation are paid reasonably well, appropriately trained, and sufficiently motivated.

7. No anti-poverty programme, in itself or by itself, would be effective unless a new professionalism of *antyodaya*, i.e., putting the last first, as advocated by Swami Vivekanand and Mahatma Gandhi, is adopted and practised by everyone concerned, directly or indirectly, with rural development.

•

11

Operation Flood

Introduction

Operation Flood (OF) can rightly be considered the world's biggest dairy development programme in terms of its coverage and longevity. It covers over 10 million rural milk-producing households all over India, and, initially launched on 1 July 1970, it is still under way. It is credited with having ushered in the 'White Revolution' in India, by creating a flood of rurally produced milk and enabling India to achieve self-sufficiency in milk and milk products. Thanks largely to OF, India is likely to emerge as the world's highest milk-producing country by the year 1998–99. The programme has also generated a lot of debate nationally and internationally about its strategy, implementation and impacts. The programme has been both applauded and criticised, but the critics are far fewer in number than the advocates. And over the last few years, some of the critics have changed their earlier stance, after having reassessed the programme more dispassionately. Now, OF is, by and large, considered a success story of global significance. This is evident from the interest shown by quite a few foreign countries in emulating the model.

This chapter is aimed at illustrating how OF contributed to the growth, development and modernisation of India's dairy industry. The goal was to establish the effectiveness of rural producers' cooperatives as instruments of promoting sustainable and equitable rural development.

The Genesis of Operation Flood

Operation Flood owes its origin to the late Prime Minister, Mr Lal Bahadur Shastri. The Kaira (Kheda)District Cooperative Milk Producers'

Union Limited, popularly known as AMUL (Anand Milk Union Limited), invited Prime Minister Shastri to inaugurate its most modern, computerised Cattle Feed Plant at Kanjari, a village situated eight km away from Anand. The Prime Minister commissioned the plant on 31 October 1964, amidst a gathering of thousands of milk producers. Abekke Boerma, Executive Director of the World Food Programme, was also present on the occasion. After having a hectic schedule in the day, beginning very early in the morning with a visit to a village milk producers' cooperative society's milk collection centre, and continuing with the inauguration of the Cattle Feed Plant, the Prime Minister chose to stay overnight with a farmer in a nearby village. Verghese Kurien, the then general manager of AMUL, selected Ajarpura village for the purpose. The village had a milk producers' cooperative society having 411 members. The Prime Minister strolled through the village, talking to villagers, asking questions and listening attentively to replies. He talked to men and women, small and marginal farmers, *harijans* and Muslims, and had his evening meal of *jowar roti*, *dal* (pulse curry) and *chhas* (buttermilk) with his host, Ramanbhai P. Patel and his family. The Prime Minister kept on talking to villagers, until he was persuaded to go to bed around two in the morning. Next morning, Kurien met the Prime Minister for the first time. The Prime Minister asked Kurien a number of questions, including what the secret of success of AMUL was. Among other things, Kurien told him that there could be an AMUL at Anand because there was a huge market for its milk in Bombay, not too far away, and that the milk producers themselves owned the AMUL dairy and operated it through competent professionals employed by them, and hence accountable to them. The Prime Minister was so convinced about the AMUL model of dairy development, that he asked Kurien to prepare a programme for replicating the model throughout India. Kurien outlined a programme, later christened Operation Flood, and sent it to the Prime Minister. On 2 December 1964, the Prime Minister sent a demi-official letter to all his cabinet ministers and to the chief ministers and governors of all states, commending the programme to all of them for implementation. The Prime Minister also approved the establishment of an organisation, the National Dairy Development Board (NDDB), with the mandate to replicate the AMUL model all over India. The NDDB was officially registered on 27 September 1965 as an autonomous government society under the administrative control of the Union Ministry of Agriculture. Prime Minister Shastri's most valuable legacy to India was perhaps NDDB, and OF, that NDDB designed and launched.

At Kurien's insistence, NDDB was headquartered at Anand. The Prime Minister appointed Kurien as honorary chairman of NDDB, a position which he held from 1965 until 27 November 1998. Officially, no guidelines were set for NDDB, beyond an echo of the Prime Minister's wish for replication of AMUL all over the country. No authority was given to NDDB to undertake projects; perhaps it was regarded as merely an advisory body. After having realised the limitations of NDDB in raising adequate funds for implementing the Prime Minister's wish, Kurien persuaded the GOI to permit NDDB to charge fees for its consultancy services. Consequently, NDDB was able to generate some funds from dairy consultancies and turnkey jobs, mostly in Gujarat. This was made possible by AMUL's expertise, placed at the disposal of NDDB. As a matter of fact, to begin with, NDDB had only an honorary chairman, honorary secretary, and honorary treasurer, who were all employees of AMUL, and NDDB's office was housed in an AMUL office building.

As it happened, after a lot of hassles, NDDB received only an initial grant of one lakh rupees from GOI. Now and then, it also received ad hoc assistance from state government agencies. But such meagre and uncertain assistance dashed NDDB's hopes of fulfilling Shastri's mandate. So Kurien thought of an innovative plan to set up a modern slaughter house and meat processing plant as a means of generating funds from export of hides and sale of meat in domestic markets. Kurien went to Rome and placed his proposal for financial assistance before the Director General of the Food and Agriculture Organisation (FAO), who at that time was an Indian, B. R. Sen. Although Kurien won over B. R. Sen, the proposal was rejected by the then Union Minister for Food and Agriculture, Jagjivan Ram: India in the mid-sixties was not prepared for such a project.

Consequently, Kurien was compelled to explore other sources of funding for NDDB. By a stroke of luck, he came to know from a knowledgeable person about an impending threat to India's dairy industry. He was told that mountains of surplus skimmed milk powder (SMP) and butter oil (BO) had been building up in Europe for quite some time, and that these surpluses would be shipped to India as free food aid, exactly when state-owned urban dairies had begun to lobby for an increase in SMP imports. Kurien feared, and rightly so, that with the donated SMP and BO being recombined into milk and sold in Indian markets, the price of fresh milk produced in India would be forced down to a level that was unremunerative to the producer, which would cripple India's infant dairy industry. Not only this, when the free aid was no longer available, doors of expanded milk markets in India would be open for multinational companies to slide in and make money. Kurien converted this threat into an opportunity. He devised a plan proposing the surplus SMP and BO be gifted to NDDB, which would then recombine them into milk and regulate the flow of that milk into the Indian market, such that the producers' price of fresh milk was not depressed below the remunerative level. The proceeds from the sale of milk made out of the gifted SMP and BO were to be used for establishing feeder balancing dairies, mother dairies, cattle feed plants, artificial insemination centres, and so on. This was the novel and brilliant idea which was translated into a project proposal by Michael Halse, an Englishman who was a graduate of the Harvard Business School, then a Ford Foundation visiting professor at the Indian Institute of Management, Ahmedabad, doing some case studies in AMUL.

In 1968, Kurien sent his proposal to GOI for financial assistance. The then Director General of FAO, Adekke Boerma, had not forgotten Kurien, nor the inauguration of the Kanjari Cattle Feed Plant by Prime Minister Shastri, four year earlier. Boerma was impressed by the very innovative proposal, when it was placed before him after having been rescued from the onslaught of the Indian bureaucracy. He guided the proposal through many vicissitudes to its final approval at the FAO General Meeting in October 1969. The project was the biggest ever undertaken by the World Food Programme of FAO, and also the first that FAO had accepted on such terms. The name given by FAO to the project—WFP 618—was not found appealing, hence NDDB substituted it with 'Operation Flood'. In November 1969, NDDB submitted to GOI a detailed plan for the first phase of Operation Flood (OF-I). OF-I was formally launched on 1 July 1970 by the newly formed Indian Dairy Corporation (IDC). IDC was a wholly GOI-owned corporation specifically set up to serve as a 'finance and promotion' house for OF. Originally, OF-I was to conclude in five years, but it had to be extended until 31 March 1981. Concurrently, OF-II was launched on 2 October 1979. It concluded on 31 March 1985. OF-III was launched on 1 April 1985, and concluded on 31 March 1996 (Table 11.1). Since 1 April 1996, OF-IV has been under way in some selected unions that are currently financially viable, but vulnerable to threats from competition of the private trade, or those that are currently sick, but can be turned around.

Table 11.1
Salient Features of Operation Flood and its Achievements, 1970–96

Features	Operation Flood (OF) phase		
	OF-I	OF-II	OF-III
1. Date when started	1 July 1970	2 October 1979	1 April 1985
2. Date when concluded	31 March 1981	31 March 1985	31 March 1996
3. Investments (Rs crores)	116.5	277.2	1,303.1
4. No. of federations/apex milk unions set up	10	18	22
5. No. of milksheds covered	39	136	170
6. No. of village DCS set up ('000s)	13.3	34.5	72.5
7. No. of members (lakhs)	17.5	36.3	92.63
8. Average milk procurement (mkgpd)	2.56	5.78	10.99
9. Liquid milk marketing (llpd)	27.9	50.1	100.2
10. Processing capacity			
Rural dairies (llpd)	35.9	87.8	180.9
Metro dairies (llpd)	29.0	35.0	38.8
11. Milk drying capacity (MTPD)	261.0	507.5	842.0
12. Technical inputs			
No. of AI centres ('000s)	4.9	7.5	16.8
No. AI done at end (lakhs/year)	8.2	13.3	39.4
13. Cattle feed capacity ('000 MTPD)	1.7	3.3	4.9

Sources:

1. *Dairy India 1997.*
2. *Quarterly and Monthly Progress Reports on Operation Flood,* NDDB, Anand, 1996.

Notes: mkgpd: million kg per day; llpd: lakh litres per day. MTPD: metric tonnes per day.

Objectives

OF was aimed at creating a virtual 'flood' of rurally produced milk in India, by helping rural milk producers in 18 milksheds in 10 selected states of India to organise Anand pattern dairy cooperatives (APDC). The basic philosophy behind OF was that milk production in the rural milksheds could be encouraged only by providing an efficient channel and a ready market for the rurally produced milk. The milk production, procurement, processing and marketing organisations were to be organised on Anand model cooperatives, which had already proved to be successful before OF.

More specifically, the main objectives of phase one of OF were as follows (WFP 1981: 4).

1. To make available wholesome milk at stable and reasonable prices to the bulk of city consumers—including vulnerable groups like pre-school children and nursing and expectant mothers—with major effects on protein intake.
2. To enable the dairy organisations involved in the project to identify and satisfy the needs of consumers and producers, so that consumers' preferences could be fulfilled economically, and producers could earn a larger share of the amount paid by consumers for their milk.
3. To improve the productivity of dairy farming in rural areas, with the long-term objective of achieving self-sufficiency in milk, thereby bringing about major increases in agricultural output and incomes, with special emphasis on the improvement of the income of small farmers and landless people.
4. To remove dairy cattle from the cities, where they represent a growing problem of genetic waste, social cost and public health.
5. To establish a broad basis for the accelerated development of the national dairy industry in the project period, as well as the post-project period.

OF-II was designed to build on the foundation already laid by OF-I. Its main objectives were to enable some 10 million rural milk producers' families to build a viable, self-sustaining dairy industry, to build up a national milk grid, and to create the necessary infrastructure to support a viable dairy industry. OF-III aimed at consolidation of the gains of the earlier two phases. The main focus of the programme was on achieving financial viability of milk unions and state federations, and facilitating widespread adoption of the salient institutional characteristics of APDCs.

Instruments Used by OF

To achieve the objectives of OF-I, the main lines of action contemplated were as follows:

1. Major increases in the capacity and throughput of dairy processing facilities, including the establishment of new city milk plants.

2. Competitive transfer of the bulk of the urban markets from the traditional suppliers of raw milk to the modern dairies.
3. Resettlement in rural areas of city-kept cattle and buffaloes.
4. Development of the basic transportation and storage network to facilitate the regional and seasonal balance of milk supply and demand.
5. Development of milk procurement systems in appropriate rural areas in order to provide raw milk a channel which was more remunerative than the traditional channel.
6. Improvement in standards of dairy farming by an improved programme of feeding and management, animal breeding, veterinary services, feed supplies and management and related extension services, thereby increasing milk yields per animal.

The AMUL Model of Dairy Development

Operation Flood sought to replicate the AMUL model of dairy development all over India. The AMUL model is based on the Anand pattern cooperative structure, which seems to be the most appropriate form of people's organisation for rural development. The Anand pattern dairy cooperatives (APDCs) formulate and implement their own policies and programmes for dairy development in their area, and hire professional managers and technicians for these purposes. The role of the government is limited to assisting the cooperatives financially, in implementing their own programmes. Government funds for dairy development are placed at the disposal of the cooperatives. The Anand pattern cooperative structure has the following salient features:

Three-tier Organisational Structure

This consists of a milk producers' cooperative society at the village level, a cooperative milk producers' union at the district level, and a cooperative milk producers' federation at the state level. This structure permits the horizontal and vertical integration of all the dairy development activities in a state, and makes it possible to realise the economies of scale in procurement, processing and marketing of milk through the use of modern technology.

Producer-elected Leadership and Decentralised Decision Making

Milk producers who are members in good standing of their village cooperatives constitute a pool from which policy makers are elected.

Management committees at the society level and boards of directors at both the union and federation levels have both powers and responsibilities for formulating their respective policies, and appointing their chief executives who are responsible for implementing the policies. This democratic and decentralised policy making structure may well be called an organisational innovation which has evolved over some 50 years since 1946, when the first Anand pattern cooperative was founded.

Cadre of Professionally Competent Managers and Technicians

Management is one of the crucial determinants of the success of a development programme. In the Anand pattern cooperative structure, special emphasis is placed on finding, attracting and retaining professionally competent managers, technicians and other supporting staff, to ensure the most efficient functioning of the system. The staff is always conscious of the fact that they are the employees of the milk producers, and hence they must work with full zeal and devotion in the best interests of their masters. A management institute called the Institute of Rural Management, Anand (IRMA) was specifically established by NDDB to meet the managerial manpower requirements of the Anand pattern rural producers' organisations in the cooperative sector.

Provision of Necessary Production Inputs and Services

Anand pattern cooperatives provide their members with all the necessary inputs and services for increasing milk production. Nutritious and well-balanced cattle feed is supplied by the unions throughout the year at a reasonable price and in adequate quantities through the village cooperatives, strictly on a cash basis. Artificial insemination to upgrade the local stock of milch animals, necessary animal health care and improved quality of fodder seeds are also provided by the unions to the members at nominal cost.

Integration of Production, Processing and Marketing

These three functions are fully integrated to derive full benefits from the backward and forward linkages between them, and to eliminate the exploitation of producers and consumers by intermediaries. The year-round assured market at remunerative prices for producers' milk provides the necessary incentive for the producers to increase their milk production.

Continuous and Concurrent Audit

Anand pattern cooperatives are subject to continuous and concurrent audit to ensure clean business and to minimise the chances of corruption.

Cash Payment for Milk Daily/Weekly/Fortnightly on the Basis of Fat Content

This has helped in meeting the day-to-day cash requirements of the members, as also in maintaining their faith in the system.

Contribution to Village Amenities

Anand pattern village cooperatives set aside a considerable portion of their annual net profits to help provide basic village amenities and facilities, like schools, health centres, libraries, panchayat *ghars*, roads and drinking water. These activities serve to win the loyalty and support of other villagers who are not members of the cooperative.

These characteristics of the Anand pattern cooperatives make them potentially suitable for dealing with the programmes of rural development as well.

Financing of OF

Operation Flood-I was financed by the funds generated from the sale of 1,26,000 tonnes of skimmed milk powder and 42,000 tonnes of butter oil donated to India by the World Food Programme (WFP), an agency of the Food and Agriculture Organisation (FAO) of the United Nations (UN). The original 1970 allocation for OF-I was Rs 95.40 crore for a period of five years, from 1970–71 to 1974–75. This was subsequently revised to Rs 116.40 crore. The funds generated from the sale of donated dairy commodities since the inception of the programme till 31 March 1981 amounted to Rs 114.68 crore, and the actual disbursements over the same period of time were Rs 116.55 crore. The donated commodities were received and sold, on behalf of the GOI, by the IDC which, as mentioned earlier, was the financing agency for the programme. The funds were disbursed by the IDC as 30 per cent grant and 70 per cent loan to the implementing agencies nominated by the participating state governments. This method of financing through aid in the form of dairy commodities was an ingenious one, inasmuch as the sale proceeds were used as investments to create the basic infrastructure needed for modernising India's dairy industry, and the donated dairy commodities used to stabilise the domestic price of milk at a level which was fair to the consumer, and remunerative enough for the producer to provide him the needed incentive to increase his milk production.

Although there were severe difficulties with regard to the quality and continuity of dairy commodities received for the programme, the funds generated from their sale provided enough liquidity, buffer and freedom to the IDC to finance the programme. The programme caused no financial strain on the Government of India's resources. Besides, the programme administrators learnt quite a few useful lessons from their experience with this form of aid, and on that basis modified the procedure of receipt of donated commodities. For Operation Flood-II, donated commodities were received directly from the donors, not through any intermediaries (as was the case with OF-I), and there were face-to-face and man-to-man dealings between the recipients and the donors.

Operation Flood-II was approved by the GOI with an outlay of Rs 273 crore. The World Bank provided a loan of US$150 million, and the balance was contributed in the form of commodity assistance from the European Economic Community (EEC). Operation Flood-III was funded by a World Bank loan of US$200 million, IDA credit of US$165 million, Rs 220.6 crore of food aid (75,000 tonnes of milk powder and 25,000 tonnes of butter/butter oil gifted by the EEC), and Rs 207.7 crore contributed by NDDB from its own resources.

Implementation

Some of the important activities of OF are briefly described below:

Increasing Milk Production and Development of Improved Milch Animals

Operation Flood provided funds to enhance milk production in the selected milksheds. In each milkshed, a technical input programme was designed to meet the particular needs of milk producers in the area, bearing in mind the anticipated scope of the cooperative union's development.

Marketing of technical inputs specifically through the farmers' own organisations was a new concept for many of the states and their implementing agencies. To help these agencies organise rural milk procurement and create a structure to provide technical inputs, the IDC, with the help of the NDDB, deployed interdisciplinary 'Spearhead Teams' to a number of rural milksheds. To help streamline the marketing of technical inputs, the IDC/NDDB prepared 'initial technical input programmes' which were implemented by the NDDB's spearhead teams, working with local teams. This initial work on technical inputs paved the way for the effective implementation of the total plan of marketing technical inputs, including mobile veterinary assistance, emergency veterinary assistance, veterinary first aid, artificial insemination through liquid and frozen semen, provision of balanced cattle feed, supply of seeds and other inputs for fodder production, and training of farmers in animal management and husbandry practices.

As a part of the technical inputs programme, the IDC helped the implementing agencies to establish balanced cattle feed manufacturing plants. In order to meet the germ-plasm requirements of the cross-breeding programme, stud farms with imported Jersey and Friesian bulls, and frozen semen banks were established. A gradual change-over from liquid semen to frozen semen has been planned in all the village cooperatives.

The minikit fodder seed programme proved an effective tool in popularising green fodder production and introducing improved varieties of fodder. With the IDC's support, the NDDB supplied improved varieties of fodder seeds for this programme, promoting cultivation of maize, *jowar*, cowpea, *guar*, *berseem*, oats, lucerne, *bajra* and *subabul*. In order to meet the ever-increasing demand, measures were also taken to produce and supply superior quality fodder seeds, using the facilities available with selected farmer producers, '*Gaushala*' farms and the farms of the NDDB. The IDC also provided funds to the Kheda District Cooperative Milk Producers' Union (AMUL) for village *gauchar* land development. A provision was also made under OF for control of foot-and-mouth disease in selected milksheds, to minimise financial losses to milk producers.

A Technology Mission on Dairy Development (TMDD) was constituted by the GOI in August 1988 to complement and supplement the efforts made under OF for dairy development. The main objective of TMDD was to optimise the use of available inputs, resources and infrastructural facilities established under OF. Under the Operational Linkage Programme (OLP) being implemented under the auspices of TMDD in 171 districts in 14 states, integrated district annual plans were prepared by the District Level Coordination Committees (DLCCs). These plans were prepared taking into account the resources available for dairy development with the state governments, the dairy cooperatives, and the NGOs concerned. The TMDD also organises orientation programmes for officers involved in implementing and monitoring OLP, conducts studies to determine the extent of incidence of various animal diseases and to evaluate various veterinary vaccines and biological production units (NDDB 1997: 34). Use of urea molasses blocks (UMB) as feed supplement was also promoted by TMDD.

As a result of these measures, there has been a remarkable increase in milk production since 1970, when OF-I was launched (Table 11.1).

Financing these animal support programmes was quite a complex matter. A major objective was to accustom the cooperative unions and village milk producers' cooperatives to support these activities out of the margins earned on milk. In each case, an agreement was drawn up whereby the union would reserve a small amount of the margin earned on each litre of milk, and these reserved monies would be contributed by the union towards the cost of the input programme. There was also an understanding that the village milk cooperatives would pay a share of the monthly salary of the lay artificial inseminators/animal first aid workers. The IDC, in turn, allocated funds to the cooperative unions on the basis of 30 per cent grant and 70 per cent loan.

Organisation of Rural Milk Procurement Systems

Since APDCs and their unions are responsible for the procurement of milk, as well as for provision of inputs for enhanced milk production, it followed that cooperatives had to be organised first, so that the producers' milk could be marketed cooperatively, and inputs could be provided to milk producers to enable them to enhance their milk production. Organisation of village milk producers' cooperatives is a specialised task. Hence, the NDDB evolved the concept of the spearhead team for the task of organising dairy cooperatives.

A spearhead team typically consists of three to four professionals—a veterinary doctor, an agronomist and a cooperative extension specialist. The team members were recruited by the NDDB, and were given training and field experience in organising new cooperatives and working with the experienced personnel of the existing APDCs. For each spearhead team, a counterpart local team called the 'Shadow Team' was recruited from each participating state/milkshed, and was given field training along with the NDDB's spearhead team. The two teams together organised APDCs and milk procurement and input supply systems in each milkshed.

Milk Marketing and National Milk Grid (NMG)

An NMG comprising four regional milk grids was set up under OF. Milk is transported to major consumption centres (including four metropolitan cities) by a big fleet of rail and road milk tankers. In March 1995, NMG had some 1,108 road and rail milk tankers and storage facilities for 33,750 tonnes of milk powder and 4,280 tonnes of butter, to facilitate the operation of NMG. Under OF-II, milk was marketed through NMG in some 148 cities and towns, with a total population of 1.5 crore. The National Milk Grid linked the consuming cities and towns to 136 rural milk sheds. In OF-III, the milk marketing infrastructure was further expanded through NMG to ensure a stable year-round milk supply. The National Milk Grid has played a crucial role in ensuring availability of milk to consumers and a remunerative price to milk producers, by levelling off regional and seasonal imbalances in supply and demand of milk.

Manpower Development and Training

To help dairy cooperatives and urban dairies to keep up with their rapidly increasing need for trained personnel under Operation Flood, training was provided by NDDB through a three-tier institutional structure comprising the following:

1. The NDDB Training and Management Development Division.
2. Four Regional Training Centres at Erode (Tamil Nadu), Bhatinda (Punjab), Mansinh Institute for Training at Mehsana (Gujarat), and Siliguri (West Bengal).
3. The District Cooperative Unions with training facilities.

NDDB's largest training centre is at Anand, where programmes are organised for the following categories of personnel:

- Executives from dairies and cattle feed plants.
- Procurement and inputs personnel.
- Personnel of other functional departments.
- Policy makers in state governments who require short-term orientation programmes.
- Personnel of the western region working in areas of procurement and inputs, dairy engineering and other skilled technicians.

There is also a Farmers' Training Institute for farmers' induction programmes. The regional training centres carry out the following kinds/levels of training:

- Procurement and inputs wings.
- Dairy engineering.
- Cattle feed plant management.
- Artisans and skilled technicians.
- Artificial insemination (AI) training for veterinarians.
- Cooperative training of village society secretaries and chairmen.
- Farmers' induction programmes.

Each regional centre is located near a district milk union, with a dairy plant and a cattle feed plant. The district unions are equipped to handle the routine and continuing training programmes for village lay inseminators and veterinary first aid workers themselves. Cooperative training of village society secretaries is carried out, together with member education programmes, in collaboration with the staff of the cooperative department of the state government concerned.

In 1979, NDDB established a national level institute, the Institute of Rural Management, Anand (IRMA) to train rural managers, primarily for meeting the managerial manpower requirements of OF. By March 1998, the institute had produced over 1,000 graduates, most of whom were working in OF projects all over the country. Informal and formal feedback received from various sources about the performance of the institute's graduates indicates that most of them are contributing significantly to professionalisation of management of the APDC and other rural producers' organisations.

Implementing Agencies

As mentioned at the outset, OF-I was designed by NDDB, and promoted and financed by IDC. The NDDB was registered under the Registration of Societies Act, 1860 and the Bombay Public Trust Act, 1950, and IDC under Section 25 of the Indian Companies Act, 1956. IDC also oversaw and monitored the implementation of OF-I in the country, in collaboration with the project authorities designated by the participating state governments for implementing the programme. The NDDB also served as a technical consultant to IDC and the project authorities, in project planning and designing Mother Dairies, feeder balancing dairies, milk chilling centres and cattle feed plants. In addition to basic designs, NDDB also provided technical advisory services in the preparation of project estimates, technical specifications, mass flow diagrams, time schedules, bidding documents, bid evaluation, supervision of procurement of equipment and materials, and of construction, erection and commissioning of dairy processing and cattle feed processing plants. Besides, NDDB also conducted short-term training programmes for managers, technicians and supervisory staff of the participating state dairy federations/unions, and induction programmes for member milk producers of APDCs. Thus, NDDB played a very important role in the implementation of OF.

With the approval of OF-I, a source of income was secured from the sale of WFP commodities, to enable the government and the NDDB to modernise the dairy industry in India. However, since NDDB was a non-governmental institution, the Government of India created the wholly government-owned IDC, with an initial equity capital of Rs 1 crore as the implementing agency for the project. Both IDC and NDDB were placed under a common chairman, Verghese Kurien. Following the Jha Committee's recommendations, the two organisations were merged in August 1987 under the general umbrella of NDDB, which then became a body corporate under an act of parliament.

The NDDB provided most of the technical inputs for projects at the instance of IDC, which controlled and managed the funds generated from the sale of WFP commodities and managed the reception, distribution, and use of these commodities. Because of their interdependence, the two organisations developed a close working relationship. They both had their national headquarters in Gujarat (NDDB at Anand and IDC at Baroda, 45 km away), and this helped to maintain consistent policy liaison. NDDB's technical capacity includes plant design and construction on a turnkey basis, training programmes for technicians, computerised management information systems, establishment of farmers' organisations, and technical advice on animal husbandry.

The relationship of NDDB and IDC with the state governments changed over time. Initially, the situation was that in most states, dairy development was in the hands of state dairy development corporations and the inter-ministerial dairy development cells. This was based on the assumption that much of the work with regard to organising cooperatives and milch animal development would be the responsibility of the state department concerned, which received funds generated from the sale of WFP commodities channelled to them by IDC.

Though dairy development is a state subject under the Constitution of India, the centre and states exercise joint jurisdiction, with the central government laying down general guidelines, within which the individual states design their dairy development policies. A significant shift in the policy took place when NDDB was established in 1965. Initially, NDDB functioned mainly as an advisory body, but it soon acquired the main responsibility for dairy development in the country. Critics argue that OF, which involved the transfer of enormous amounts of dairy aid from the EEC, was responsible for this change. Doornbos and Gertsch (1994: 918) note that NDDB enjoys considerable autonomy, because of its intermediary position between the donor agencies and Indian state governments, in addition to influencing dairy policy at the centre.

Mascarenhas (1988: 99–100) notes that since the state governments have the responsibility of actually implementing OF, NDDB promotes its dairy development policies through a process which involves considerable networking with the states. He describes:

> By adopting a strategy of persuasion, negotiation and bargaining with the implementing states, the NDDB has adopted a collaborative rather than a controlling role. Such collaboration takes several forms [and] is supported by a system of incentives to encourage state agencies to adopt new types of programmes.

It now appears that the state governments have come to accept that dairy development functions are better carried out directly by the producers' cooperatives, with technical inputs provided directly by NDDB. This really means that the technical inputs are channelled directly from NDDB to these organisations, and that NDDB negotiates its financial arrangements directly with cooperative unions and federations, although state governments continue to be party to (and signatories of) such agreements, and guarantors of loans.

Major Achievements of OF

The phase-wise salient features of the OF programme and its achievements have been presented in Table 11.1. Operation Flood projects were well under way in 170 milksheds covering 267 districts in 23 states/union territories in the country by the end of 1995–96. Except Arunachal Pradesh, Meghalaya, Manipur and Mizoram, all the states originally envisaged for coverage under the OF programme had been covered. Over 92.63 lakh milk producing families were participating in the programme, and over 72.5 thousand village milk producers' cooperatives (VMPCs) had been established in the country.

By 31 March 1996 (the end of OF-III), the average milk procurement under OF had increased nearly two times, as compared to the level of production at the end of OF-II. Almost the same rate of increase was observed during the OF-II period. The average growth in milk procurement in the OF and IDA-assisted projects areas was over 20 per cent per annum during the 16-year period, from the base year of 1980–81. By the end of 1995–96, the total milk processing capacity in the OF milksheds had gone up to 21.97 million litres per day, with an annual growth rate of over 14 per cent per annum since the end of OF-I (1980–81). In many milksheds in states like Rajasthan, Maharashtra and Tamil Nadu, the capacity created had fallen short of the requirement, especially in the peak flush months, when milk procurement had to be discontinued to contain the flow of milk to the plants. All together, by the end of OF-III, the dairies under OF recorded an average milk processing capacity utilisation of nearly 67 per cent during the peak milk procurement month (January 1996), and 55 per cent on an annual basis.

As in March 1996, OF dairies had their milk distribution network in over 778 cities (including 175 metro and Class I cities) out of the total of 3,700 cities and towns in the country. The average daily liquid milk supply from all sources in the metro cities by the end of March 1995 was 9.42 million litres, of which the cooperative dairy sector organised through OF contributed 3.47 million litres. During the year 1994–95, OF projects produced nearly 2,68,000 MT of milk powder (including SMP, WMP, baby food), 40,000 MT of butter and 130,000 MT of ghee. The milk powder manufacturing capacity in the country increased from 58.50 MT per day in 1970 to 842 MT per day in 1995–96, and the use of imported SMP came down from 19,000 MT in 1970 to 700 MT in 1993 (Table 11.1). The share of imported SMP and BO in India's total throughput of milk in 1950–51 was 67.3 per cent, and in 1993–94 it came down to 0.09 per cent.

The growth in total milk production in India had more than trebled to 68.6 million MT between 1969–70 and 1996–97, registering an average increase of over 8 per cent per annum. The per capita milk availability increased from 107 gm per day to 200 gm per day over the same period. In 1995, the USA was the world's number one milk producer, with its production at 72 million MT. In 1998–99, when India's annual milk output was estimated at 74 million MT, it would overtake the USA to be number one. The increase in milk production had been due more to *increase in milk yield per animal* than to increase in the milch animal population.

According to a conservative estimate, by March 1996, OF had reached more than 40 million rural people. Over the period 1970–1995, a huge sum of Rs 1,706 crore had been invested in creating rural milk processing facilities (Rs 874 crore), urban marketing facilities (Rs 373 crore), milk production enhancement schemes (Rs 205 crore), training and research (Rs 176 crore), and cooperative education (Rs 78 crore) (Patel 1996: 37).

Impact of OF

Several WFP inter-agency evaluation missions have assessed the progress and achievements of OF-I. The fourth UN inter-agency mission (WFP 1981), which was the Terminal Review Mission, visited India in February/March 1981 and prepared a terminal report on Operation Flood I. This mission observed that Operation Flood has shown that:

Dairying in India to be a powerful development tool...by creating a stable outlet for milk produced in rural areas, incomes in villages in many cases have been doubled...standard of living in rural areas under project...improved, extra income from the milk sold was used for buying cheaper foods...consequently food energy (calorie) and protein intakes of milch cattle owners were 15 to 20% higher than those of non-owners...had the project not been implemented, milk in metropolitan cities would have been severely rationed and price for milk from private vendors would have increased substantially, creating problems for the lower income groups.

In February 1984, the Government of India (Ministry of Agriculture) constituted a committee under the chairmanship of L.K. Jha to evaluate, *inter alia*, the performance of IDC and NDDB with specific reference to the objectives of OF-II (GOI 1984). The committee took note of the positive impact of OF-II on the returns to the milk producers, mainly due to the higher and more stable producer price of milk throughout the year than before. The committee pointed to the need for devoting more resources to milk production enhancement activities, for making timely payment to milk producers in most states in the north and east, and for stepping up the utilisation of the capacity created, particularly in the case of powder manufacturing and cattle feed production. Contrary to a widely-held view that OF deprives the rural population, particularly children, of the milk they need, the committee observed that for the poor, milk had been primarily a source of income, less an article of consumption and that, thanks to OF-II, the poor milk producer had higher income and wider options to meet family needs. The committee, while giving credit to the NDDB and IDC for all that they had achieved through close cooperation, recommended that the two organisations be merged into one.

The above-mentioned observations notwithstanding, there has been a lot of controversy about the impact of OF. Although quite a few sample surveys have been conducted to assess the impact of OF using the 'with and without' approach, there exist no studies which measured its precise impact using both the 'with and without' and 'before and now' approaches. Given the vast size and diversity of India, it is not methodologically sound to generalise on the basis of small scale area-specific studies. However, such studies are valuable in that they provide useful indicators of location-specific impact. Drawing upon a sample of micro-level studies, we describe below the impact of OF on milk production, and on a few selected socio-economic parameters.

Impact of OF on Milk Production

Operation Flood can be expected to increase milk production through its impact on (*a*) milk yield per animal; (*b*) the size of the milch herd; and (*c*) the proportion of lactating animals. Very few scholars have studied the impact of OF on these three parameters, using appropriate measurement techniques.

Micro-level studies conducted by Singh and Das (1982), Alderman et al. (1987), Singh and Acharya (1986: 9, 206) and Mascarenhas (1988) report that milk production per household in the sample project villages was substantially higher than in the control villages. On the basis of an econometric analysis of data from nine project villages and three control villages in Madhya Pradesh, Mergos and Slade (1987: 85) conclude that milk production over a five-year period was about 17.5 per cent higher in project households than in control households.

At the national, i.e., macro-level, the evidence of significant increase in milk production due to OF is very clear. Milk production in India had been stagnant around 20 million metric tonnes (mmt) for decades before OF was launched in July 1970. But it took a quantum jump from about 21 mmt in 1968–69 to about 69 mmt in 1996–97, registering an average increase of about 8 per cent per annum, in contrast to the average annual growth rate of 0.85 per cent over the period 1940–41 to 1969–70. Similarly, per capita availability of milk also increased significantly from

112 gm/day in 1968–69 to 200 gm/day by 1996–97. A large part of this phenomenal increase in milk production could be attributed to OF.

Impact on the Weaker Sections

Operation Flood has been criticised by many scholars, mostly social scientists associated with the Indo-Dutch Programme on Alternatives in Development. The critics include Alvares (1985), Doornbos et al. (1987, 1990), and George (1987, 1988). Many of the critics arbitrarily ascribe miscellaneous objectives to OF, and then criticise it for not achieving them. For example, these critics maintain that OF did not succeed in eliminating or reducing rural poverty, and improving the nutritional status of the poor. Singh and Acharya (1986: 206) reach a very different conclusion on the basis of their Madhya Pradesh study, which covered 12 villages in three milksheds. Of these villages nine had a DCS, and the other three were used as control villages. The analysis is based on a randomly selected sample of 604 and 265 households in the DCS and control villages respectively. The authors conclude that in villages exposed to OF, the landless and poorer households had 'markedly higher milk production per household than their counterparts in the control villages.' They add that 'The lower caste and SC/ST households had higher milk production per household than the upper caste households.' From his study of two large cooperative milk unions in Bihar, Singh (1996: 137–45) concludes that more than three-fourths of cooperative members belong to the 'weaker sections.'

But the moot point is that OF was primarily a marketing programme: it never had 'reduction in poverty' or 'improving the nutritional status of the poor' as its objectives, although it is true that millions of the poor milk producers have benefited from it. But now there is a consensus that OF, on balance, had a positive impact on milk production, income and employment, and that 60 per cent of those who have benefited are landless or marginal and small farmers (Nalini Kumar 1997: 14). OF also had a positive impact on women engaged in milk production (ibid. 34–35).

Impact on Women

Women play an important role in India's animal husbandry and dairying subsector: they do 60 to 80 per cent of the work involved. Duly recognising women's role in dairying, NDDB launched a special programme in the late 1980s to enhance women's participation in the control and governance of dairy cooperatives. Under the programme, women were educated, trained and motivated to manage dairy cooperatives. **They** are encouraged to contest for membership of management committees, and in some states, seats have been reserved for them on the boards of village dairy cooperatives and district level dairy unions. Consequently, about 6,000 out of over 72,000 dairy cooperatives in India are women's cooperatives. The percentage of women members has increased from about 14 in the mid-eighties to around 20 in 1997–98. Some critics argue that commercialisation and modernisation of dairying under OF has increased the work burden for women (Shah 1992: 152, Sharma and Vajnani 1993). However, advocates argue that after OF, drudgery of women involved in churning milk and making ghee has decreased, and their awareness of the need for hygienic milk production increased.

Singh and Acharya (1986), in their study of Madhya Pradesh, found no significant increase in employment of women labour in milk production under OF. To conclude, we can say that OF provided many opportunities for women to improve their economic, social and political status, and to develop their leadership qualities (Somjee and Somjee 1989).

Impact on Sustainability

Operation Flood sought to lay the foundation of a modern dairy industry in India, using dairy aid as an instrument for achieving self-reliance in milk production. The programme received aid from a variety of international agencies, namely, WFP and EEC. In addition, OF received bilateral assistance through the GOI from several countries. Five loans from the World Bank provided additional funding. Doornbos and Gertsch (1994: 935) discuss the reason why donors and recipients are interested in foreign aid. They observe that donors consider aid to be either an investment, a means of disposing of their surplus, or an instrument of development. They explain that the European Community, initially, thought of OF as a means of disposing of its surplus and promoting its exports. In the 1980s, the EEC came to look upon aid as an instrument of development. India saw aid as a means of strengthening and achieving self-sufficiency for its dairy sector, and improving its balance of payments situation.

The Dependency Debate

A key issue, which has been the subject of much debate in the literature on the subject, is whether OF has built dependency into the system. In our opinion, OF is an example of successful utilisation of food aid as an investment for rural development. In the words of Kurien (1992: 26), 'The overriding objective of all aid should be to eliminate the need for aid, and that the use of food aid as an investment would seem to be the most likely way to achieve that objective.'

To conclude, we could say that OF had, on balance, a positive impact on milk production, income and employment of milk producers, and on women engaged in milk production. It also enabled India to attain self-sufficiency in milk and milk products, as contrasted to its neighbouring country, Pakistan, which, despite its better milch animals, is still dependent on imports of dairy commodities.

Major Points

From the foregoing description of the salient features and the review of the major achievements and impact of OF, a number of important points can be extracted:

1. An appropriate institutional-organisational structure is the most important prerequisite for the success of a rural development programme. The structure should be capable of providing all the essential inputs and services, to each and every constituent of the target population efficiently and effectively. The Anand pattern cooperative structure is a living example of an institutional structure which has successfully catered to the needs of a growing and modernising dairy industry.

2. Appropriate technology is necessary to obtain greater output from a given amount of land, labour, capital and management. Improved technology can be used in production, processing or marketing, or in all these three. The new technologies of increasing milk yield, procurement and processing of milk, packaging and marketing of milk and milk products followed under OF, seem to be appropriate under the prevailing agro-climatic and socio-economic environment. The modern milk processing technology available now has significant economies of scale, and this is the rationale for its adoption by Anand pattern dairy unions. The technologies used under OF led to substantial improvement in the socio-economic condition of milk producers, were simple to understand, adopt, and maintain, and made full use of locally available resources. Besides, they were conducive to the generation of community cooperation and participation.

3. Equitable access to the total package of all necessary production inputs and services, including credit, is another prerequisite for the success of a production-oriented programme. In the absence

of this, all producers would not be able to contribute their utmost to production, and therefore the full production potential existing in the area concerned would not be realised. Meeting this requirement also helps in improving income distribution, and increasing employment.

The experience of OF-I has been that production inputs and services are most efficiently provided by a single agency, owned and controlled by the producers themselves, and managed by competent managers hired by the producers. To help the producers with necessary credit facilities, the producers' union should work in close cooperation with banks and other institutions, such as the district rural development agencies, which are engaged in the task of financing agricultural and rural development programmes.

4. A producer-owned and controlled integrated system of production, procurement, processing and marketing is necessary to derive full benefits from the backward and forward linkages that exist among these activities, and to minimise the exploitation of producers and consumers by intermediaries. Here again, the Anand pattern of ownership, operation and management of these activities is worth emulating. Therefore, the policy should provide for setting up such a system as part of the development programme.

5. Experience of OF demonstrated that external aid in the form of food commodities could be used productively to create, expand and modernise the production, processing and distribution facilities in the country, such that dependence on foreign aid is eventually eliminated. It also demonstrated that food aid need not necessarily depress domestic prices below the levels which are low enough to kill the domestic producers' initiative to produce more.

6. Operation Flood represents a good example of how a joint venture involving the Government of India, the state governments, NDDB, rural producers' cooperative unions and federations, and UN/FAO-WFP could be successfully executed and managed.

7. Operation Flood has also shown that Anand pattern dairy cooperatives are powerful instruments of socio-economic development. They can improve income, employment and nutrition of the participating households, and can also contribute to the improvement of village amenities.

•

12

Integrated Rural Development Programme

Introduction

Progressive reduction and ultimate eradication of poverty has been one of the major goals of India's economic policy since the beginning of the Fifth Plan. Although group-specific and area-specific rural development programmes were initiated during the Fourth Plan, the basic strategy of combining the minimum needs programme with programmes for employment and income generation took concrete shape towards the end of the Fifth Plan, when the Integrated Rural Development Programme (IRDP) was launched. The Sixth Plan launched a direct attack on the basic problems of rural poverty and unemployment. The Seventh Plan gave a wider base to IRDP, by integrating it more effectively with agricultural and other rural development programmes. IRDP continued to receive a high priority in the Eighth Plan.

IRDP is the single largest anti-poverty programme currently under way in all the community development blocks in the country. It was launched in 1978–79 in 2,300 selected blocks in the country, and was extended to all the blocks in the country with effect from 2 October 1980. It aims at providing income-generating assets and self-employment opportunities to the rural poor, to enable them to rise above the poverty line once and for all. IRDP, in effect, seeks to redistribute assets and employment opportunities in favour of the rural poor, and thereby reduce income inequality.

Target Group

IRDP's target group consists of the poorest of the rural poor—small and marginal farmers, agricultural and non-agricultural labourers, rural artisans and craftsmen, Scheduled Caste (SC) and Scheduled Tribe (ST) families who live below the poverty line. The Government of India Manual (GOI 1980: 3–4) defines the target group of beneficiaries as follows:

- **Small farmer:** A cultivator with a landholding of five acres or less is a small farmer. In the case of Class I irrigated land, as defined in the State Land Ceiling Legislation, a farmer with 2.5 acres or less will also be considered a small farmer. Where the land is irrigated but not of the Class I variety, a suitable conversion ratio may be adopted by state governments, with a ceiling of five acres.
- **Marginal farmer:** A person with a landholding of 2.5 acres or less is a marginal farmer. In the case of Class I irrigated land, the ceiling will be one acre.
- **Agricultural labourer:** A person without any land, but with a homestead and deriving more than 50 per cent of his income from agricultural wages is an agricultural labourer.
- **Non-agricultural labourer:** Persons who derive their income partly from agriculture and partly from other sources can also be brought under this category, provided at least 50 per cent of their income is from non-agricultural sources. They need not have a homestead, but must be residents of the village in which they are identified.

Small farmers and marginal farmers should themselves be cultivators. Ownership for this purpose implies having transferable and heritable rights over land. For purposes of identification of beneficiaries, the family should be taken as a unit. Persons connected by blood and marriage and normally living together should constitute a household. Where members of the same family are living separately and as independent units, they should be identified as separate units. The income of the wife and minor children should also be taken into account and added to that of the head of the family in determining the status of the head of the family as a small or marginal farmer. Where share-croppers are concerned, only such of them as have recorded rights should be identified as small and marginal farmers.

With a view to ensuring that the benefits of IRDP reach the vulnerable sections of society, it is stipulated that in the identified target group, at least 50 per cent of the assisted families should belong to the SC and ST, with a corresponding flow of resources to them. Further, to ensure better participation of women in the development process, it has been decided that at least 40 per cent of those assisted should be women. Three per cent of the assisted families are to be from amongst the disabled. Priority in assistance is also to be given to the families belonging to the assignees of surplus land, Green Card holders of the Family Welfare Programme, and freed bonded labour.

These definitions of the target groups may be used to identify the beneficiaries for assistance under IRDP. These definitions are, however, only working definitions, and are to be used for the purpose of preparing a list of beneficiaries, which should be further scrutinised by holding detailed inquiries regarding their income. Screening of this list of beneficiaries would be necessary to identify the families living below the poverty line, and to design suitable economic programmes to raise these families above the poverty line. As IRDP has its main focus on raising families above the poverty line, the basic criterion to be used for identifying the families should be the income of the family. The poverty line for the Eighth Five Year Plan was set at an annual household income of Rs 11,000, at the 1991–92 prices.

Approach and Strategy

IRDP employs the cluster approach to select villages for implementing various components of the programme, the *antyodaya* approach to select beneficiaries within the selected villages, and the package approach to assist the selected beneficiaries. The cluster approach ensures that the supporting infrastructure is either already available in the selected villages, or can be made available at a relatively low cost. The *antyodaya* approach makes sure that the poorest of the poor are selected first, and the package approach assures the beneficiary full benefits from the complementarity between various inputs and services.

In this sense, IRDP's strategy represents a synthesis of the various approaches tested and found effective in India's rural development programmes, especially: the Intensive Agriculture District Programme's package approach; the Small Farmers and Marginal Farmers Development Agency's target group concept; the Drought-Prone Area Programme's and the Command Area Development Agency's cluster approach; and the *Antyodaya* Programme's *antyodaya* concept.

Table 12.1
Targets and Achievements under IRDP, 1980–81 to 1996–97

Year	Physical target (lakhs)	Achieve-ments (lakhs)	Allocation (Rs crores)	Utilisation (Rs crores)	Credit mobilised (Rs crores)	Investment (subsidy + credit) (Rs crores)
1980–81	30.07	27.27	250.55	158.64	289.05	447.69
1981–82	30.07	27.13	300.66	264.65	467.59	732.24
1982–83	30.07	34.55	400.88	359.59	713.98	1,073.57
1983–84	30.54	36.85	407.36	406.09	773.51	1,179.60
1984–85	30.27	39.82	407.36	472.20	857.48	1,329.68
Total	151.02	165.62	1,766.81	1,661.17	3,101.61	4,762.78
1985–86	24.71	30.60	407.36	441.10	730.15	1,085.17
1986–87	35.00	37.47	543.83	613.38	1,014.88	1,525.61
1987–88	39.64	42.47	613.88	727.44	1,175.35	1,779.13
1988–89	31.94	37.72	687.95	768.47	1,231.62	1,855.27
1989–90	20.09	33.51	747.75	765.43	1,220.53	1,835.38
Total	160.38	181.77	3,000.27	3,315.82	5,372.53	8,080.56
1990–91	23.71	28.98	747.31	809.49	1,190.03	1,858.18
1991–92	22.52	25.37	703.61	703.09	1,147.34	1,805.07
1992–93	18.75	20.69	662.22	693.08	1,036.80	1,616.48
1993–94	25.70	25.39	1,093 43	956.65	1,408.44	2,209.26
1994–95	21.15	22.15	1,098.22	1,008.32	1,450.58	2,268.88
1995–96	—	20.89	1,097.21	1,077.16	1,701.33	2,571.53
1996–97	—	18.96	1,097.21	1,131.53	1,957.43	2,856.91
Total	111.83	162.43	6,499.21	6,379.32	9,891.95	15,186.31

Source: GOI. 1998. *India 1998*. New Delhi: Publications Division, Ministry of Information and Broadcasting, Government of India: p. 350 (Table 17.1).

Financing

Being a centrally-sponsored scneme, IRDP is funded on 50 : 50 basis by the centre and the states. The total amount of subsidy disbursed (centre + states) and credit mobilised under the programme since 1980–81 is shown in Table 12.1.

IRDP beneficiaries are assisted through viable bankable projects which are financed partly by subsidy and partly by bank loans. The beneficiary could select a project suited to his background, skills and personal preferences from a shelf of schemes in the fields of agriculture, irrigation, animal husbandry, village industries, the tertiary sector and others. In order to enhance the viability of a project, differential rates of subsidy are admissible on the total cost of the project. The capital cost of the assets is subsidised to the extent of 25 per cent for small farmers, 33.33 per cent for marginal farmers, agricultural and non-agricultural labourers and rural artisans, and 50 per cent for tribals. A non-tribal beneficiary may receive a subsidy of up to Rs 4,000 in non-Drought-Prone Area Programme areas and Rs 5,000 in DPAP areas, and SC, ST, and disabled beneficiaries up to Rs 6,000 each.

Recently, a new category of trained literate youth has been introduced for which the admissible subsidy is 50 per cent of the project cost, or Rs 7,500, whichever is less. Further, with effect from 1 January 1996, the amount of subsidy to groups of five persons or more living below the poverty line has been increased to 50 per cent of the project cost, or Rs 1.25 lakh, whichever is less.

Banks have been advised by the Reserve Bank of India/NABARD to provide loans up to Rs 5,000 without any security cover or guarantee. Banks have also been instructed to dispose of loan applications within a reasonable time, and they are required to give a report of the position in respect of disposal of loan applications to block development officers every month. Back-up facilities in infrastructure, community works and assistance to voluntary agencies interested in supporting the programme are also provided.

In view of the very important role assigned to various financial institutions in IRD programmes, effective coordination between them and the government agencies is necessary. In many states (including Gujarat), the desired coordination was achieved through the consultative committees at the state, district and block levels. Besides, the Reserve Bank of India has instructed the lead banks to formulate credit plans for their districts in collaboration with the government officers concerned. It was intended that the district credit plan would have separate credit plans for the blocks incorporated in it, and would indicate the shares of various nationalised banks and cooperative banks in financing the IRD programmes.

It is possible that the financial institutions involved may not be fully equipped with the required personnel, vehicles, etc., to afford the needed credit support on such a large scale. The state governments are expected to provide such support as may be necessary. The government machinery is also expected to assist the banks to find land and buildings to set up new branches, and to recover outstanding loans from IRDP beneficiaries.

There is substantial participation in the dispensing of credit by NABARD through the nationalised banks, regional rural banks and co-operative banks. With a view to facilitate quick disposal of loans cases,

NABARD has issued instructions to its regional offices to prepare block level banking plans in collaboration with the state and district administration. These plans will be treated as loan proposals by NABARD and the banks participating in the NABARD schemes, and will obviate the need for preparing separate schemes for sanction by the banks.

During 1996–97, total credit mobilisation by the financial institutions was of the order of Rs 1,957.43 crore, and the amount of subsidy disbursed was Rs 899.48 crore. Thus the total investment amounted to Rs 2,856.91 crore (Table 12.1). The total amount of investment in IRDP over the period 1980–81 to 1996–97 was Rs 28,029.65 crore, and the total number of beneficiaries 509.82 lakh. Thus, the average investment per beneficiary works to Rs 5,498, which is not sufficient to generate enough income for the average beneficiary to rise above the poverty line once and for all.

To ensure adequate and timely flow of credit for IRDP, the Union Ministry has shifted its emphasis from setting physical targets, to credit mobilisation in higher quantities. Accordingly, state-wise credit mobilisation targets have been fixed. The average level of investment per family during the Ninth Plan is being targeted at a level that would enable the beneficiary family to attain an annual income of at least Rs 24,000 by the end of the plan (GOI 1997a: 21). Besides, multiple doses of credit would be made available to beneficiaries in a bigger way under the Family Credit Plan that was introduced in 40 districts on a pilot basis in 1991–92, extended to 213 districts in 1996–97, and would be extended to more districts during the Ninth Plan period.

Organisational Structure and Implementing Agencies

The organisational structure of IRDP is not markedly different from the standard bureaucratic form, the only difference being the establishment at the district level of an autonomous agency called the District Rural Development Agency (DRDA). At the national level, the Department of Rural Employment and Poverty Alleviation of the Ministry of Rural Areas and Employment is responsible for the release of the central share of funds, policy formulation, overall guidance, direction, coordination, monitoring and evaluation of IRDP.

Government circulars constitute the most important means employed by the Ministry to fulfil its responsibilities. Through these circulars, the Ministry has sought to revise, clarify, and supplement the original guidelines and instructions incorporated in its manual on IRDP. A perusal of these circulars would show that most of them had been issued in response to the feedback, comments and suggestions received by the Ministry from various sources from time to time. This shows that the Ministry has been sensitive, open, and responsive in its approach to the planning and implementation of IRDP. This structure and its modus operandi seem to be appropriate to meet the policy and planning needs of IRDP at the national level.

At the state level, in most cases, the Department of Rural Development is responsible for policy planning, implementation, coordination, supervision and monitoring of IRDP. In a few states like Gujarat, a Commissionerate of Rural Development, which is headed by the Secretary, Rural Development as its Commissioner, has also been established to ensure proper implementation, supervision, monitoring and evaluation of IRDP. The central ministry has recommended this as a model for emulation by the remaining states as well. A State Level Coordination Committee (SLCC), which is chaired by the chief secretary/agricultural production commissioner/principal secretary(agriculture), reviews, sanctions, coordinates, monitors, and evaluates all schemes of IRDP in each state. Members of this committee include heads of the concerned departments, namely, agriculture, animal husbandry, cooperation, irrigation, forestry, fishery, finance, industry and planning; representatives of the GOI in the Ministry of Agriculture and Rural Development; the Reserve Bank of India; NABARD, and the cooperative and commercial banks. The committee normally meets once in three months.

At the district level, an autonomous agency called the District Rural Development Agency is responsible for planning, implementing, coordinating, supervising and monitoring IRDP. The DRDA is constituted under the Societies' Registration Act and the Public Trust Act and is chaired by the district collector/district development officer. The governing body of the DRDA consists of the local MP and MLAs, the chairman of the zila parishad or his representative, district level heads of technical departments, representatives of concerned cooperative and commercial banks, and representatives of the weaker sections and rural women. The chief executive of the DRDA is normally a senior state administrative cadre officer, designated the Project Officer or Director. He is assisted by eight or nine assistant project officers in various relevant areas, like agriculture, animal husbandry, credit, monitoring, industries, etc. Some supporting ministerial staff is also provided. The governing body usually meets once in three months, but emergent meetings may be called as and when necessary to discuss urgent matters.

Coordination with financing institutions is achieved through a District Level Coordination Committee (DLCC) which is chaired by the district collector. This committee reviews and monitors the progress of institutional credit support to programme beneficiaries.

At the block level, there is a complete tie-up with the existing planning and implementation machinery, and the programme is wholly dealt with by the BDO. The block structure varies from state to state, but the guidelines from the Union Ministry have underlined the need to strengthen the block machinery by appointing one additional extension officer and 10 VLWs, and to upgrade the status and salary of the BDO. To ensure proper coordination with financial institutions at the block level, some state governments (Gujarat, for example), have provided for the constitution of a block level consultative committee on the pattern of the district level consultative committee.

After the coming into force of the 73rd Constitution Amendment Act 1992, the organisational structure may change at the district and block levels, with the panchayati raj institutions being delegated more financial and administrative powers. But as of May 1998, the structure was the same as described above.

Planning and Implementation Processes

Under IRDP, a Community Development Block has been accepted as the unit for planning and implementation. The IRD plan is intended to be a component of a comprehensive block plan, which is supposed to be formulated as per the guidelines issued by the Planning Commission. Generally speaking, however, block level planning has not been done systematically anywhere in the country. This is because the block staff as provided at present is inadequate, and lacks expertise in formulating comprehensive development plans and projects. Even for the purpose of effective implementation, it would be necessary to supplement the existing block level machinery suitably. It seems the provision of one additional extension officer (EO) and 10 additional VLWs per block under IRDP is inadequate for core planning and implementation functions.

The following is a brief discussion of the major steps involved in the planning and implementation of IRDP:

Selection of Villages

Under the operational guidelines for implementation of IRDP, it is laid down that a cluster approach should be adopted in the selection of villages. The cluster approach requires, *inter alia*, the existence, in the villages to be selected, of programme-specific supporting infrastructure, including credit institutions. This approach is justified in terms of economic efficiency, i.e., returns from scarce financial and administrative resources invested in the selected clusters. But by denying the benefits of the programme to the poor families living outside the selected clusters, this approach does not fulfil the criterion of equity.

This lacuna of the cluster approach was identified very early in the implementation of IRDP, and necessary remedial action was taken by the GOI. It issued a clarification to its earlier guidelines that not more than 50 per cent of the IRDP outlays in a block may be spent in selected clusters, and the remaining funds may be utilised for poor families in as many villages as possible outside the selected clusters. Thus, a compromise was made with the economic efficiency criterion, i.e., to improve equity, some efficiency was sacrificed.

This new policy stipulation, although politically and socially more appealing than the pure cluster approach, proved to be difficult to administer, and led to the spread of scarce resources rather too thinly over a large number of villages which lacked the supporting infrastructure, as a result of which no tangible impact was made on the beneficiaries. An important implication of this new policy for society is that we should bear with the 'small benefits to many' approach, which has been deliberately preferred by our policy makers, to the alternative approach of 'large benefits to a few'. Given our limited resources, we cannot have the largest benefits for the largest number of poor people at the same time.

Selection of Beneficiaries

Selection of IRDP beneficiaries is expected to be made by the VLW by following the *antyodaya* principle, i.e., selecting the poorest of the poor first. In actual practice, however, the *antyodaya* principle is not strictly followed. This is due partly to some genuine difficulties in following this principle, and partly to some deliberate manipulations on the part of the VLWs. The genuine difficulties include reluctance and/or inability of the poorest of the poor to be able to purchase (with bank loans and IRDP subsidy) one of the assets identified for him at the time of the household survey and manage the asset. This may be due in part to the lack of managerial ability of the householder, and partly to his inability to bear the risk involved in purchasing a loan-financed asset. This means that we need to identify and formulate bankable projects that would suit the managerial and risk bearing ability of the poorest of the poor.

In our opinion, the expertise needed for this purpose is not available at any level in the district, either with the DRDA or with the banks concerned. This is one of the critical areas in which it would be worthwhile to seek consultancy assistance from some reputed public or private organisations engaged in rural development management.

So far as deliberate manipulations by the VLWs are concerned, we believe that the VLWs have a lot of scope for arbitrary action in selecting beneficiaries. Lack of income-generating norms for various activities, and lack of rigorous scrutiny by the block level and district level authorities of the income estimates prepared by the VLWs, lead to wrong selection of beneficiaries by the VLWs. Whereas some flexibility in the selection procedure is desirable, opportunities for corrupt practices need to be minimised by the state governments, by prescribing income-generating norms for various activities and ensuring intensive and rigorous scrutiny by higher officials of the household income estimates prepared by the VLWs. Further, the VLWs and EOs need training in how to estimate income, and motivation through economic and non-economic incentives to do their job well. The VLWs and EOs seem to be extremely frustrated. Typically, a VLW has to work in the same capacity for 15 to 20 years before he can be eligible for promotion to the post of EO, while for an EO there are very few, if any, prospects for further promotion. In the absence of many of the basic and civic amenities of life in the villages in which they live and work, and with uncertain promotion prospects, the VLWs could not be expected to do a better job than at present. The existing system of reward and promotion needs to be rationalised.

According to the GOI instructions, *gaon sabhas* are to be involved in the process of selection of beneficiaries. Although the involvement of *gaon sabhas* in the process of selection of beneficiaries seems to be desirable, in the sense that it ensures the public scrutiny of the selections made by government functionaries, it opens the floodgates of political intervention in the process of selection, which may lead to unnecessary delays and disputes. However, in our opinion, an honest and impartial VLW should not have any serious problems in adhering to this requirement, and therefore it should be strictly enforced by the DRDA officials.

Formulation of Household Plans

The GOI instructions require a detailed household plan to be formulated for each selected beneficiary. A format for the plan is also prescribed. This plan is supposed to be prepared by the VLW concerned on the basis of a household survey of the beneficiary. The plan format provides for inclusion of such details of each of the schemes proposed to be executed by the beneficiary as estimated cost, subsidy, and loan to be provided, loan repayment period, amount of loan instalment and estimated additional net income over a period of time. The plan is intended to be comprehensive enough to include all feasible economic activities necessary to enable the beneficiary to cross the poverty line over a period of five years or so.

In actual practice, however, detailed household plans for selected beneficiaries are not prepared as per the GOI instructions. In our opinion, this is due partly to the non-availability of adequate expertise and manpower for the purpose, and partly to the lack of clear instructions on this subject. In our opinion, a properly formulated household plan could be an important instrument in helping the selected beneficiary rise above the poverty line, and in monitoring the progress of the implementation of the programme. Therefore, we suggest that a detailed household plan be prepared for each selected beneficiary in triplicate—one copy to be retained by the beneficiary, one to be kept by the VLW, and one to be attached with the bank loan application. For this purpose, the village, block and district level staff need to be properly trained and motivated.

Preparation of Village and Block Plans

The GOI Manual on IRDP specifies that the village and block plans under IRDP are to be based on the detailed household plans of the beneficiaries. In practice, however, village and block plans are not prepared according to the instructions contained in the manual. This is because the requisite manpower and expertise is not available. What is done in the name of a village plan is merely the aggregation of requirements of various inputs, services, credit and subsidy based on the household plans.

Similarly, a block plan is prepared by aggregating the village-wise requirements of inputs, services, credit, etc. No serious attempts are made to identify the infrastructural gaps, to integrate the IRDP plans with plans for the other sectors, and to establish forward and backward linkages with other agencies. A serious management gap in this area of activity is the lack of an appropriate organisational structure which can translate the policy decisions into actions. The existing organisational structure is incongruent with the strategy of IRDP.

Preparation of a District Plan

At the district level as well, the picture is not very different from the block level. Although the Planning Commission's Guidelines for Block Level Planning provide for the constitution of a three-member planning team at the district level, consisting of an economist/statistician, a credit planning officer, and a small and cottage industries officer, there is only one official, the Assistant Project Officer, responsible for formulating the district level IRD plan. A draft district IRD plan is to be prepared every year as per the guidelines issued by the Union Ministry.

The draft IRD plan contains the scheme-wise physical and financial targets broken down by blocks. The IRD plan is not integrated with the comprehensive district plan, hence the complementarities between the two are not taken advantage of. The harmonisation of targets communicated from the state level and those worked on the basis of block level plans is supposed to take place at the district level, but it rarely happens. Block targets are sent to the BDO concerned for his comments and the draft district plan is revised, if necessary, in the light of the comments received from the BDO. The annual district IRD plans of all the districts in a state are reviewed and approved by a state level coordination committee, which is chaired by the Agricultural Production Commissioner or the Principal Secretary, Department of Agriculture and Rural Development, and includes as members all the heads of technical departments, chairmen of DRDAs, representatives of banks and the Union Ministry of Rural Areas and Employment.

Provision of Loans and Subsidies

As mentioned earlier, IRDP beneficiaries are assisted through viable bankable projects which are financed partly by subsidies, and partly by bank loans. The present guidelines stipulate subsidies at differential rates, ranging from 25 to 50 per cent of the capital cost of the scheme, subject to a maximum of Rs 4,000 in non-DPAP and Rs 5,000 in DPAP areas; for an SC/ST or disabled beneficiary the limit is Rs 6,000.

NABARD has advised the participating banks to provide IRDP beneficiaries loans upto Rs 5,000 without any security cover or guarantee, and to dispose of the loan applications within a reasonable period of time. However, in most cases, banks insist that prospective borrowers furnish some security cover, and the time taken to dispose of the loan applications is inordinately long. Besides, it has also been observed that in many cases, banks try to recover the loans in fewer instalments than prescribed.

It has also been noticed that the bulk of loan applications are rushed to the banks in the last two or three months of the financial year. This places an avoidable burden on both the banks and the field functionaries. It would, therefore, be desirable to ensure the even flow of applications to the banks every month, keeping in view the seasonality and availability of assets.

Acquisition of Assets

The IRDP beneficiaries are assisted by the EOs/VLWs in acquiring the desired assets. In many states, purchase committees have been consti-tuted at the block level to assist the beneficiaries in acquiring the chosen assets. However, it has been observed that in most cases, the assets are purchased by the beneficiaries alone, without consulting the other mem-bers of the committee concerned. This is because it is only rarely that all the members of the committee are available when required. Thus, this procedure does not seem to be practicable. Besides, there have been numerous cases where no assets were purchased, but certificates to that effect were issued by the committee members in return for bribes.

There have also been cases where sub-standard assets have been sup-plied at prices higher than the market rates by the authorised dealers in collusion with the banks. Purchase procedures have to be streamlined to minimise the incidence of corrupt dealings. The central government has already issued instructions to the state governments that each and every asset acquired with IRDP assistance be verified physically. This is being done now in most cases.

Provision of Inputs, Services and Marketing Facilities

After having acquired the income-generating assets, the beneficiaries need considerable assistance in terms of supply of raw materials, mar-keting support, technical advice and training, to be able to fully realise the potential benefits from the assets. It has been noticed that in the case of milch animals, there is a steep fall in the yield of milk after the beneficiary has acquired the animal, mainly because of lack of adequate and nutritious feed and neglect in the care of the animal. Year-round and assured marketing facilities at remunerative prices for the produce of the beneficiaries is also lacking, and has been another serious constraint in their realising the full benefits from these assets.

Enlisting People's Participation

The implementation of IRDP has suffered to some extent as a result of the inadequate response from the rural people including the target group, and their consequent lack of involvement in its activities. Like its predecessors, IRDP is also considered to be the 'government's programme'.

What is imperative is to reorient it such that it becomes a 'people's programme', with the government's *participation*. To make this happen, beneficiaries would have to be motivated to organise themselves formally or non-formally, so that they can gain access to the nation's economic and political systems. If a viable organisation of IRDP beneficiaries is established in each state, then it could assist the administration in various ways—in the identification of new beneficiaries, selection of appropriate projects for beneficiaries, upkeep of the assets acquired, and monitoring and concurrent evaluation of the programme. The beneficiaries, when organised, can prevent the field functionaries from indulging in corrupt practices, and can demand what is in their interest. Unfortunately, the task of motivating and organising the beneficiaries cannot be effectively performed by any government agencies. This could be done better by local NGOs of repute.

Mechanism for Coordination and Policy Interaction

To ensure a close liaison between the banks and the implementing agencies, institutional arrangements for coordination have been made at various levels. At the national level, there is a High Level Committee on Credit Support (HLCC) for IRDP under the chairmanship of the Secretary, Department of Rural Employment and Poverty Alleviation. The other members of the committee are the state secretaries of rural development, senior officers from the RBI, NABARD and banks. Similar coordination committees have been constituted at the state, district and block levels to review progress and sort out problems in implementation at their levels. The Union Ministry is also represented in various other fora dealing with institutional credit, like the National Cooperative Development Corporation, NABARD, and the High Level Committee of RBI.

Pursuant to a recommendation made by the Mehta Expert Committee on IRDP (1994), the RBI has constituted a Standing Committee on

Recovery in 1996. The committee has been entrusted with the function of periodically reviewing the existing status of recovery of loans advanced under IRDP, and to suggest measures for improving the recovery.

Training under IRDP

The IRDP provides for training of both beneficiaries and functionaries at all levels. Beneficiaries are trained in how to manage the new assets or projects so as to derive the maximum benefits from them. The full cost of training the beneficiaries is met out of the programme funds.

Training is imparted in both agriculture and allied activities, and industrial activities. Training in agriculture and allied activities is conducted in gram sevak training centres, farmers' training centres, krishi vigyan kendras and agricultural universities. Industrial training institutes, polytechnics and other training schools run by the Khadi and Village Industries Commission. The All India Handicrafts Board and other organisations provide training in artisan activities and the establishment of rural industries.

Besides this, a special scheme called 'Training of Rural Youth for Self-Employment' (TRYSEM) was initiated in 1979, with the principal objective of removing unemployment among rural youth. TRYSEM is an integral part of IRDP, and is concerned with equipping rural youth in the age group of 18 to 35 years with the necessary skills that would enable them to be self-employed. Any rural youth below the poverty line is eligible for selection, but preference in selection is given to SC, ST and women candidates. TRYSEM training would be sharply focused on trades whose products have high potential demand, and can lead to sustainable IRDP projects. Linkages of IRDP with TRYSEM would also be strengthened in the Ninth Plan.

Suitable training programmes have been designed for the functionaries of IRDP at all levels. The objective is to train them in the philosophy and operational details of IRDP, so that they could discharge their responsibilities effectively. At the national level, training seminars and workshops for district level officers and bankers are either organised directly by the Ministry, or conducted at its instance by various training institutions, such as the National Institute of Rural Development, Hyderabad; College of Agricultural Banking, Pune; Indian Institute of Public Administration, New Delhi, and the Institute of Rural Management, Anand, to mention a few.

Orientation and training programmes are also held from time to time at the state, district and block levels. Senior officers of the Ministry are deputed to participate and clarify points raised by the participants.

Monitoring of IRDP

The IRDP provides for monitoring both the benefits actually accruing to its target group, as well as the achievement of its physical and financial targets. A family-based approach has been adopted under the programme to monitor the income status of the beneficiary. This approach provides for comparing the actual income accruing to the family through various schemes under IRDP, with the baseline income of the family assessed at the time of conducting the household survey for selection of beneficiaries. However, such a system of monitoring is not yet fully operational.

A new system to monitor the financial and physical progress under the programme has been evolved, and requires the completion of the following reports:

1. Block level annual report for monitoring the per capita annual income of the beneficiary households.
2. Block level quarterly report for monitoring the financial progress.
3. Block level quarterly report for monitoring the physical progress.
4. Block level quarterly report for monitoring the beneficiaries and employment content.
5. Block level quarterly narrative report.
6. District/agency level monthly report of selected beneficiaries.

The proforma for these reports and the guidelines for collecting/reporting the information are given in the manual. State governments have been advised to strengthen the existing arrangements at the district level, and to set up a suitable cell at the state level to ensure effective monitoring of the progress of IRDP.

Concurrent Evaluation and Impact Studies

The Union Ministry of Rural Areas and Employment has provided for concurrent evaluation and impact studies of IRDP as an aid to administer the programme effectively. State governments have been advised to undertake evaluation studies from time to time to ascertain the impact of the programme, and to measure the extent to which the beneficiaries have directly derived additional income and employment from the investments made under the programme. The state governments may make use of their own evaluation machinery, wherever practicable, to undertake concurrent evaluation and impact studies, or they may entrust this work to selected academic/research institutions of standing and repute in this field.

The Union Ministry has been undertaking concurrent evaluation of IRDP since 1985. The latest (fourth) round of evaluation was carried out all over the country during the period September 1992–August 1993. Some 44 independent and reputed research institutions conducted the evaluation. The survey covered 18,246 beneficiary families in 924 sample blocks in 463 districts of the country. Kumar and Pal (1998) used the data generated by the survey to examine the correlation between the success of the programme and the efficiency of the delivery system. They identified the following six parameters:

- The difference between the actual cost of the asset and the cost as per the opinion of the beneficiary.
- Adequacy of assistance for acquiring the asset.
- Amount spent on visits to various offices, including the loss of wages.
- Purchase of asset with the consent of the beneficiary.
- Quality of assets.
- Aftercare and support by the government.

The information on these parameters for the 25 states covered under the evaluation was summarised in a Delivery Index, by giving equal weightage to each parameter and using an acceptable methodology of aggregation. The value of the index varied from a minimum of 0.479 to a maximum of 0.836 on a scale of zero to one. The authors found that the index had a positive correlation (0.45) with the performance under IRDP, measured in terms of the proportion of old beneficiaries who crossed the new poverty line of Rs 11,000. Similarly, the authors also found that the initial endowment of the beneficiary in terms of income, and the level of investment under IRDP, both had positive correlation with the index.

In September 1993, the RBI constituted an Expert Committee under the chairmanship of D.R. Mehta, former deputy governor, RBI, to review the performance and current policies and procedures of IRDP, and make recommendations for improvement. The committee submitted its report in October 1994, and the GOI accepted most of the recommendations of the committee. The RBI issued instructions to banks on the recommendations accepted concerning them. The recommendations accepted include the following:

- Identification of projects with higher investment.
- Working capital assistance.
- Realistic repayment schedule.
- Greater freedom to banks in implementation of IRDP.
- Involvement of voluntary organisations.
- Loans for acquisition of land.
- Extension of family credit plan.
- Cash Disbursement Scheme and supplementary dose of assistance to IRDP beneficiaries who were unable to cross the poverty line through the initial dose of assistance.

Impact of IRDP on Alleviation of Poverty

Now we proceed to examine the impact of IRDP on the incomes of its beneficiaries and on alleviation of rural poverty. There have been four major all-India evaluation studies of IRDP carried out by NABARD, the RBI, the Programme Evaluation Organisation (PEO) of the Planning Commission, and the Institute of Financial Management and Research (IFMR). All the studies suffer from two major limitations. First, they all relate to the first two-and-a-half years of the programme, which is too short a period to draw any definite conclusions about the impact of the programme. Second, their coverage was rather small. Bandyopadhyay (1988) critically reviewed the methodology and results of all the four studies, and cautioned against the uncritical acceptance of the findings of the studies.

The Public Accounts Committee (PAC) of the Indian Parliament made some recommendations in its report about reshaping IRDP. The PAC report points to the following major inadequacies of IRDP (Hirway 1988):

- Inadequacy of the IRDP approach to achieve the set goals. The committee recommended that the approach should be business-like and more focused, and that overlaps with other programmes should be avoided.
- Casualness of the Union Ministry, as reflected in the design and implemention of the programme. According to the committee,

the programme was launched in haste, without proper preparatory measures.

- The per capita investment (loans plus subsidy) was too low to generate enough income to bring the beneficiary family above the poverty line.
- Inadequate infrastructural support for various income generating activities.
- Inadequate representation of the concerned agencies on the governing body of the District Rural Development Agency (DRDA).
- Absence of people's participation in the programme.

The survey conducted by NABARD in 1984 was the most comprehensive of all the four studies so far. According to the survey, 47 per cent of the sample beneficiaries had been able, through IRDP, to increase their family incomes at current prices, enough to rise above the poverty line set at an annual family income of Rs 3,500 at 1979–80 prices for a family of five members. If the effect of inflation on family income since 1979–80 is neutralised, the number of beneficiaries crossing the poverty line slumps to 22 per cent (Rath 1985: 20–21).

Major Points

This review of IRDP brings to light the following important points:

Better Implementation

Implementation of IRDP deserves much more in the form of resources and attention than it has received so far. Better implementation can be ensured only if those responsible for the actual implementation are paid reasonably well, trained appropriately and motivated sufficiently. Given the magnitude and the severity of the problems of rural poverty and unemployment, I would suggest that all state administrative service officers start their careers working at the village level for a minimum period of two years. There is very little hope of improving the implementation with the existing staff.

Critical Minimum Effort

To enable a poor household to rise above the poverty line once and for all, it is necessary that the household be assisted sufficiently, so that the critical minimum level of investment required to generate sufficient income is attained. Needless to say, the critical minimum level of investment would vary from family to family, depending upon the family's initial resource endowment, type of asset/scheme identified, and access to basic infrastructure.

Supporting Infrastructure

To enable a beneficiary to realise the full potential benefits from the chosen asset/scheme, it is necessary to ensure timely and adequate availability of all necessary inputs, services and raw materials at reasonable prices, as also an assured and year-round market for the produce. This can be achieved by establishing effective forward and backward linkages with other sectoral programmes that are currently under way in the country.

Organising the Rural Poor

The government must seek the help and cooperation of local NGOs of repute to help the rural poor organise themselves around some viable economic activity, and within an institutional framework that gives them access to modern technology, institutional credit, resources, markets, professional management and the political system. These are all crucial determinants of the success of an economic enterprise.

Provision of Basic Necessities and Civic Amenities

As compared with their urban counterparts, the rural poor are at a great disadvantage in terms of the availability of the basic necessities of life, such as food, fuel and clothing at fair prices, and of such civic amenities as education, health care, drinking water and police protection. Lack of such civic amenities or facilities creates severe handicaps and erodes their meagre incomes. Therefore, the government must protect the purchasing power of the rural poor by providing these facilities and services on a high priority basis, and at fair prices.

Changing Evaluation Criteria

Excessive pressure for immediate results, as measured by the achievement of physical and financial targets, diverts the attention of IRDP functionaries from making the beneficiaries self-reliant, and makes it difficult for them to move beyond a welfare approach to poverty; distribution of milch animals is a lot faster than enabling beneficiaries to derive full benefits from them and to become self-reliant. The performance of a rural development programme is better judged in terms of its output than its inputs. This means that what is needed is a simple and quick system of monitoring, and concurrently evaluating the impact of IRDP on income and employment of its beneficiaries, rather than merely reporting the number of beneficiaries covered and the amount of subsidies and loans disbursed.

13

Planning for Rural Development

Introduction

A plan is a blueprint for action—it points out a precise way to reach a predetermined goal or a set of goals within a predetermined period of time with the means that are available with the planner and under the prevailing circumstances. Planning is a process of formulating a plan. Development planning as a process involves the application of a rational system of choices among feasible courses of investment and other development possibilities, based on a consideration of economic and social costs and benefits. In the context of a quantitative planning model, planning may be defined as a process of determining an optimal mix of alternative investment activities, so as to maximise the objective function under the given constraints. Howsoever we define planning, it implies an organised, conscious and continued effort to achieve specific goals in the future.

In every country, some development always occurs naturally (autonomous development), but it may not be sufficient to maintain a socially desirable level of living in the country. Therefore, some sort of government intervention in the economic system is needed in almost every country to initiate and foster a higher rate of development (induced development). These days, governments in virtually all countries are engaged in one way or another, and to a small or large extent, in planning and regulating their economic activities. However, planning makes a positive contribution only if, through it, the objectives are achieved more rapidly and more efficiently, than if development followed natural forces. Planning can contribute to development mainly through direct provision and allocation of scarce resources by the government, regulation and direction of resource allocation decisions in the private sector, coordination of public and private actions, and guiding the use of private resources through the manipulation of market forces.

Levels and Functions of Planning

Problems in planning can be identified, and consequently planning can be carried out, at the national and state levels (macro-level), at the level of the individual unit of production (micro-level), and at an intermediate level (meso-level). The planning function at the national and state levels consists mainly of defining the goals of development effort, projecting population growth and demand and supply of important goods and services, estimating and mobilising the necessary domestic and foreign resources of money and skills, and allocating them to those specific uses among different sectors of the economy which seem likely to make the greatest contribution to achieving the national goals. Macro-planning is, of necessity, based on highly aggregated data and on considerations that are usually of broad significance. Planning at the district and block levels may be considered as meso-level (intermediate) planning. The main function of meso-level planning is to translate the macro-level plan into concrete and operational programmes and projects, taking into consideration the peculiar characteristics and requirements of the district/block concerned.

Micro-level planning refers to planning at the level of the basic unit of production, which may be a farm, a factory, a household enterprise, or any other production/service unit. Micro-planning is concerned with the what, how much, how, when, and where questions relating to production, consumption, credit and marketing. In a nutshell, micro-level planning is concerned with the allocation of the resources of the planning entity concerned, to maximise whatever goals the entity may have.

In the context of rural development planning, micro-level planning has the following major roles to play:

1. To reveal the prospective needs of farmers (or any other rural producers) for production inputs and credit, so that a suitable supply scheme could be designed.
2. To determine the best alternatives for reorganisation of the rural business units, so as to utilise the public services and facilities completely.
3. To furnish basic information for formulation and evaluation of rural development projects.

4. To aid in projecting the effects of changes in technology, prices, and public programmes and policies, on rural production, income and employment.
5. To serve as an aid to the rural development extension worker in establishing an effective working relationship with rural producers, and in educating them in scientific methods of farming.

If micro-level planning is to play an effective role in the modernisation of India's rural economy, it must be treated as an integral part of development planning. Micro-planning, in and of itself, is not of much use in the formulation and implementation of national development plans and policies. Micro-plans should be vertically integrated with national plans via the regional/area planner. He is at an intermediate level between micro- and macro-planning systems, and his job should be to blend them together, relying on his knowledge of the overall plan and his familiarity with the micro-details of the region. It is his task to bring about a synthesis of macro- and micro-planning in such a way that what is desirable at the national/state level, will be made worthwhile and feasible for the individual producer and consumer.

Horizontal integration embraces inter-sectoral coordination between different sectors—agriculture, industry and services—within a specific spatial framework. Micro-plans should be horizontally integrated with the plans for supply of production inputs and credit, marketing, infrastructure development, and industrial development for the area.

India's approach to development planning has been predominantly macro-oriented, emphasising national goals and priorities. The national planners really do not know whether their targets can, in effect, be achieved and what it takes to achieve them. And the planners at the sub-national levels do not know what the effect of their plans would be on aggregate input requirements and aggregate output of the country as a whole. Thus, for successful and effective planning, it is necessary that the macro- and micro-plans are harmonised at some intermediate (region/area) level. In a nutshell, to make development planning effective, we must follow a two-pronged approach, working simultaneously and in a coordinated way from the grassroots level up, and the national level down.

The term 'area planning' is highly fashionable nowadays, and is widely acclaimed in both advanced and developing countries. The term is used in many different ways and in vastly divergent contexts. We shall use the term to refer to planning for the overall development of a single area, within the broad framework set by national development planning. In essence, we imply by this term a multi-level and decentralised planning approach to the overall development of an economy.

Rural development is the end result of interactions between various technological, economic, social and institutional factors. For example, to increase total output from an individual farm, it is necessary to introduce new technology adapted to local ecological and socio-economic conditions, to educate and train the farmer in its use, to provide him with sufficient resources at the proper time and place, and to create the necessary infrastructure of service facilities for supply and marketing. Ultimately, however, it is the response of the individual producer to these measures that determines the success or failure of the development plan. The area approach to development planning, therefore, emphasises the role of the people, their potentialities and their motivations. Besides, this approach is integrative, in the sense that it assesses the significance of all the factors affecting the development process.

The area approach to development planning can contribute to the achievement of the following main objectives of national planning in India:

1. To accelerate the development of lagging areas.
2. To reduce inter-regional disparities in development and growth.
3. To provide the basic disaggregation of national planning with respect to agriculture and other sectors of the economy.
4. To facilitate coordination and integration of planning and implementation at various levels.
5. To coordinate agricultural and rural development with overall area development plans.
6. To facilitate the wider involvement of people in the process of preparation and implementation of development projects.

In view of different agro-climatic, techno-economic, and sociocultural factors obtaining in different regions of India, national planning, to be realistic and effective, has to be decentralised to sub-national/sub-state levels. Decentralisation or regionalisation of planning and development is a logical step for a democracy. This is a movement which permits the wider involvement of people in the process of planning and implementation, reduces discrepancies between national and sub-national plans which arise from regional or area characteristics that differ from national assumptions.

The need for decentralisation was recognised in the Fourth Plan, and a modest beginning was made in the direction of extending planning to the state, regional and district levels. In September 1969, the Planning Commission issued detailed instructions to the state governments on how to formulate district plans. In the Fifth Plan, special emphasis was laid on the area/regional approach to development planning, particularly in the backward areas. In November 1977, the Planning Commission appointed a Working Group under the chairmanship of M.L. Dantwala to draw up guidelines for block level planning. The group submitted its report in 1978, which emphasised the need for strengthening the planning team at the district level, and for the integration of the block plan with the district plan. In 1979, the Union Department of Rural Development prepared a brochure on the methodology for planning and implementation of IRDP.

There have also been quite a few attempts by state governments and other organisations to frame block level plans. Having taken cognisance of all these efforts, in December 1979 the Planning Commission issued 'Guidelines for Block Level Planning'. These guidelines cover only some broad and essential aspects of block level planning, and it was understood that the Union Ministry of Rural Development and the state governments would supplement and elaborate these guidelines further from time to time, as considered necessary.

In 1980, the Union Ministry of Rural Reconstruction prepared a 'Manual on Integrated Rural Development Programme', which includes, *inter alia*, procedures and formats for preparing household, village and block plans (GOI 1980). The block and district level plans for IRDP were to be formulated as per the Planning Commission's 'Guidelines for Block Level Planning'. In April 1982, the Union Ministry of Rural Development issued 'Operational Guidelines on Block Level Plans for Integrated Rural Development Programme' in consultation with the Planning Commission, the state governments, and other organisations involved in rural development. These guidelines are in the nature of a broad frame of reference, to enable those who are engaged in the implementation of IRDP to draw up sound and locally appropriate programmes and action plans. The guidelines envisage preparation of a five-year development profile, or a perspective plan as well as an annual action plan for each block.

The block level perspective plans were to be aggregated at the district level, based on practical possibilities of development in the primary, secondary and tertiary sectors. The IRD block plan was to be integrated with the development programmes of other departments, and it was eventually to be a component of the comprehensive block development plan. A five-year credit plan and an annual credit plan were also to be prepared for each block, and were to be a part of the IRD block plan. The procedures and formats for the preparation of the five-year perspective plan, block credit plan, cluster plan and household plan are specified in the guidelines.

Methodology of Micro-level Planning in Agriculture

Micro-planning is essentially a two-stage process of diagnosis and prescription. The first stage consists of a preliminary survey of local farm conditions for an appraisal of natural and human resources, institutions, and infrastructural facilities and services available in the area, and to obtain a proximate view of the organisation and management of individual rural enterprises, including farms and their major handicaps and shortcomings. The second stage is to work out improved farm plans for representative types and size groups of rural enterprises.

To be successful and effective, micro-planning requires an interdisciplinary approach. The technical agricultural scientists—the agronomist, the horticulturist, the agricultural engineer—and the social scientists should work together to identify the major possibilities of, and kev constraints on, increasing production and income in the area, to design appropriate research and action programmes to remove or minimise the constraints, and to exploit the potentialities, and to test, on a limited scale, these programmes under real world conditions.

The important components of a sound micro-planning programme can be elaborated as follows, with special reference to the farm subsector:

Farm Planning and Programming

The first step necessary to implement this component of the programme is to identify and delineate major farming areas of the country. Two types of areas may be identified to meet different agricultural planning needs. One is crop regions which would be appropriate for central production planning of major crops. The second is agro-climatic regions/areas which could be used for overall agricultural planning by the district, state and central governments.

In India, several attempts have been made in the past to delineate areas based on several criteria. The most comprehensive and recent work on agro-climatic classification of the country is the one done by the Agro-Climatic Regional Planning (ACRP) Unit of the National Planning Commission. The unit has recommended the adoption of the ACRP approach for bringing about balanced, sustainable agricultural and rural development. The ACRP approach is based on optimum utilisation of land and water resources through decentralised and participatory planning, which has been facilitated by the 73rd and 74th Constitution Amendments. The ACRP project was launched by the Planning Commission in 1988. The project has generated a large volume of high quality research-based information useful for agricultural planning (Basu and Guha 1996; Basu and Kashyap 1996). The moot question now is: How to institutionalise the ACRP approach and ensure that it becomes an integral part of overall national and regional development planning?

For each major agro-climatic region or area, a sample of 50–100 typical farms may be selected, on the basis of their representativeness of the most important farm type (with respect to soils, farm size, etc.) of the area. In cooperation with these farmers, a farm business survey is conducted, and information about input-output coefficients, resource availability, and kind and level of predetermined activities is collected. Cooperation with agronomists is necessary to acquire information on improved crop varieties, and their yield response to fertilisers—with animal scientists for information on high-yielding breeds of milch animals and appropriate feeding practices, and with agricultural engineers on the technical feasibility of using tractors and machinery for various field operations and transportation. This information may be generated by conducting sample trials and demonstrations on farmers' fields. On the basis of these technical data and the data obtained from the sample farmers, a set of alternative farm plans are worked out, indicating the range of different crops and livestock combinations which are technically feasible.

Linear programming is by far the most commonly used tool for micro-level planning. This technique can be used to determine: (*a*) the most profitable combination of crop and livestock activities under varying assumptions about the level of technology, resource availability and input and output prices; (*b*) the optimal amount of outside financing needed to maximise returns to farmers' fixed resources; (*c*) the least-cost methods and techniques of production to employ in those cases where alternative techniques are available; (*d*) the sensitivity of the farm plans to variations in the values assumed for various economic factors included in the model; and (*e*) the shadow prices of scarce resources/inputs which would serve to direct the type of investment which should be made.

The inputs and outputs from the farm plans are aggregated for the major farming areas and the nation, and are evaluated with respect to national production needs and the possibilities of meeting the supply requirements for various inputs and services. Not many details are required, and only a few selected major products and input items are handled.

Harmonising Local Farm Plans and National Production Targets

The farm management specialist works out a set of farm plans for a certain area, without reference to what the effect of the farm plans so prepared would be on aggregate output and aggregate supply requirements of the various farming areas and the country as a whole. On the other hand, the macro-economist works out a set of production targets on the basis of past production records, prospective demand, nutritional needs, foreign exchange requirement, etc., none of which are based on the particular agricultural resources and the potential production capacity of various agricultural areas of the country. Hence, the national planners really do not know whether their production targets can, in effect, be achieved, or what it takes to achieve them. The farm management researchers really do not know what effect the adoption of a series of specific improvements in farming methods and enterprise combinations would have on the aggregate output of various products, on the aggregate requirements of inputs, and on the total supply and demand, and the import and export situation of the country.

Harmonising local farm plans and national production targets requires a tentative breakdown of the national production targets into the major farming areas, and comparison with the aggregated farm plans for the farming areas and the nation as a whole. Major discrepancies between the national plan targets and the national production (aggregated from farm plans for important individual agricultural products) are harmonised by working out alternatives acceptable both from the point of view of the national needs and local production feasibility. Similarly, the aggregate input requirements derived from the farm plans are evaluated in the context of national supply prospects, financial feasibility and foreign exchange considerations. Infrastructural investments needed for the facilities of transport, marketing, storing and processing are stressed, as this makes the required supplies of inputs available to the farms in various areas, and moves the increased output efficiently through the market channels.

Improving External Environmental Conditions

Changes in the external socio-economic and institutional conditions affecting farmers' incentive to adopt a desirable farm plan, and their ability to implement it are explored in each farming area. We must identify those external factors which impede the implementation of the farm production plans, and indicate the specific incentives required for farmers to improve their production efficiency. Among these factors, prevailing tenure arrangements, cost-price relationships, marketing facilities, availability of inputs at the farm level, nature and effectiveness of extension and other government services, cooperatives, etc., are of crucial importance.

Methodology for Block- and District-level Planning

Almost all past efforts at development planning are characterised by the lack of an appropriate methodology for both planning and implementation at the sub-national levels. Conscious of this fact, the Planning Commission constituted a Working Group in 1977 under the chairmanship of M.L. Dantwala, in order to draw up detailed guidelines for block level planning. The Dantwala Working Group mentioned in its report that no serious attempt had been made so far to induct technical skills in planning at the district level, even in states which have set up some sort of district planning machinery. The Working Group recommended the following guidelines for planning at the block and district levels (GOI 1978b: 4):

1. Prepare and analyse resource inventories to assess the prevailing level of development, potential for further development, and to identify constraints on further development.
2. Determine priorities of various programmes proposed for the area, and identify a catalytic programme.
3. Formulate programmes and projects for development, and establish their spatial and temporal linkages within an integrated framework.
4. Devise a plan for fuller utilisation of manpower resources.
5. Assess the availability of financial resources from various sources, such as the district budget, banking system and private sector, and mobilise the same.
6. Provide for monitoring and concurrent evaluation, or parallel audit of development plans and their modification from time to time in the light of experience.

These guidelines define the scope of the functions of the planning team alright, but they are of little help to the planner as far as the actual mechanics of formulating, evaluating and integrating various projects is concerned. The planner needs a framework which could guide him in collection and processing of data, and in formulating, ranking and combining various projects in optimal proportions, given a set of technical, economic, and institutional constraints and a choice criterion.

We now make a modest attempt to outline such a framework. The planning framework consists of a number of components, which are described below.

Delineation of Viable Areas for Planning

This is the first logical step in the process of area development planning. Several factors, such as cohesiveness, locus of economic activities, an adequate resource base for self-sustained growth and the nature of the development programmes, need to be considered in identifying and delineating areas for planning.

The question of an appropriate basic planning unit still continues to be controversial. But it seems that the Community Development (CD) Block has been accepted as the primary unit for local planning. But block level planning will have to be built in a framework of district level planning, which has to be adjusted to the state plan. The state plan already forms a part of the national plan. On the other hand, the use of the district as the basic planning unit is advocated on the grounds that time series area and production data are not available in published form for any units smaller than the district.

In the present situation in India, the block may be a convenient administrative unit for the planning and implementation of area development programmes, with clusters of villages delineated on the basis of micro-watersheds/command areas within the block serving as the ultimate units for micro-level planning. The framework for integrated planning outlined in this paper is based on the concept of multi-level planning, with clusters of villages (sub-areas) serving as the ultimate units of micro-level planning.

Determination and Quantification of Plan Objectives

This is the second step in the process of area planning. The objectives set for the area plan should represent the collective needs of the people living in the area, and should be realistic and operational. From past experience with planned development, it has become abundantly clear that it is no longer appropriate to formulate the principal objectives of a plan in terms of a specific target of growth only. The rate of growth in income and production that is achieved during a plan period is of little importance, if it does not result in a reduction of the worst forms of poverty and unemployment. The essential point is that a high rate of growth has been, and is not, any guarantee against worsening poverty and unemployment. How much is produced and how fast is not as important in our present situation, as what is produced and how. Keeping this in view, we can specify the following as the main objectives of planning at the block and district levels:

1. Maximising production in agriculture and allied activities in the rural areas.
2. Removal of unemployment and significant underemployment.
3. An appreciable improvement in the level of living of the poorest sections of the population.
4. Provision by the state of some of the basic amenities, like drinking water, elementary education, adult literacy, health care, rural roads, rural housing for the landless, etc.

Identification of Target Groups

To achieve the plan objectives, a comprehensive and integrated area plan covering the entire rural population is called for. For the purposes of planning, the target population can be broadly classified into four categories, as follows:

1. Farm households possessing land holdings of economic size.
2. Farm households possessing land holdings of uneconomic size.
3. Landless agricultural labourers.
4. Rural artisans.

The population falling in the first category would require technical assistance and guidance, as well as supply of inputs and institutional finance in order to be able to adopt the new farm technology appropriate for the area. If farmers in this category adopt new farm technology, it will substantially increase farm production, and will also generate considerable employment opportunities to absorb a significant proportion of rural unemployed.

For the households in the second category, high-value and labour-intensive crops will need to be identified, and their production and marketing facilitated. Besides crop production, some complementary and supplementary enterprises, like dairying, poultry, bee-keeping, pisciculture and sericulture, will also need to be introduced on these farms to supplement their income.

For landless agricultural labourers and rural artisans, a set of cottage and small-scale industries and rural crafts will need to be identified and evaluated in terms of their technical and economic feasibility and social acceptability. A massive programme of appropriate rural crafts and industries would require upgrading traditional skills, setting up a chain of training-cum-production centres, supply of raw materials and credit, and institutional arrangements for marketing the output.

In the first two years of the plan, the first category of target population may be left out of the plan fold, and the resources available for development may be devoted to the betterment of the quality of life of the lowest three strata of the population.

Resource Appraisal and Identification of Constraints on Development

After identifying the target groups, the next step in the process of area planning is to appraise the quantity and quality of natural, human and artificially created resources available in the area, and those likely to be available from outside the area for implementation of the plan. The process of resource appraisal would also facilitate the identification of constraints on any further development of the area. Resource appraisal is a multi-disciplinary endeavour, requiring the collaboration of meteorologists, hydrologists, plant scientists, animal scientists, soil scientists, agricultural engineers and social scientists.

Technical scientists appraise the environmental attributes (land, water, plants, fish, livestock and mineral resources) and the available technologies to exploit them, whereas social scientists appraise the attributes of human resources, institutions and organisations. The end product of this appraisal is a comprehensive resource inventory of the biophysical and socio-economic phenomena. The use of a proforma facilitates the resource appraisal exercise and the preparation of resource inventories.

Most of the information required for preparing a resource inventory is usually available with various government departments and other public and private agencies and organisations. Some of the information, such as input use, yield rates, income and expenditure patterns, sources and structure of employment, etc., will need to be collected afresh from a representative sample of the target population. Preparation of a preliminary plan format would help in gathering the right kind of information and should, therefore, precede data collection.

The resource inventory should be analysed to identify the major constraints on the achievement of the objectives of area planning. Some of the constraints may be technological, others economic and institutional, and still others social and cultural in nature. The constraints may be identified by direct contact with the people, area leaders, extension workers and programme administrators. Some of the constraints may be such as could be removed, or relaxed within the plan period, with the resource, technology, and institutional framework already available in the area.

On the other hand, there could be some other constraints that may require a longer time to be removed than the proposed plan period. Their alleviation may require further basic and/or applied research and/or a new institutional structure, which may not be feasible during the proposed plan period. After their identification, the constraints should be listed according to (*a*) their significance, as measured in terms of economic losses suffered by the people when they are present; and (*b*) the relative ease with which they can be removed within the plan period.

Identification and Selection of Development Projects

The next step in the process of area planning is to prepare a list of all technically feasible activities/enterprises which could be taken up in the area. This is again a multi-disciplinary endeavour. Insights gained from resource appraisal would prove helpful in the identification of (agro-technically) appropriate activities for the area. The activities would include those which are already prevalent in the area, as well as those found successful under similar conditions elsewhere. The following four criteria seem to be appropriate in identifying such projects:

1. The activities should be technically and organisationally feasible.
2. The activities should directly or indirectly contribute to the objectives of the plan.
3. The activities should be legally permissible.
4. The activities should be, by and large, socially acceptable.

The criteria for selection of projects for an area are largely furnished by the values and preferences of the people living in the area. Generally speaking, four criteria—efficiency, equity, employment and sustainability—can be used to make a choice from amongst a shelf of projects initially identified as appropriate.

Formulation of Development Projects

After having identified and selected various projects for inclusion in the plan, the next step is to formulate detailed projects for the activities so selected. Each of the projects should specify the following:

1. Title of the project.
2. Rationale for the project.
3. Duration of the project.
4. Objectives of the project.
5. Location of the project.
6. Target groups to be covered.
7. Details of the technology to be adopted.
8. Cost-benefit calculations.
9. Indicators of success.

    a) Increase in production of major produce.
    b) Increase in income.
    c) Incremental employment.
    d) Distribution of project benefits among the target groups.
    e) Impact on environment and ecology.
    f) Sustainability.

10. Financing strategy.

    a) Total financial outlay needed.
    b) Amount likely to be available from the target groups.
    c) Amount likely to be available from other ongoing government projects.
    d) Amount likely to be available from various institutional sources.
    e) Balance to be met from fresh allocations.

11. Linkages with other projects.
12. Implementation: organisational structure, staffing, flow of funds and work schedules.
13. Arrangements for supplying inputs and disposing output.
14. Arrangements for monitoring, feedback and control.
15. Anticipated externalities and conflicts and procedures for their resolution.

It is important that a separate project be formulated for each distinct process or activity. For example, if wheat can be produced by three different methods (*a*) with a complete package of improved inputs and practices, (*b*) with 50 per cent of the recommended dosage of nitrogen, phosphorous and potash and all other improved practices, and (*c*) with no fertilisers and no other improved practices, then three separate projects would need to be formulated for it. Similarly, if two different scales of a cottage industry are to be considered, two different projects should be formulated.

The task of project formulation is highly technical in nature, and therefore can be handled satisfactorily only by a multi-disciplinary team of experts. Expertise in project formulation is not usually available at substate levels, and therefore this very crucial phase of planning remains, by and large, neglected. The competence of the planning staff at all levels in the areas of project formulation and appraisal needs to be upgraded. This should be done through special in-service training programmes.

Determining Optimal Mix of Development Projects

After having formulated detailed projects, the next step in the process of area planning is to determine the optimal mix or combination of various projects, so as to attain the objectives of the area plan under the given conditions of resource availability and the technical, economic, institutional and social constraints. A number of quantitative techniques are now available for planning at the macro-level. But of all the planning techniques, linear programming is by far the most powerful and flexible tool that can be used for area planning. This technique can facilitate: (*a*) annual re-planning exercises within the framework of a five-year rolling plan; (*b*) testing the effects of changes in projected resource availability, prices and government policies on plan objectives through sensitivity analysis; (*c*) estimation of the amount of outside financing needed to meet the objectives of the plan; (*d*) estimation of the amount of labour employment that would be generated as a result of the plan; and (*e*) investment planning on the basis of shadow prices generated in the linear programming solutions.

A multi-period linear programming model can be used to determine the optimal mix of various activities/projects for an area, a block, a district, or a watershed. The model is constructed essentially in a linear programming framework, adding to it the appropriate dynamic equations characterised by flexibility coefficients on the lines of so-called Recursive Linear Programming. These dynamic equations reflect the dynamic structure of agricultural production, and the psychological and cautious responses of producers to innovations. The formal structure of the model can be presented in its mathematical form as follows (Ramakrishnaiah 1980).

1. Maximise $Z(t) = \sum_{j=1}^{n} C_j(t) X_j(t) (j = 1, \ldots, n$ and $t = 1, \ldots, 5)$

Subject to the constraints:

2. $\sum_{j=1}^{n} a_{ij}(t) X_j(t) \leq b_i(t), (i = 1, \ldots, m)$

3. $\sum_{j=1}^{n} a_{ij}(t) X_j(t) = b_i(t), (i = m + 1, \ldots, p)$

4. $\sum_{j=1}^{n} a_{ij}(t) X_j(t) \geq b_i(t), (i = p + 1, \ldots, r)$

5. $X_j(t) \leq (1 + \bar{\beta}_j) X_j(t - 1)$

6. $X_j(t) \geq (1 - \underline{\beta}_j) X_j(t - 1)$

7. $\sum_{j=1}^{n} X_j(t) \leq (1 + \bar{\alpha}) \sum_{j=1}^{n} X_j(t - 1)$

8. $\sum_{j=1}^{n} X_j(t) \geq (1 + \underline{\alpha}) \sum_{j=1}^{n} X_j(t - 1)$

9. $X_j(t) \geq 0$

In the above,

$Z(t) =$ returns over variable costs in rupees in a year (t),

$C_j(t) =$ returns over variable costs per unit of the jth activity in rupees in a year (t),

$X_j(t) =$ units of the jth activity in a year (t),

$a_{ij}(t) =$ requirement $(a > 0)$ or contribution $(a < 0)$ of the jth activity for the ith constraint,

$b_i(t) =$ the ith constraint level of supply—a resource capacity in equation (2), an accounting balance in equation (3), and a requirement to be met in equation (4),

$\bar{\beta}_j =$ upper flexibility coefficient with respect to the jth activity,

$\underline{\beta}_j =$ lower flexibility coefficient with respect to the jth activity,

$\bar{\alpha} =$ upper flexibility coefficient with respect to a group of related activities, and

$\underline{\alpha} =$ lower flexibility coefficient with respect to a group of related activities.

This model was used for formulation of a set of five-year agricultural development plans for a small watershed in the hills of Uttar Pradesh. The objective function of the model was to maximise the aggregate returns over variable costs for the watershed, subject to various constraints. The model included 72 activities and 47 constraints. On the whole, the model was found to be a very powerful and highly flexible tool for formulating multi-period integrated development plans at both micro- and macro-levels.

Concluding Remarks

India's approach to development planning has so far been predominantly macro-oriented, emphasising national goals and priorities. This has reduced planning to a set of sterile exercises, where plans and programmes are formulated mechanically without considering the resource base, development potential and needs and aspirations of people at the grassroots. Also, the requisite degree of people's participation in the formulation and implementation of development programmes has not been sought seriously. Decentralisation is, therefore, needed to make plans realistic, and to permit wider involvement of people in the process of planning.

However, the task of decentralised and multi-level planning has not yet been taken up systematically and seriously. Household, village (cluster), and block plans are not prepared as per the guidelines issued by the Union Ministry of Rural Areas and Employment. This is largely due to lack of appropriately trained staff for this purpose at the block and district levels. With the decentralisation of rural development planning after the 73rd Constitution Amendment Act, 1992, strengthening of rural development planning expertise at the district and block levels is all the more necessary to realise the full benefits from decentralisation. It is hoped that with the introduction of computers at the district level, preparation of household, cluster, block and district plans would be facilitated. However, a computer cannot be a substitute for trained and experienced rural development planners, who are a scarce resource at present in India.

14

Organising for Rural Development

Introduction

By 'organising for rural development', we mean: (*a*) designing appropriate organisational structures; (*b*) facilitating desirable human behaviour within the organisation; and (*c*) organising the clientele of a programme, such that the stated goals of the organisation and/or the programme under consideration are achieved as efficiently as possible.

The term 'organisation' is derived from the Greek word *organon*, which means a tool or an instrument. An organisation may be thought of as the coordinated actions of two or more people for the purpose of meeting an objective. In the context of management, we may conceptualise an organisation as a concrete and tangible entity, comprising men, machines and material resources that are organised and interrelated in a particular manner. The main purpose of an organisation is to transform something—materials, people, information—in a manner that adds value to what is transformed, and allows the organisation to survive and prosper.

The term organisation is also used to refer to any government, or governmental sub-division or agency, corporation, trust, estate, partnership, cooperative or association. In this sense, it connotes various forms of organisation. An organisation becomes an institution with an absence of indispensable people.

An organisational structure may be thought of as made of goals, tasks, resources, relationships, reward-and-punishment systems, communication systems, authority systems, etc. The net effect of 'structure' is a specific set of behavioural patterns. Therefore, any structural change basically involves a behavioural change. In the human being, however, behaviour must be consistent with attitudes. When there is inconsistency or dissonance, unpleasant tensions arise which the individual seeks to resolve. When he cannot alter his behaviour (because he cannot leave the structure), he changes his attitudes to attain consistency.

The rationale of organising the programme clientele is based on the 'Participative Model' of organisations. According to the proponents of this model, 'the over-all objective of the organisation is to achieve satisfactory integration between the needs and desires of the members of the organisation and the persons functionally related to it such as shareholders, suppliers, consumers' [programme beneficiaries] (Lorsch and Lawrence 1972: 12).

This chapter briefly presents a few organisational models first, then lists a few criteria of designing an appropriate organisation for rural development, and finally evaluates critically the suitability of various forms of organisations for rural development.

An organisation performs a variety of functions. Some of the important organisational functions are as follows:

- Formalising rules and procedures for establishing a repetition of desired actions.
- Ensuring that desired actions will fit together in a systematic way, and that these will be coordinated.
- Making the behaviour of organisation members predictable.
- Storing information and 'learning' in the course of their existence.
- Establishing an identity independent of the people within it, thereby ensuring its existence in spite of members who leave it.
- Allocating rewards to contributors and claimants.

Thus, the failure to organise properly can result in wasted energy and resources, the inability to accumulate knowledge, a dependency on the presence of certain people for existence, and a failure to provide incentives for contribution by its members.

To understand and interpret information about an organisation, a manager should adopt the following three elemental strategies:

1. Measures of events—a case study of an organisation.
2. Measures of association—determining the correlation between two measures.
3. Measures of causation—identification of causal variables by using experimental procedures.

A Detour to Organisational Models

Like the person who solves problems in other fields, the rural development manager concerned with organisational issues needs analytical tools and models that can help him analyse the problems he faces, and evolve solutions to the problems. When a manager wants to build an organisation, or when he sets out to change an existing organisation, he has in mind a theoretical model of what the reorganised structure should resemble. A manager can be more effective if he is explicit about the organisational models he chooses to use. We shall briefly review some important organisational models.

Gouldner (1959: 404–6) defines two types of organisational models.

The Rational Model

In the rational model, the organisation is regarded as a rationally conceived instrument or means to the realisation of group goals. It assumes that decisions are made on the basis of a rational survey of the situation and well-received knowledge with an orientation to a legal framework. Basically, the model is 'mechanical', with explicit focus on legal structures or 'blueprinted' patterns which can be inspected and rationally manipulated with a view to realise the group goals. Individual organisational elements can be subjected to successful and planned modification, and the organisation as a whole can be brought into conformity with explicitly held plans and goals. This model is widely used by managers in analysing issues of organisational design.

The Natural-system Model

This model regards the organisation as a 'natural whole' or system which is oriented to the realisation of group goals. Its elements are seen as interdependent and emergent institutions, which can be understood only in relation to the diverse needs of the total system. The organisation continues to strive to survive, and to maintain its equilibrium even after its goals have been attained, and thus it becomes an end in itself with its distinct needs which have to be satisfied. Changes in organisational patterns are considered the results of cumulative, unplanned, adaptive responses to threats to the equilibrium of the system as a whole. The organisation is seen as growing organically, with a natural history of its own which is modifiable only at great cost, if at all.

Buckley (1967: 36–41) has criticised the mechanical rational model and the biological natural-system model and has offered an alternative modern system theory, which he feels is more consistent with the observed functioning of organisational systems. He points out that organisations are more like 'sociocultural systems' than either mechanical or biological systems. To many managers, both the rational and the natural-system models may seem inappropriate. Yet many, if not most, managers implicitly or explicitly rely on one, particularly the rational model, and sometimes on an eclectic mixture of both, when they think about issues of organisational design.

To understand why these two models are so widely used, it would be helpful if we develop a general understanding of the 'classical' and 'participative' models which have a clear connection to Gouldner's 'rational and natural-system' dichotomy, and the 'socio-technical' and 'cognitive' models which have captured more of the complexity of organisational phenomena.

The Classical Model

This model focuses primarily on the relationship between management and workers. Workers are viewed as instruments, solely motivated by economic incentives, and existing to carry out organisational objectives. Managers, on the other hand, are characterised as rational, omniscient, and possessing outstanding personal qualities, such as kindness and fairness. However, despite these qualities, the manager's role defines that he be firm with workers. Because of the model's view of the worker as an 'economic man', rewards and punishments to the workers should be economic in nature. An astute classical manager would give detailed instructions to his subordinates. Then, according to the model, he must measure or assess exactly what has been done by the workers, and whether the employee should be rewarded or punished for his performance in executing the task. The essence of this model is: fitting the 'right' man into the 'right' job. This fit is to be defined by personal characteristics such as physical strength, manual dexterity, or specific craft skill.

The classical organisation pattern resembles a pyramid. Within this structure, both the chain of command and the channels of communication are vertical. The vertical chain of command stipulates that each person in the organisation is to have only one superior or boss. Similarly, each member is to have authority delegated to him, which is equal to his responsibility.

The Participative Model

Whereas the classical model is derived from an analysis of the experience of practitioners, the participative model is derived from the work of behavioural scientists. According to the proponents of this model, the individual in the organisation is engaged in a multidimensional process of development. Within this dynamic developmental process, the individual is seen as moving through the process of maturity. As he matures, this individual's needs, goals and desires tend to move in a specific direction. The individual seeks to be in a position of relative independence, in which he has some level of self-determination about his future. He begins to seek deeper, more constant, and increasingly complex interests with which to be challenged. And he also seeks a greater depth to his behavioural interaction within the organisation.

According to participative theorists, the overall objective of the organisation is to achieve a satisfactory integration between the needs and desires of the members of the organisation, and the persons functionally related to it, such as consumers, shareholders and suppliers. It is assumed that the management can make full use of the potential capacities of its human resources, only when each person in the organisation is a member of one or more effectively functioning work groups, thus participating in the overall organisational effort. Further, it is required that these groups have a high degree of group loyalty, effective skills and goals of high performance.

The organisations that perform best, according to this model, are those which motivate the individual to *cooperate*, not compete. In achieving this cooperation, the group leader is accountable, and must accept final responsibility for the performance of the group. However, in spite of the leader's responsibility for group performance, he must consider accepting those group decisions with which he does not concur, if he feels he could adversely affect group loyalty by neglecting to take the group's decisions into account.

Socio-technical Model

This model views the organisation as a system interacting with its environment—a system in which behaviour is influenced by human, technological, social and organisational inputs. All these variables are interdependent, so that a change in one influences the others.

In this model, the organisation is seen as an open system, exchanging resources with its environment in the form of an input-conversion-output process. The enterprise takes in raw materials, energy and manpower, and converts them into output of goods and services. The ability of an organisation to satisfy and adapt to its environment determines its success or failure, in terms of accomplishment of the 'primary task' for which it is built.

In this model, the organisation is viewed as consisting of a 'formal organisation' and an 'informal organisation', and both these components are expected to be as congruent as possible. The major strength of this model is in its systematic treatment of the complex realities of organisation life, thereby allowing us to identify the diverse causes of behaviour in organisations. The model is very useful for thinking about division of work and organisation 'fit' to primary tasks. Its limitation is that it is difficult to use as a design tool without practice and formal training (Lorsch and Lawrence 1972: 22).

The Cognitive Model

This model is also known as the Behavioural Theory of Decision Making. This approach to the analysis of complex organisations was developed by Herbert Simon, James March and their colleagues at the Carnegie Institute of Technology, mainly to aid them in building quantitative models of the decision process (March and Simon 1958). Their model assumes that price and output decisions are made by a group of managers whose goals are often in conflict with each other, and who possess very imperfect information, rather than by an individual entrepreneur who has perfect information, as presumed under the economic theory of the firm. In their opinion, organisations tend to 'satisfice' rather than optimise profit by the very nature of their decision processes. They view the organisational decision process as built around the development of alternative courses of action and execution of a choice from amongst these alternatives, on the basis of available information and under constraints imposed by the environment, as well as the structural aspects of the situation.

Although the cognitive model may seem overly complex, it provides a number of useful insights into the functioning of complex organisations. As an analytic approach, it leads us to view organisation as a *process* which evolves from the interaction of structure, human cognitive mechanisms, and the nature of the decisions that must be made. In this sense, it is a dynamic model, which emphasises the development and adaptation of organisational systems under varying conditions.

The Search for a New Paradigm

Unfortunately, the organisational models reviewed in the preceding section are not very helpful in designing appropriate organisational structures for rural development in India, as also in other developing countries. This is mainly because these models were all built out of the Western experience, which, to begin with, was confined to relatively simple and well-defined organisational activities, since the state functions were essentially of regulation and maintenance. Under those conditions, it was relatively easy to develop an administrative theory capable of analysing, through both inductive and deductive systems, the various organisational issues. Having done that, it was also possible to design an operating system capable of performing various tasks.

In a developing country like India, with a mixed economy, it is difficult to observe any uniform pattern either in the activities or in the behaviour of a development organisation. In the fields of agriculture, community development, health, family planning and in many other areas of social welfare, it is virtually impossible to establish clear-cut roles for social, economic, political and administrative organisations. Under these circumstances, it has not been possible to identify the behavioural patterns which have to be changed, or the methods by which they can be changed. Nor has it been possible to design an administrative structure which can bring both the change agent and the clientele system in any kind of effective working relationship. As a result, the various organisations engaged in rural development criss-cross each other, causing a great deal of confusion in the operations, and wastage of resources in the process.

Even so, the organisational models serve considerable purpose in their applications to discrete projects, such as those relating to fertiliser production, power generation, irrigation, etc. In these projects, the functions, activities and tasks to be performed can be fairly accurately measured and identified, making it easy to prescribe what is to be done organisationally to achieve them. However, when it comes to diffused programmes such as agricultural and rural development programmes, where the goals are intertwined with different sets of forces and are not so easy to describe, it has not been possible to develop appropriate organisational structures for effective implementation and management. Therefore, the search for appropriate organisational designs and structures for rural development still continues.

Numerous individuals and institutions are searching for new paradigms of development, based on structures which meet the criteria of efficiency, sustainability, equity, well-being and participation. Toffler (1980: 368), among others, argues that sustainable social development should be based on exploitation of the one resource that is inexhaustible—information and the human capacity for creative imagination. The structures of social institutions must be designed with the intention of gaining complete advantage of the potentials of this resource. This is basic not only to sustainable and equitable material well-being, but to the non-material advancement of human beings as well.

Berger and Neuhaus (1977: 2–3) suggest policy actions to strengthen the role of intermediate human institutions such as the family, the neighbourhood, the self-managing work group, the voluntary agency, etc., which perform a mediating role between the individual and the megastructure (government bureaucracies, big corporations, etc.), providing a source of personal support and recognition, and facilitating solutions to problems at the local level and creative innovation.

Korten (1981: 610) asserts that

...the answer rests not in abolishing society's megastructures since they are basic to the functioning of any modern society. Rather it rests in substantially reforming them, in loosening central control and strengthening the feedback systems that increase potential for self-direction and direct participation at local levels consistent with the well-being of the larger society. It will be necessary to move beyond more primitive forms of bureaucratic organisation, able only to control or to substitute for local action, to substantially more sophisticated forms which can work to strengthen capacities for creative local self-help action and self-control. Though most calls for greater reliance on local level solutions to global problems look to such action as a substitute for bureaucratic action, it is neither so easy to dismiss their stifling regulatory power or to achieve effective problem solving on the scale required without access to their massive resources.

In the Introduction to a series of studies on bureaucracy, Littrell (1980: 263) concludes:

Although many critically important problems face us today, most of the problems as well as proposals for their solutions are defined and shaped in bureaucratic organisations. Our capacity to understand and modify bureaucracy in the present decade will greatly determine our capacity to solve our problems and thus shape the decades to come.

Criteria for Designing an Appropriate Organisation

While the organisational structure for rural development may differ from state to state, depending upon the variations in the role assigned by the states to NGOs and the panchayati raj institutions for agricultural and rural development, an ideal rural development organisation should satisfy the following criteria:

1. It should provide for effective coordination of macro-planning and micro-planning, i.e., vertical integration of planning.
2. It should provide for the formulation of inter-sectoral plans, programmes, and projects and their horizontal integration.
3. There should be a mechanism for maintaining a dynamic relationship between planning and implementation.
4. The delivery system should be in a position to channelise the benefits of development programmes to the target groups, and should be strong enough to resist vested interests that have in the past stood in the way of these benefits reaching the poor.
5. It should have a high degree of technical and professional competence.
6. It should provide for the maintenance of a direct and continuing relationship between the planners and the people, and for the meaningful participation of the people in the process of development planning and implementation.
7. It should provide for checks, balances and correctives, so that target groups belonging to the weaker sections are not deprived of the benefits meant for them.
8. It should be sensitive to the needs of its clientele, and responsive to changes in its external environment.
9. It should provide for participation of its target group(s)/clientele in making its policies that affect them.
10. It should be financially viable and sustainable.

Now we briefly describe the salient features of various forms of organisations engaged in rural development in India, and critically appraise their suitability for the purpose.

Government Organisations

The government has been, still is, and will continue in the near future to be an important organisation in the field of agricultural and rural development in developing countries, including India. Development is seen as the specific responsibility of the government in all such countries. This has far-reaching implications for the role of public bureaucracy, which is the arm of the state responsible for carrying out the wishes of political leaders. In most of these countries, efforts to bring about improvement in the quality of life of rural people depend heavily on government administration and bureaucrats. According to Bauer (1991: 190–91), economic development is not the result of forced mobilisation of people's resources, forced modernisation of attitudes and behaviour of people, of large-scale state-sponsored industrialisation or of achievement of political independence. It is the result of individual voluntary responses of millions of people to emerging or expanding opportunities, brought to their notice primarily through the operation of the market. The government has a limited role to play in this process, and does not have to incur huge expenditure of public funds. The primary role of the government should be to create and nurture an institutional set-up that provides needed incentives and facilities to economic agents to do what they want to do, and which is flexible and adaptable to changing social and economic conditions. Besides, the government should also establish mechanisms for coordination of the activities of atomistic economic agents, and for removing uncertainty about human behaviour or solving the assurance problem which characterises the classic prisoner's dilemma. More specifically, the main functions of governmental organisations/institutions can be seen at the following six levels:

1. Facilitating policy formulation.
2. Harmonising the actions of various economic agents and coordinating programme implementation.
3. Providing incentives for collective action and self-regulation.
4. Enforcing regulations and policing.
5. Resolving conflicts and providing arbitration.
6. Providing technical assistance.

After Independence, certain changes were effected in the administrative system with a view to reorient it to meet the needs of development. The nation-building departments of agriculture, rural development, education and health have expanded considerably. New development agencies and corporations have been set up. The district is the focal unit of rural development administration, and developmental activity is one of the numerous responsibilities of the district collector. His prime responsibility is and will, in the foreseeable future, continue to be the maintenance of law and order. He is so preoccupied with this that it is impossible for him to do justice to the developmental responsibility. The district collector leans heavily on the District Development Officer (DDO) for the purpose, but as all the authority vests in the district collector, the DDO only plays second fiddle and is not able to achieve what is desired. Further, hierarchically, the DDO, being lower than the district collector, is unable to provide the requisite leadership and obtain the cooperation of, and adequate input from, the officers of other departments/disciplines, which is so vital for coordinated development.

Due to the unethical value system and highly inflammable sociocultural environment in which we are operating, the law and order situation has deteriorated over the years, requiring greater attention from the district magistrates, which in turn means less attention both quantitatively and qualitatively for developmental activity. The result is that the goals of development have become mirages. There is yet another aspect of this matter. The machinery charged with the responsibility of law and order cannot handle the development portfolio adequately. The qualities required for the efficient discharge of the responsibility of law and order are just the ones which hinder developmental responsibility. For example, the efficient discharge of the law and order responsibility requires qualities of evasiveness, toughness, circumspectness and capacity to dispense expedients. For developmental work, however, one needs to be receptive, open-minded, communicative, empathetic, and have the capacity to go deep and find real and lasting solutions. In these days of specialisation, how can one be expected to become adept at simultaneously handling varied responsibilities requiring contrasting skills?

It is, therefore, not surprising that even after more than four decades of development planning, rural administration still displays serious faults. It generally fails to deliver services and supplies promptly, efficiently, and equitably. The failure is due partly to inadequate resources, partly to an elitist bias, and partly to a lack of coordination. And rural administration generally fails to secure popular participation. Traditional attitudes have prevented any synthesis with local institutions, or a real partnership with the people.

From a management perspective, the central challenge of our times is to understand and modify bureaucratic organisations by building into them a capacity for innovative learning, leading to a fundamental orientation in their purposes and modes of operation. This is what is called Bureaucratic Reorientation (BRO). What we need most urgently now are operational prescriptions for rural development organisations which may want to implement the new strategy of BRO. Unfortunately, very little is known at present to advise a development agency about what it should do to achieve BRO and how.

Korten (1981: 610) suggests that BRO should give priority to the management of systems over the management of projects, to innovation over compliance, and to methodologies for continuous self-monitoring and rapid self-correction over formalised planning and evaluation methodologies. To achieve these, he suggests the formation of social learning clusters and networks within the system, linking together those individuals who have commitment to appropriate action, and providing them mutual support and operational methodologies needed to translate their good intentions into effective action.

Jesus (1984), on the basis of action-research activities of the Asian Institute of Management through its Rural Development Management Programme (RDMP) team with three agencies undertaking BRO, has attempted to construct a conceptual framework to capture the process of BRO. The salient features of his framework are as follows:

1. BRO assumes a decision by the agency to initiate a fundamental change in its objectives, or a radical shift in its strategy. Only the strongest present or imminent pressures from the external environment are likely to budge bureaucracies from their settled ways.
2. Once the new strategy is identified and accepted, the BRO process can begin. Access to the top management of the agency is a precondition for any attempt at BRO to get started and prosper.
3. BRO takes a long time, possibly longer than the tenure of the executive who starts the process. His departure from the scene inevitably results in some disruption of the BRO process.
4. For the purposes of triggering and sustaining the BRO process, it is vitally important that some source of external funds, such as a foundation or an international development agency, be associated with the agency undertaking BRO. As with the stimulus for changes, resources for bringing about BRO have to come from outside the agency.
5. Training of agency personnel seems to be a tactically sound first step in the process of BRO. A training programme can serve not

only to develop skills, but also to initiate or sustain the process of change.

6. A manager aiming to elicit certain behaviour patterns from his staff ought to focus on changing the structures within the organisation, rather than the attitudes of the people. But this assertion holds more strongly for private enterprise than for a government or public sector organisation. Public sector managers place a high premium on convincing people to change their views about their work. Not everyone will respond to the appeal for an attitude change, but not everyone will need to. A few 'champions' can have pervasive effects.

Panchayati Raj Institutions

It was Gandhiji who realised the importance of village panchayats as important instruments of rural development, and of promoting and nurturing democracy at the grassroots. He asserted that unless panchayats were invested with adequate powers, villagers cannot have real swaraj. Article 40 in Para iv of the Constitution of India was introduced at his insistence. The article states that: 'The State shall take steps to organise village panchayats and endow them with such powers and authority as may be necessary to enable them to function as units of self-government.'

In January 1957, the GOI appointed a committee under the chairmanship of Balwantray Mehta to study the working of the Community Development Programme, and suggest how best it could be maintained and implemented. The committee recommended a three-tier system of local government, christened 'Panchayati Raj' by Jawaharlal Nehru. At the grassroots or village level were to be formed village panchayats, at the middle or block level were to be panchayat samitis and at the apex or district level zila parishads were to be formed. The new bodies were to have wide powers and adequate finance. The committee offered two broad directional thrusts: (*a*) it argued that there should be administrative decentralisation for effective implementation of development programmes, and (*b*) the decentralised administrative system should be under the control of elected bodies. The three-tier structure of panchayati raj institutions was brought into existence after the Mehta Committee scheme was approved by the National Development Council (NDC) in January 1958. The NDC affirmed the objectives behind the introduction of democratic institutions at the district and block levels, and suggested that each state should work out the structure which suited its conditions best.

The new system of Panchayati Raj Institutions (PRIs) was first adopted in Rajasthan and Andhra Pradesh in 1959, and thus PRIs have been in existence in India since then. However, there were inter-state variations in structural pattern, tenure and responsibilities entrusted to them. With a view to grant constitutional status to PRIs in the country and to bring about uniformity, the Indian Parliament passed the Constitution (73rd Amendment) Act, 1992 in December 1992. This act came into force with effect from 24 April 1993. It envisages the establishment of panchayats as units of local self-government in all states and union territories, except the tribal areas in the states of Nagaland, Meghalaya and Mizoram, and certain other scheduled areas. Subsequently, in December 1996, the provisions of the 73rd Amendment were extended to the tribal and other scheduled areas also through an act of Parliament. Adequate powers and responsibilities would be devolved upon the PRIs at the appropriate levels, to enable them to prepare and implement schemes for economic development and social justice, as entrusted to them under the items listed in the Eleventh Schedule to the Constitution. Significantly, the 73rd Amendment does not have a provision for constitution of gram sabhas, but their powers and functions have to be specified by the state legislatures. However, in the extended act, constitution of gram sabhas is mandatory.

The salient features of the Constitution (73rd Amendment) Act, 1992 are as follows: (*a*) The gram sabha has been envisaged as the foundation of the panchayati raj system. It shall perform such functions and exercise such powers as may be entrusted to it by the state legislatures. (*b*) There shall be three tiers of panchayats, at the village, intermediate and district levels. Only states having population not exceeding 20 lakhs will have the discretion to not constitute panchayats at the intermediate level. (*c*) Seats in a panchayat at every level are to be filled by direct election from territorial constituencies demarcated for this purpose. In addition, there would be ex officio members also, as provided in the state legislation. (*d*) Seats shall be reserved at every level of panchayat for Scheduled Castes and Scheduled Tribes in proportion to their population in a given panchayat area, and for women to the extent of not less than one-third of the total number of seats. Reservation for offices of chairpersons of panchayats at every level shall also be made for SC/ST, in proportion to the total number of chairpersons of panchayats at each level as the population of the SC and ST in the state bears to the total population of the state, and for women to the extent of not less than one-third of the total number of offices of chairpersons in the panchayats at each level. (*e*) The term of office of panchayats shall be for five years, and elections must be completed before the expiry of its duration; if dissolved earlier, elections must be completed within six months from the date of dissolution. (*f*) A State Finance Commission shall be constituted in every state, to go into the principles governing the distribution and devolution of financial resources between the panchayats and states. (*g*) The superintendence, direction and control of the preparation of electoral rolls and conduct of all elections to panchayats shall be vested in a state election commission. (*h*) The Eleventh Schedule has been added to the Constitution, which denotes 29 subjects/functions which could be entrusted to the PRIs. Elections to the PRIs in most states have been held. About 25 lakh people are expected to be in position in the PRIs, out of which one-third would be women. The central government is assisting the states in orienting the elected representatives and officials towards their new responsibilities through training.

A national committee of state panchayat ministers has been constituted by the central government to review the progress of implementation of the constitutional provisions and guide and advise the states in this regard.

While PRIs have been, on one hand, considered as having generated tensions, factions and party politics in village communities, they have been, on the other hand, considered as the only hope for achieving people's participation, which is the soul of the democratic system. Whereas the introduction of panchayati raj in the year 1959 was in itself a major landmark in the history of administrative reforms, the system was not implemented faithfully in most of the states, due largely to the indifferent attitude of bureaucrats towards it. Consequently, there have been more failures than successes. After the operationalisation of the Constitution (73rd Amendment) Act, 1992, it is hoped that PRIs will emerge more strong and dynamic to face various challenges and problems that still lie ahead of them. Their success in the future will depend on the extent of transfer of rural development functions, and devolution of financial and administrative powers to them by the state governments. If the deliberations of the conference of chief ministers and panchayat raj ministers held in New Delhi on 3 August 1997 are any guide, the new panchayati raj structure will take a long time to be fully functional. A major concern expressed at the conference was the slow pace of devolution of powers, functions and responsibilities to PRIs. The conference recommended that the process of devolution of powers be completed latest by the end of December 1997, but it seems that this has not been done by most of the states yet. Similarly, the district rural development agencies have not been restructured to permit the PRIs to perform their intended functions effectively and efficiently.

While it is too early to assess the impact of the constitutional status given to PRIs, the report of the first concurrent evaluation survey of the Jawahar Rozgar Yojana, which covered 448 districts in the country, throws some light on certain aspects of elected village panchayats, and the people who head them. The evaluation covered a one-year period from January to December 1992. The survey was conducted before the introduction of the 73rd Amendment to the Constitution. Some of the major findings of the evaluation are as follows: In West Bengal, as many as 89 per cent of the elected panchayat heads were landless and marginal farmers, whereas in states like Maharashtra, Punjab and Andhra Pradesh, over 25 per cent of the *pradhans* were big farmers, owning at least 10 hectares of land. As expected, a majority of the panchayat *pradhans* (77 per cent) were from the upper classes. Only 7 per cent of them were from the SC, and another 15 per cent from the ST. About 3 per cent of the sample panchayats were headed by women, of whom 41 per cent belonged to the SC. Of the panchayat pradhans, 13 per cent were graduates, about 24 per cent had education up to primary level, and 7 per cent were illiterate. The level of deliberations in the panchayat level meetings was extremely poor. During the 12-month period preceding the survey, 39 per cent of the sample panchayats did not meet even once (Gangrade 1997: 755–56). In a study conducted in Orissa, it was found that women entered panchayat politics due to persuasion of their family members, or pressure from the village community or political parties. However, the women who reluctantly entered politics showed greater maturity in outlook, enthusiasm, political consciousness, and consciousness about their role and responsibilities (Panda 1997: 663). Given these features of panchayats and their elected heads, there is need for building the capacity of elected leaders through education and training. This is all the more necessary, given a variety of administrative and financial functions expected to be performed by the elected leaders, as also the ambivalent attitude of the bureaucracy and the reluctance of the state leaders to part with power.

Cooperatives

If the goals of agricultural and rural development are to be achieved, it will be necessary that the people are organised within an institutional structure that gives them access to the national economic and social systems. Organising people is a political act, because it alters the distribution of power within the community by increasing the number of people who are making decisions.

Governments in most developing countries are afraid of altering and expanding their power base. The apprehension is, however, unfounded, because these governments may not endure unless the rural elite are willing to bridge the gap between themselves and the masses. For the endurance of the state, it is necessary that the people believe that they belong to it, and that because of their own personal interests they have a stake in its survival. If a state is to create a sense of belonging among the great mass of the people, then it must decentralise the decision making process.

The problem in many Third World countries is that governments, far from viewing decentralisation as a way of winning the support of the people, view it as a loss of control, a splintering and weakening of the political system. What is needed is an understanding of how decentralisation can be used, both to stimulate local initiative and strengthen central governments (Owen and Shaw 1972: 18).

Both the central and state governments in India have so far followed a paternalistic approach to rural development, which presumes that rural people are incapable of helping themselves and that everything must be done for them. This has increased a 'dependence syndrome' wherein rural people depend on the government, to the extent that most of them now believe that rural development is the sole responsibility of the government.

Instead, the government should help rural people organise themselves within an institutional system. The art of organising people lies in allowing decisions to be made at the appropriate level—national, regional, or local—and helping them design effective problem-solving systems. This is possible only if the government moves away from its traditional detailed control over local activities, towards policy determination and general supervision.

The key to releasing the energies of the people lies in designing effective problem-solving systems. This would admit them into a world from which they have always been excluded—the world of knowledge and control of their destinies. The question now is how to establish a working system to solve problems. Owen and Shaw (1972: 23–20) identify the following six principles for creating such a system:

1. Identifying regional and local functions.
2. Defining a national policy framework.

3. Setting minimum standards of performance.
4. Setting up new institutions for solving local problems.
5. Creation of a large number of leadership positions.
6. Transferring loyalty to modernising institutions.

The experience of Taiwan, which has established local problem-solving bodies to carry out agricultural development projects, is relevant to India. The Taiwanese government has set up township offices, farmers' associations and irrigation associations to bridge the gap between the national government and individual farmers. The farmers' association is a non-governmental cooperative society organised by the farmers themselves, run by professional managers who are employees of the farmers. It is dedicated to the promotion of farmers' interests, advancement of farming techniques and knowledge, and improvement of rural living conditions. Its service activities include cooperative marketing and processing of farm products, purchase of farm supplies, extension of farm loans and acceptance of farm deposits, distribution of fertilisers, and sponsoring agricultural extension services and other rural welfare services. In India also, cooperatives could play an important role as instruments of promoting rural development.

A cooperative is generally viewed as a socio-economic organisation that can fulfil both social and economic objectives of its members, and that has its members' interests truly at heart. A cooperative is based on certain values and principles of its own, which distinguish it from other forms of organisations.

Cooperation has three dimensions, that is, economic, social and moral, which are equally crucial for its success. The very motto of cooperation, 'each for all and all for each', signifies loyalty, trust, faith and fellowship. A cooperative is a perfect democratic institution of the members, for the members, and by the members, and is based on the 'one member, one vote' system of decision making.

The International Cooperative Alliance (ICA) Congress held in Manchester on 23 September 1995 adopted the following seven principles:

1. Voluntary and open membership.
2. Democratic member control.
3. Members' economic participation and limited interest on share capital.
4. Autonomy and independence.

5. Provision of cooperative education, training and information.
6. Cooperation among cooperatives.
7. Concern for the community.

The cooperative as a business organisation is similar in many ways, and different in many other ways, from other forms of organisations. The similarities are in the domain of roles and functions, and the differences in the manner in which the roles and functions are performed. Cooperatives are expected to reflect in their day-to-day practices the principles and values of cooperation, which emphasise, *inter alia*, equality, equity and mutual self-help.

Like any other business organisation, cooperatives are expected to ensure efficiency and profitability in their operations. But unlike other business organisations in the private and public sectors, the cooperative is both a social organisation and a business enterprise, and therefore has a dual purpose: it serves both a social as well as an economic function. A cooperative manager must be concerned not only with the economic aspects, but also with the social obligations of his organisation.

Cooperatives have higher comparative advantage over other forms of organisations, in involving people in their activities, in mobilising people's resources and political power for achieving their goals, in identifying and developing local leaders through democratic processes, in securing vertical and horizontal integration of production, procurement, processing and marketing functions, and in facilitating equitable distribution of benefits of development. All these advantages can help cooperatives in improving their competitive position as a business organisation vis-à-vis their competitors.

The economic rationale for a cooperative organisation lies in its endeavour to secure for its members advantages of modern technology and economies of scale. A cooperative organisation that does not want or cannot secure these two advantages is doomed to failure sooner or later. Theoretically speaking, there is hardly a better organisational structure than the cooperative for achieving the dual goal of social and economic development, but final success depends on the level of operational efficiency achieved (Dulfer 1974).

The major difference between cooperative management and management in other organisations, is the greater need for cooperatives to involve directors, members and staff in key positions in problem solving and decision making. This is no small task. Managers trained in traditional management schools, when confronted with a difficult situation, feel they must think it through for themselves and find a solution. That is what they have learnt in management courses. Cooperative theory requires a different response. Cooperative managers are expected to take the problem out to the members and staff, and involve various interest groups in the development of solutions.

Cooperatives occupy an important place in India's rural economy, in terms of their coverage of population and their share in the total supply of agricultural inputs, including credit. India can rightly claim to have the largest network of cooperatives in the world. In India, as of 31 March 1994, there were 3.95 lakh cooperatives, having a total membership of some 1,896 lakh and working capital of Rs 118,699 crore (NIRD 1996: 105). Cooperatives now account for 62 per cent of the total credit supplied in rural areas, and 34 per cent of the total quantity of fertilisers distributed in the country. The two giant cooperative fertiliser plants, Indian Farmers' Fertiliser Cooperative (IFFCO) and Krishak Bharati Cooperative (KRIBHCO), manufacture 21.1 per cent of the fertilisers produced in the country.

Of all the types of cooperatives, the Anand pattern dairy cooperatives are considered to have been most successful in serving their members, as well as society at large. Growth and development of milk producers' cooperatives in Kheda (Kaira) district of Gujarat, under the umbrella of the Kaira District Cooperative Milk Producers' Union Ltd, popularly known as AMUL, during the fifties and sixties demonstrated the potential of cooperatives as instruments of dairy development. The then Prime Minister Lal Bahadur Shastri was convinced about the suitability of the Anand model, and advised the GOI to set up an organisation under the chairmanship of V. Kurien to replicate the Anand pattern dairy cooperatives in India. Consequently, the National Dairy Development Board (NDDB) was established in 1965 with its headquarters in Anand. NDDB designed a programme called Operation Flood (OF) to replicate Anand pattern cooperatives in the country. Operation Flood is perhaps the world's largest dairy development programme in terms of its scope, coverage and longevity. (See Ch. 11 for details of OF.)

Despite their overwhelming importance in India's rural economy, most of the rural cooperatives are not financially viable due to mismanagement. Cooperatives need to be managed by professional managers, if they are to survive and grow in the wake of India's new economic policy characterised by deregulation, delicensing, privatisation and globalisation. Several obstacles hinder the professionalisation of management of agribusiness cooperatives—lack of professional managers having values and ethos congenial to cooperative management; excessive government control and interference; lack of good leadership; small size of business and hence inability to hire professional managers; lack of performance-based reward systems; and internal work culture and environment not congenial to professionalisation of management.

Voluntary Agencies/Non-governmental Organisations

Voluntary action in India is as old as the emergence of organised society itself. It originated as pure philanthropy or charity, and this motivation sustained the effort all through history. Even the establishment of the Indian National Congress in 1885 was a voluntary effort initiated by Allan Octavian Hume, acclaimed as its 'father and founder'. Addressing an open letter to the graduates of Calcutta University in 1883, Hume gave a clarion call to the educated youth (Maheshwari 1987; 560–61):

> You are the salt of the land. And if amongst you the elite, 50 men cannot be found with sufficient power of self-sacrifice, sufficient love for and pride in their country, sufficient genuine and unselfish heartfelt patriotism to take the initiative, and if needs be, devote the rest of their lives to the cause, then there is no hope for India. Her sons must and will remain mere humble and helpless instruments in the hands of foreign rulers, for they who would be free themselves must strike the blow.

More recently, emphasising the role of voluntary agencies in rural development, the Working Group on Block Level Planning (1978) shares the view that

> the country's social and economic problems are so vast and multifarious that the Government's administrative machinery alone cannot tackle them. The establishment of a self-reliant society implies progressive curtailment of people's dependence on the Government. From times immemorial, voluntary agencies in our country have played a significant part in promoting people's welfare .... The planning team at the district level should consult and actively seek the assistance of the voluntary agencies in their area while preparing the plan and selectively entrust to them the implementation of some sectoral plans in which they may have requisite expertise and experience (GOI 1978b: 45).

Voluntary agencies (VAs) or Non-Governmental Organisations (NGOs) can (and some of them do, in fact) play a very important role in rural development. They can enthuse the rural population to prepare meaningful plans for rural development, as also to take part in their implementation. There are now quite a few voluntary agencies in the country which have the requisite technical and managerial resources available with them to undertake rural development projects, and to manage them successfully. For example, the Bhartiya Agro-Industrial Foundation (BAIF) of Urlikanchan (Maharashtra) has acquired a high level of technical competence in the field of animal husbandry, and is implementing a number of projects in this field in many areas in the country. Similarly, MYRADA of Bangalore has developed expertise in the fields of irrigation, wastelands development, watershed development, and resettlement of released bonded labourers, and it has a number of projects in these fields in operation in the southern states of the country. There is a definite need to support genuine voluntary effort in rural development.

At the national level, the Council for Advancement of People's Action and Rural Technology (CAPART) is the nodal agency responsible for promoting voluntary action in rural development. CAPART was registered under the Societies Registration Act, 1860 on 1 September 1986, with its headquarters in New Delhi. It aims at encouraging, promoting and assisting voluntary action for rural development. In pursuance of these objectives, CAPART makes available financial assistance to VAs/NGOs under the following schemes: (*a*) promotion of voluntary action in rural development; (*b*) Development of Women and Children in Rural Areas (DWCRA); (*c*) Accelerated Rural Water Supply Programme (ARWSP); (*d*) Central Rural Sanitation Programme (CRSP); (*e*) organisation of beneficiaries of anti-poverty programmes; (*f*) Integrated Rural Development Programme (IRDP); (*g*) Jawahar Rozgar Yojana (JRY) consisting of watershed conservation and development programmes, village link roads, and rural housing and social forestry; (*h*) Advancement of Rural Technology Scheme (ARTS); (*i*) Panchayati Raj (PR) and (*j*) disability rehabilitation.

Its funds mainly consist of grants from the Union Ministry of Rural Areas and Employment. The council can also obtain grants from various central and state government departments, and accept donations and contributions from other sources. CAPART had sanctioned about 16,553 projects worth Rs 441.03 crore by 31 March 1997 (GOI 1998a: 352). CAPART has set up six regional committees at Jaipur, Ahmedabad, Hyderabad, Bhubaneswar, Guwahati and Lucknow to decentralise its functioning. These committees have been given the mandate to sanction and monitor projects involving an outlay of upto Rs 5 lakh.

The 1990s have witnessed a proliferation of development initiatives taken by NGOs. It is no longer an issue of concern for the elite. Now, development action is perceived as an alternative career option even by the common person. The idea of undertaking socially meaningful activities as a full-time occupation is not an alien concept for a large majority of those working with NGOs. Ideological fervour, or a sense of nationalism in society as a whole, has been waning gradually over time.

Large-scale support from government has also necessitated routinisation of development interventions. This has also been encouraged by the fact that many common people, who are not innovators, are involved in delivery of goods and services, which are not adequately catered to by the state or market institutions.

Most new organisations that are coming up now are those promoted by common people. They do not attract highly trained or highly competent personnel. Most old, large organisations, which attracted some of the best brains during the phase of innovation, are either saturated at the top (with a small group, if not one, of development innovators at the helm of affairs), or have routinised functions to an extent that they have ceased to remain attractive for competent youth. However, the liberalised market economy now offers much more attractive opportunities to talented youth, as compared to the development initiatives that they had even a few years ago.

The present generation of NGO worker has a very different set of aspirations and motivation, from those of the leaders of the NGO sector a decade ago. Many of the norms of personal need (gratification, accountability and transparency) evolved around people of high social motivation. These norms need changes in the present context, with people having different sets of motivations and aspirations.

With development funding agencies re-focusing their attention on supporting small organisations, the small NGOs have received a boost. This has also made it necessary for funding agencies to take a more proactive role than they did earlier. Many of them now play the role of a resource centre, contributing to the planning and implementation of programmes and competence building of the NGO teams.

The known processes of development interventions have become more complex with enhanced understanding of the development process itself. Though in the 1950s service delivery was the focus of development initiatives, by the 1960s development activists were talking about transfer of technology. By the 1970s, it was recognised that technology transfer remained inadequate, unless backed with competence building. By the 1980s, the initiatives concentrated on multiple or comprehensive sets of services, backing up technology transfer with training, credit and market linkages. But by the 1990s it had been recognised that the development inputs, to be sustainable in an eco-friendly manner, have to have much more than this. The ability of NGOs to deliver high quality development services has also been recognised by the state machinery. This has also led to fairly high expectations from these organisations.

But now most of the NGOs are left with poor quality manpower to address this even more complex task. This may have serious implications for the quality of services being delivered by these organisations. Though substantial weightage is being given to building the competence of development teams by various support agencies, developing human resources is also being seen as one more task by a large majority of these organisations.

Corporations and Rural Development

Corporations could make a significant contribution to rural development in India, through establishing and/or supporting institutions that bring corporate resources, new technologies, modern management and expertise to bear on the problems of rural development. There are at least the following four reasons why involvement of corporations in rural development is desirable (Raymond 1996):

- **Win-win Outcome.** Promoting the involvement of corporations in rural development is a classic 'win-win' strategy. Corporations gain by demonstrating their commitment to rural communities, thereby building their credentials as good corporate citizens. This improves their image in the market place and contributes to their commercial success. The rural people benefit from new expertise and resources used by corporations to solve their problems and fulfil their felt needs. The government wins because corporations supplement limited public resources available for rural development.
- **Stable Democracy.** The involvement of business houses in rural development—and the emergence of non-profit institutions such as charitable trusts and societies—boosts institutional pluralism and people's participation in the policy making process. Indeed, independent private institutions are vital to ensuring the stability

of democratic processes in times of political change and economic crisis.

- **Sustainability.** Government-funded rural development programmes are vulnerable to changes in policy and budgetary allocations. Involvement of private corporations and their executives, who are not affected by political changes, in rural development projects could help make those projects sustainable. Sustainability depends on both availability of funds, as well as commitment of institutions and their employees over the long term. Commitment of government employees to rural development is often short-lived, as compared to that of their counterparts in private sector development organisations. How many Kuriens of Anand and Anna Hazares of Ralegon Siddhi can you find in government organisations?

- **Locking-in Economic Reforms.** When economic reforms fail to bring any real benefits to rural people, rural voters may throw the political party which introduced the reform out of power. Cuts in subsidies on fertiliser, irrigation water, electricity and withdrawal of social welfare programmes can erode the electoral support for reforms. If policy makers respond by slowing down the process of reforms, the result may be a decline in investment and the rate of economic growth. In contrast, successful economic reforms make private corporations and enterprises more robust, and then corporate voluntarism delivers the benefits of growth and prosperity to the underprivileged and poor people.

In India, the government provides many incentives to the corporate sector for making contributions to the cause of rural development. Through the Finance Act 1978, two new Sections, 35 CC and 35 CCA, were added to the Income Tax Act 1961. These sections provide fiscal incentives to corporations and cooperatives to undertake rural development activities, directly as well as to promote indirectly such activities through rural development agencies approved by a prescribed authority notified by the Central Board of Direct Taxes. These sections stipulate that the expenditure incurred by a corporation or a cooperative on rural development activities would be considered as normal expenditure, and would be deductible from the income of the tax payer (donor) to compute the taxable profit. The Finance Act of 1983 has amended Section 35 CCA to provide for setting up of a National Fund for Agricultural Development for providing financial support to voluntary agencies to undertake rural development work. However, Section 35 CC has been retained, and private companies and business houses can avail the tax concession by undertaking rural development activities directly.

Fortunately, India's corporate sector, with its powerful economic status, is able to influence the policy makers in the country. Most business houses in the past have confined their roles to their business and in maximising profits. Nevertheless, some business houses do make attempts to address the problems of the community. This is, however, in no way adequate. When the majority of India's population is struggling for survival, how can corporations turn a blind eye and plan for their progress and prosperity? The corporate sector cannot continue to prosper, unless the economy and quality of life of our common people is improved.

In all the programmes implemented by both the governmental and non-government organisations, good management is the critical input for success. It is here that the corporate sector can play a major role. Transfer of management skills from business houses to the agencies in charge of rural development can easily enhance the productivity of natural resources.

Business houses like the Tatas, Godrej, Hindustan Lever, Escorts, Lupin, IPCL, Usha, Martin, Excel and Arvind Mills have established their own trusts to take up agricultural and rural development work in selected rural areas. There are other industrial houses, such as the Mafatlal Group, who have been funding professionally managed public trusts. Business houses with experience in management can assist the rural people directly, or through local voluntary organisations, to generate employment and to improve the quality of life.

Some of the important areas where industry can support the development of the rural areas are as follows:

1. Arranging financial assistance in the form of grants and loans, to invest in various income and employment generating activities.
2. Direct procurement of produce as industrial raw material, or for the consumption of their employees. In this process, middlemen can be eliminated at various levels.
3. Imparting management skills to field workers and village leaders involved in rural development to improve their project management skills.

The Confederation of Indian Industry (CII) can play an important role by persuading medium-sized companies to undertake rural development work in their neighbourhoods, where basic facilities and amenities are lacking and the people are poor.

To begin with, a corporate house can start work in villages where its plants are located. By constructing roads, installing hand pumps, starting primary schools and a health centre, corporates can not only earn goodwill, but it will also help them in establishing good relationships with the people.

Subsequently, corporates can spread their work to nearby areas. A good example to emulate is furnished by Tata Steel, which started rural development work in rural areas in Jamshedpur, Bihar. As a result, the company earned a lot of goodwill of the beneficiaries, as well as of the government.

The private sector can also join hands with government agencies like the Khadi and Village Industries Commission (KVIC) and the Council for Advancement of Public Action and Rural Technology (CAPART) to develop rural areas. These agencies not only provide cheap funds, but their wide network can also prove useful for new entrants.

After having said this, we would like to mention some points. First, corporations do not come forward spontaneously to take up rural development activities; public policy must create a congenial legal and policy environment for them to get into this arena. Tax relief and other incentives for rural development endeavours are pivotal. Second, both the corporations and the community must be partners in identifying felt needs, and formulating programmes that are beneficial to both the parties involved. Third, socially-oriented corporations having good credentials and hands-on experience will need to provide leadership and advice to other interested companies and enterprises. Last, leaders in the public and private sectors must support the establishment of well-managed non-profit rural development organisations.

Concluding Remarks

Rural development should be looked upon and treated as a joint venture of the public, corporate, cooperative and private sectors, and a systems approach followed to bring about all-round and balanced development of the economy. Although it is true that the government has been, still is, and will continue in the future to be the most important actor in the field of rural development in India, it alone cannot effectively tackle all the problems of rural development. Panchayati raj institutions, cooperatives, voluntary agencies and private companies and corporations can all play important roles in the process of development, by complementing and supplementing the functions and activities of the government. The role of the government should be to define the roles of other agencies, coordinate, and, if necessary, regulate their activities, and provide such infrastructural facilities and services as cannot be provided by other agencies. Above all, the government should help organise the rural poor within an institutional framework that can give them access to the nation's economic and political systems.

Panchayati raj institutions can help achieve the goal of local self-governance, thereby realising Gandhiji's dream of swaraj. Cooperatives that are owned and controlled by their members and managed professionally can ensure to the producer a fair share in the consumer's price, and supply of good quality products at reasonable prices to the consumer. NGOs have a special advantage over other forms of organisations in educating and training rural people, in enlisting their participation in rural development programmes, and in working closely with them. Corporations could make a significant contribution to rural development through establishing and/or supporting institutions that bring corporate resources, new technologies, modern management and expertise to bear on the problems of rural development.

15

Financing Rural Development

Introduction

The capital requirements of agricultural and rural development are tremendous. Capital is required not only for on-farm investment to improve the production apparatus and to provide various farm inputs and services, but also for a vast array of supportive infrastructural facilities, such as power, roads, transportation, communication, markets, storage, education, training, research and extension. Capital is also required for creation of non-farm jobs through the provision of factories and their complement of machinery and equipment. There are no precise estimates available about the capital requirements of agricultural and rural development in India. But the amount required is in hundreds of thousands of crores of rupees. Funds for investment in rural development projects come from two main sources: domestic and foreign. Further, in each category, there are institutional and non-institutional sources (Figure 15.1). Domestic institutional sources include the government, government undertakings including public enterprises, the Reserve Bank of India (RBI), NABARD, cooperative banks, commercial banks and Regional Rural Banks (RRBs), and private companies and corporations. Non-institutional sources include households, moneylenders, traders and friends and relatives. Foreign institutional sources include foreign governments, development agencies, the World Bank, the Asian Development Bank, the International Monetary Fund (IMF), foreign banks, multinational corporations, and so on. Foreign non-institutional sources include Non-Resident Indians (NRIs), and foreign nationals.

In countries like India, which are both poor and nationalistic, neither sacrifices from current consumption nor heavy reliance on foreign aid and investment is popular with the electorate as means of financing

Figure 15.1
Sources of Funds for Rural Development

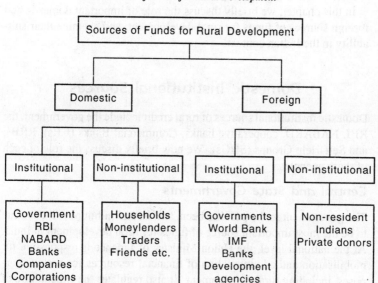

development. However, there are no other alternatives for the government but to follow these painful paths to development. Without a certain amount of national sacrifice, economic development will not occur.

The sacrifice may take one, more, or all of the following forms:

1. Working harder and more efficiently.
2. Saving voluntarily to finance development investment, public or private.
3. Paying higher taxes to finance development investment.
4. Controlling inflation, with whatever hardships it may cause to the people (deficit financing).
5. Encouraging foreign investment, no matter what temporary sacrifices of opportunities for national businessmen may be involved.
6. Accepting foreign aid, with whatever commitment is required as a condition for receipt of such aid.
7. Changes in sectoral terms of trade.

Working harder and better is not 'finance' in the ordinary sense, and it will not raise standards of living very much unless accompanied by

292 • *Rural Development: Principles, Policies and Management*

capital formation. Therefore, the government depends on the other six sources of financing development.

In this chapter, we briefly discuss the role of important domestic and foreign sources of funds for rural development, and examine their suitability in the Indian context.

Domestic Institutional Sources

Domestic institutional sources of rural credit include the government, the RBI, NABARD, cooperative banks, Commercial Banks (CBs), RRBs, and Self-Help Groups (SHGs). We now briefly discuss the role of each of these agencies.

Central and State Governments

The government in the past has been, still is, and in future will continue to be the most important source of funds for rural development in India. At the national level, the Union Ministry of Finance is responsible for mobilisation and administration of financial resources for various purposes, including rural development. It also regulates the expenditure of the government, including transfer of resources to the states. Power to raise and disburse public funds has been divided under the Constitution of India between the union and state governments. The sources of revenue for the union and states are, by and large, mutually exclusive, if shareable taxes and duties between the two are excluded. The Constitution provides that: (*a*) no tax can be levied or collected except by authority of law; (*b*) no expenditure can be incurred from public funds except in the manner provided in the Constitution; and (*c*) executive authorities must spend public money only in the manner sanctioned by parliament in the case of the union and by the state legislature in the case of states.

All receipts and disbursements of the union are kept under two separate heads, namely, the Consolidated Fund of India and the Public Account of India. All revenue received, loans raised and money received in repayment of loans by the union form the Consolidated Fund. No money can be withdrawn from this fund except under the authority of an act of parliament. All other receipts, such as deposits, service funds and remittances go into the Public Account, and disbursements therefrom are not subject to the vote of parliament. To meet unforeseen needs not provided in the Annual Appropriation Act, a Contingency Fund of India has been established under Article 267(1) of the Constitution. The Indian Constitution provides for the establishment of a Consolidated Fund, a Public Account and a Contingency Fund for each state.

The main sources of the union tax revenue are customs duties, union excise duties, corporate and income taxes. Non-tax revenues largely comprise interest receipts, including interest paid by the railways and telecommunications ministries, dividend and profits. The main heads of revenue in the states are taxes and duties levied by the respective state governments, a share of taxes levied by the union, and grants received from the union. Property taxes, octroi and terminal taxes are the mainstay of local finance. Devolution of the resources from the union to the states is a salient feature of the system of federal finance of India. Apart from their share of taxes and duties, state governments receive statutory and other grants, as well as loans for various development and non-development purposes.

An estimate of all anticipated receipts and expenditure of the union for the ensuing year is laid before the parliament. This is known as the Union Budget, and it covers the central government's transactions of all kinds in and outside India occurring during the preceding year, the year in which the statement is prepared, as well as the ensuing year, or the 'Budget Year', as it is known.

Government funds are made available in the form of investment, grants, subsidies and loans. Allocations are made through the annual budgetary process. The total public (government) sector expenditure on agriculture and allied activities, including rural development programmes under the five year plans is given in Table 15.1. As shown in the table, the total expenditure on agriculture and allied activities in the public sector since the beginning of the planning era (1951–52) until the Eighth Plan (1992–97) aggregated Rs 76,528 crore. As a percentage of the total plan expenditure in the public sector, it varied from around 12 to 17, with an overall average of 15.87 for the entire period.

In India, the government is probably the oldest institutional source of rural credit. The government provides financial assistance by granting loans to the cultivator under: (*a*) the Improvements Loans Act of 1883; and (*b*) the Agriculturists' Loans Act of 1884. Such loans are known as *taccavi* loans. The act of 1883 authorises the grant of long-term loans by the taluka/tehsil level officers of the government for effecting permanent improvements on land, such as construction of wells, land levelling, protection of lands from floods or erosion, etc. Such loans are generally granted for periods extending over 25 years, on the security of landed property at a relatively low rate of interest.

Table 15.1

***All-India Pattern of Outlay and Expenditure in Public Sector
on Agriculture and Allied Activities***

(Rs in crores)

Five Year Plan	Agriculture and allied activities[1]		Total		Share of agriculture and allied activities (%)	
	Plan outlay	Actual expenditure	Plan outlay	Actual expenditure	Plan outlay	Actual expenditure
First Plan (1951–56)	354	290	2,378	1,960	14.9	14.8
Second Plan (1956–61)	510	549	4,500	4,672	11.3	11.7
Third Plan (1961–66)	1,086	1,089	7,500	8,577	14.5	12.7
Annual Plan (1966–69)	1,037	1,107	6,665	6,625	15.6	16.7
Fourth Plan (1969–74)	2,728	2,320	15,902	15,779	17.1	14.7
Fifth Plan (1974–79)	4,766	4,865	39,322	39,426	12.1	12.3
Annual Plan (1979–80)	1,815	1,996	12,601	12,176	14.4	16.1
Sixth Plan (1980–85)	12,539	15,201	97,500	1,09,292	12.9	13.9
Seventh Plan (1985–90)	22,233	31,509	1,80,000	2,18,730	12.3	14.4
Annual Plan (1990–91)	9,142	8,542	64,717	58,369	14.1	14.6
Annual Plan (1991–92)	10,058	9,060	72,317	6,475	13.9	14.0
Eighth Plan (1992–97)	63,642	–	4,34,100	–	14.7	–
Total	1,29,910	76,528	9,37,502	4,82,081	13.86	15.87

Source: GOI. 1997. *Agricultural Statistics at a Glance.* Directorate of Economics and Statistics, Department of Agriculture and Cooperation, Ministry of Agriculture, Government of India, March. p. 134.
Note: 1. Includes animal husbandry and dairy research and education, forestry and wildlife, plantation, agricultural marketing and rural godowns, food storage and warehousing, rural development, cooperation, and special area programmes.

Under the act of 1884, short- and medium-term loans are granted by the government to meet the current agricultural needs, such as purchase of seeds, fertilisers and small tools and implements. Such loans are repayable over a period of six months to one year, mostly after the harvest. The rate of interest charged on these loans is lower than the rate charged by commercial banks and cooperatives.

The record of taccavi loans has been rather poor. Some of the draw-backs are the inadequate amount, inordinate delays in sanctioning the loan, lack of supervision, poor recovery and lack of coordination. In view of the rapidly expanding role of cooperative credit institutions, CBs and RRBs in the sphere of rural credit, the relative importance of taccavi loans has been declining over the years.

With a view to encouraging individuals, corporate and non-corporate bodies to participate in the national effort of rural development, a National Fund for Rural Development (NFRD) was established in the Union Ministry of Rural Development in February 1984. The fund is managed by a committee under the chairmanship of the Prime Minister.

Donations made by all categories of taxpayers to the NFRD are deductible while computing taxable income under Sections 35 CCA and 80 CCA of the Income Tax Act, 1961.

NFRD projects can be executed through an implementing agency, having the legal status of:

1. an irrevocable public charitable trust registered under the Income Tax Act, 1961, or
2. a society registered under the Societies Registration Act, 1860 or under any law corresponding to that act in force in any part of India, or
3. a company incorporated under Section 25 of the Companies Act, 1956, or
4. a corporation established by or under a central/state act concerned with development of rural areas.

Donors, while making donations, may recommend their preference for the area or locality and the rural development programmes for which the donations may be utilised, as also the implementing agency through which the programme may be undertaken and implemented. The recommendations, if any, of the donors, are given due consideration to the extent deemed appropriate by the government management committee of the fund.

The Reserve Bank of India

The RBI was established under the Reserve Bank of India Act, 1934 on 1 April 1935, and nationalised on 1 January 1949. The RBI is the sole authority for issue of currency in India, other than one rupee coins and subsidiary coins and notes. As the agent of the central government, the RBI undertakes distribution of one rupee notes and coins as well as small coins issued by the government. The bank acts as banker to the central government, state governments, commercial banks, state cooperative banks, and some of the financial institutions. It formulates and administers monetary policy, with a view to ensuring stability in prices, while promoting higher production in the real sector through proper deployment of credit. RBI plays an important role in maintaining the stability of the exchange value of the rupee, and acts as an agent of the government in respect of India's membership of the International Monetary Fund (IMF). The RBI also performs a variety of developmental and promotional functions.

The RBI was a pioneer central bank in the sphere of rural credit. Its founding act of legislation, and subsequent amendments, entrusted to it the responsibility for enlarging the availability of rural credit. The bank shouldered this responsibility rather reluctantly until 1947, when, after Independence, this responsibility was reinforced and became a major responsibility of the bank. The activities of the RBI in the sphere of rural credit can be broadly divided into three categories: (*a*) financing functions; (*b*) promotional, advisory and coordinating functions; and (*c*) regulatory functions. The first category covers the provision of long-term loans to state governments from the National Agricultural Credit (Long-Term Operations) Fund, to enable them to contribute to the share capital of the cooperative credit institutions; provision of medium-term loans to the state cooperative banks to refinance the seasonal crop (short-term) loans of credit cooperatives; granting medium-term loans to the state cooperative banks from the National Agricultural (Stabilisation) Fund to enable them to repay their short-term loans to the RBI under conditions of drought or famine; and short-, medium- and long-term loans to NABARD. Its promotional and coordinating functions include formulation of programmes for cooperative credit under the five-year plans, annual reviews of the progress of various credit schemes, and assistance to the central and state governments and cooperative credit institutions in tackling their problems in implementing various credit schemes. The regulatory functions include establishing credit limits and credit norms for various purposes, and control of advances by commercial and cooperative banks.

Though the flow of credit to the agricultural sector has improved from Rs 11,202 crore in 1991–92 to Rs 28,653 crore in 1996–97 and an estimated Rs 34,274 crore in 1997–98, the RBI perceives that investment in agriculture, particularly non-farm investments in agriculture, have not kept pace with demand. To encourage credit flow to the agricultural sector, therefore, the RBI governor, Bimal Jalan, has appointed R.V. Gupta (a former deputy governor of the RBI), to look into the matter and suggest ways and means to increase the flow.

NABARD

A major landmark in the history of development of rural credit in India was the establishment of the National Bank for Agriculture and Rural Development (NABARD) in July 1982, by merging the Agricultural Refinance and Development Corporation, the Agricultural Credit Department of the RBI, and the Rural Credit and Planning Cell of the RBI. The RBI owns 50 per cent of the share capital of NABARD, and the rest is held by the GOI. As on 31 March 1997, NABARD had a share capital of Rs 500 crore. In addition, it received Rs 500 crore from the GOI and another Rs 500 crore from the RBI during the year 1996–97 towards its capital. The Union Finance Minister announced in his Union Budget 1998–99, speech that the share capital of NABARD would be further augmented by another Rs 500 crore in the year 1998–99, with Rs 100 crore coming from the budget, and Rs 400 crore to be contributed by the RBI.

The main functions of NABARD include refinance (short-, medium-, and long-term) to the cooperative and regional rural banks, refinance to commercial banks against term lending (medium- and long-term), short-term accommodation for special cases, and overall policy, planning, coordination and monitoring of all agricultural and rural lending activities in the country. Besides, it also undertakes training, research and consultancy relating to rural credit. The sources of NABARD's funds mainly consist of the National Rural Credit (Long-Term Operations) Fund and the National Rural Credit (Stabilisation) Fund transferred to it by RBI at the time of its establishment, and annual contributions from RBI and NABARD thereafter, and borrowings from the RBI, the GOI and the market. The GOI also provides to NABARD funds received from the World Bank, the Swiss Agency for Development and Cooperation (SDC), and other external agencies under various credit projects.

The main objective of the establishment of NABARD was to provide institutional credit through banks for promotion of agriculture, small-scale industries, cottage and village industries, handicrafts and other rural crafts and allied activities in rural areas. NABARD provides refinance facilities to commercial banks, State Cooperative Banks (SCBs), State Land Development Banks (SLDBs now known as State Cooperative Agricultural and Rural Development Banks) and regional rural banks, to enable them to advance short-term, medium-term and long-term loans for specified bankable projects. Commercial banks and SLDBs are supported only for term (medium and long) loans. Financial assistance is also provided by NABARD to state governments to enable them to contribute to the share capital of cooperative credit institutions. From the financial year 1995–96, NABARD has also entered the area of direct financing. Initially, it proposes to directly finance big high-tech projects only.

Hitherto, the farm sector had been the major focus of rural development. The Non-Farm Sector (NFS) has of late assumed importance in view of its potential for employment generation in rural areas. Several refinements in policies relating to credit for the farm sector, as well as new initiatives relating to the NFS have been introduced by NABARD. Even after considerable expansion of the network of the formal credit institutions, certain sections of the population have not been reached. The bank has actively supported innovations in credit delivery, to extend the outreach of credit to these sections.

NABARD works in close cooperation with various central government agencies to refinance various priority schemes, such as watershed development and management, dry land farming, wastelands development, forestry, aquaculture, the Integrated Rural Development Programme (IRDP) and other poverty alleviation programmes. Besides, it has made quite a few innovations in both the structures and methods of delivering rural credit. A few of its innovative schemes include: Vikas Volunteer Vahini (VVV) programme; promotional grants to VAs and NGOs; establishment of a cooperative development fund; establishment of a Rural Infrastructure Development Fund (RIDF); and promotional schemes for non-farm sectors and financing of rural health services.

Cooperative Credit Agencies

Cooperative credit societies entered the field of rural finance with the adoption of the Cooperative Societies Act of 1904. Since then, the government has been making deliberate attempts to nurture the cooperative movement in the country in the larger interests of the rural people. Credit cooperatives have been recognised as the best institutions to provide rural credit to the farmer, because they satisfy all the important criteria of sound agricultural credit.

Credit cooperatives have many advantages over other sources of credit. First, being located right in the rural areas where their borrowers reside, they are in close proximity to their clients. Second, they have more intimate knowledge of the character and abilities of their members than any other financial institution. Third, they can easily supervise the use of credit, so that it is used for productive purposes. Fourth, the credit provided by cooperative societies is bound to be cheap, due to their lower administrative costs and lower cost of their funds. Last, the credit provided by the credit cooperatives is neither too rigid nor too elastic; it is also safe, as it assists, and does not hamper, the borrowers' stability and productive capacity.

Despite these positive aspects, cooperative credit suffers from the following weaknesses:

1. The tendency of cooperative credit has been to flow mainly towards larger cultivators. In many parts of the world, the smallest farmers have been handicapped in their access to cooperative credit, both for current inputs and viable investment.
2. The experience of cooperative credit in many countries shows that despite improvements over the years, the proportion of cooperative credit to total borrowings of cultivators appears to have continued to be small in absolute terms.
3. The orientation of cooperative credit to production needs has, by and large, been inadequate.
4. The cooperative credit system has given rise to increasing overdues from year to year.
5. A large number (over 65 per cent) of primary agricultural credit societies are neither viable, nor even potentially viable, and must be regarded as inadequate and unsatisfactory agencies for dispensing production-oriented credit.
6. Cooperative credit has frequently fallen short of standards of promptness, adequacy and dependability. This has been due to various reasons, including paucity of resources, lack of eligibility, time consuming and cumbersome procedures, poor management and efficiency in working methods.
7. Coordination between the authorities and agencies in charge of cooperative credit, and those in charge of supplies and extension under agricultural programmes, has generally been inadequate.

The cooperative credit system in the country comprises short-term (ST) and long-term (LT) credit structures. The short-term cooperative credit structure, as on 31 March 1997, comprised 28 State Cooperative Banks (SCBs), 366 District Central Cooperative Banks (DCCBs) and 92,682 Primary Agricultural Credit Societies (PACS, including Large-sized Adivasi Multi-Purpose Society [LAMPS] and Farmers

Service Society [FSS]), operating at the apex, middle and ground levels respectively.

The long-term cooperative credit structure in the country consisted of 19 State Cooperative Agriculture and Rural Development Banks (SCARDBs), originally known as Land Mortgage Banks/Land Development Banks, having a unitary structure in eight states and a federal/mixed structure in 11 states, operating through 2,960 units (including 733 PCARDBs). In Andhra Pradesh, there is an integrated structure where the units of the short-term structure provide all types of agricultural credit under a 'single window' credit delivery system. In the north-eastern region, only three states are served by the LT structure.

As far as short-term credit is concerned, the share of the cooperative credit societies was 59 per cent in 1995–96. For the same period, commercial banks accounted for 35 per cent, and RRBs accounted for 6 per cent. Regarding medium- and long-term credit requirements, commercial banks were the major providers, accounting for 58 per cent, while the cooperative credit societies' share was 35 per cent, and that of RRBs 7 per cent, for the period 1995–96.

Commercial Banks

As in January 1997, the commercial banking system in India consisted of 334 scheduled banks (including foreign banks) and two non-scheduled banks. Of the scheduled banks, 223 were in the public sector, and they accounted for about 80 per cent of the deposits of all scheduled banks. In July 1969, 14 major CBs were nationalised, and another six in 1980. Now there are 28 public sector banks having a mandate to provide credit to rural people. In addition, 246 private CBs are also operating in the country. These CBs provide short-term, medium-term and long-term credit for various agricultural and rural development activities. Until the nationalisation of major commercial banks in 1969, the official policy was to give a fillip to the cooperative system, as the channel best suited for institutional credit for agriculture. Before their nationalisation, CBs supplied only a negligible share of rural credit: 0.9 per cent in 1951–52 and 0.6 per cent in 1961–62. Even after nationalisation, they were a bit hesitant in going full steam ahead in financing agriculture; four years after nationalisation, their share in total rural credit was only 5 per cent in 1973–74.

However, during the last couple of years there has been a substantial increase in their involvement in agricultural lending. As in June 1995, there were some 34,949 rural branches of various scheduled commercial banks spread over the countryside. These accounted for 56 per cent of the total branches of these banks in the country. The share of CBs in direct agricultural advances went up from 1.3 per cent of bank credit in July 1969, to 13.2 per cent in March 1984, and to 33.2 per cent as on 31 March 1995 (NIRD 1996: 102).

In the years to come, the Indian banking system has a strategic role to play in increasing the national savings rate, in canalising the available savings to finance high priority investments, in better utilisation of available capacities both in agriculture and in industry through adequate supply of credit as working capital, and in promoting the cause of social justice, by increased emphasis on the credit needs of the hitherto neglected sectors and sections of population, as also by providing finance for such anti-poverty programmes as IRDP.

Regional Rural Banks

RRBs were established consequent to the acceptance by the GOI of the recommendations of a Working Group on rural banks appointed by the Union Finance Ministry in July 1975, under the chairmanship of M. Narasimham. The first five RRBs were established on 2 October 1975, following the promulgation of the RRBs ordinance by the GOI on 26 September 1975. The ordinance was subsequently replaced by the Regional Rural Bank Act, 1976. The issued and paid up share capital of each RRB at Rs 25 lakh (subsequently raised to Rs 100 lakh in March 1996), is held by the GOI, the sponsor bank and the concerned state government in the proportion of 50 : 35 : 15 respectively. The management of each RRB is vested in a board of directors headed by a chairman (usually an officer of the sponsor bank and appointed by the GOI). As in March 1997, there were 196 RRBs, covering 436 districts, with a network of 14,450 branches in the country. Their loans and advances stood at Rs 7,852.70 crore as on 30 September 1996.

Initially, RRBs were mandated to cater to the credit needs of the weaker sections of the rural community comprising small and marginal farmers, agricultural labourers, artisans, small entrepreneurs, etc. With effect from December 1993, their mandate has been expanded to include non-target group borrowers also. These RRBs were intended to be low-cost 'small man's banks', combining the advantages of cooperatives (close rapport with villagers), and commercial banks (business acumen). To enable RRBs to keep their costs down, the salary and perks of their staff were fixed at par with those of the comparable district level staff of the state government concerned. The Statutory Liquidity Ratio (SLR) was fixed at a lower level as compared to commercial banks, and low cost refinance from NABARD and sponsor banks up to prescribed levels was permitted.

The RRBs advance short-term, medium-term and long-term loans for various rural development activities, including crop production, purchase of tractors, setting up of small village industries, village crafts, various artisans' activities, retail trade, consumer durables, house construction, purchase of mini-buses, etc.

The RRBs were established as a new set of state-sponsored, rural-oriented, region-based, low cost banks, having the ethos of cooperatives and business acumen of commercial banks for providing credit in the rural areas, particularly to the relatively weaker sections of society. It would be fair to say that RRBs have succeeded in spreading banking services to far-flung rural areas, mobilising rural savings, opening up more avenues for rural poor through institutional credit and generating employment opportunities. However, their mandate of financing only the target group borrowers, coupled with an administered interest rate structure, poor recovery performance, increasing establishment costs, and low level of operational efficiency have resulted in RRBs incurring losses and losing their financial viability right from their inception. In 1995–96, of the 196 RRBs in India, 164 made losses and the remaining 32 made profits. The extent of loss in 1995–96 was Rs 425.65 crore, and the accumulated losses till then Rs 1,686.81 crore (Deshpande et al. 1996: 22–23).

With a view to enabling RRBs to achieve current and sustainable financial viability, several policy measures were initiated including revamping of RRBs by infusion of capital. The concept of Development Action Plans (DAPs) was initiated by NABARD and RRBs and sponsor banks signed a Memorandum of Understanding (MoU) for ensuring performance obligations/commitments. Initially, 49 RRBs and subsequently another 53 were selected for restructuring during 1994–95 and 1995–96 respectively. Financial support aggregating Rs 747.14 crore was provided for the purpose. During 1996–97, an additional 36 RRBs were selected, and the central government provided Rs 149.77 crore for strengthening their financial position. Further, a second dose of assistance was also provided to 16 RRBs during 1996–97, aggregating Rs 50.23 crore. An equal amount is required to be contributed by the sponsor banks and state governments. The central government made a further provision of ·Rs 270 crore in the 1997–98 budget and Rs 265 crore in the 1998–99 budget to carry forward the process of rehabilitation and recapitalisation of RRBs. As a result of all these measures taken under the direction of

NABARD, perceptible improvement in the performance of RRBs in all spheres has been observed (NABARD 1997: 47)

Self-Help Groups (SHG)

An SHG is a small group of individual members who voluntarily come together and form an association for achieving a common objective. In most cases, SHGs are constituted by persons known to one another and coming from the same village, community, or neighbourhood. That is, SHGs are small in size with membership ranging from 10 to 25, are homogeneous and have certain pre-group social binding factors. The purpose for which SHGs are formed varies from managing a common pool resource, such as an irrigation facility and tree plantation on common land, to providing such basic amenities as a school, health centre, and so on. In the context of micro-finance, SHGs are formed around the theme of savings and credit. In February 1992, NABARD launched a pilot project on 'Linking SHGs with Banks' after consultations with the RBI, selected banks and NGOs. The main objective of the project was to develop innovative participatory and self-sustaining credit delivery systems for improving the access of the rural poor to institutional credit. The systems are intended to complement and supplement the role of the formal rural credit system. Under the project, credit is provided to SHGs by banks using a simplified procedure that requires a minimum of documentation.

As in March 1997, 18 states and two UTs were covered under the programme with the participation of 29 commercial banks, 79 RRBs and 12 cooperative banks. The programme had benefited nearly 1,50,000 rural poor families.

Under the SHG–Bank Linkage Programme, three linkage models have broadly emerged. Under the first mode, banks are directly linking SHGs without the intervention of the NGOs. In the second mode, banks are providing credit to SHGs, and NGOs act as Self-Help Promoting Institutions (SHPIs). Under the third mode, NGOs are acting both as Self-Help Promoting Institutions and financial intermediaries for channelising credit from banks to SGHs. As on 31 March 1997, the SHGs linked to banks under the three models numbered 1,105, 3,889 and 3,604 respectively, and the bank loans advanced to them were worth Rs 11.84 crore (NABARD 1997: 69).

NABARD has been networking with a large number of NGOs. As on 31 March 1997, around 220 NGOs had, as SHPIs, participated in the linkage programme. These NGOs acted either as facilitators, or both as facilitators and financial intermediaries, in effecting linkage of SHGs with banks.

With a view to increasing the involvement of NGOs/SHGs in improving the outreach of credit to the rural poor, the RBI constituted a Working Group in November 1994 under the chairmanship of the managing director, NABARD. Based on the recommendations of the working group, banks were advised to consider lending to SHGs as a normal business activity under the priority sector, and internalise training of their officers. As a follow-up measure, NABARD constituted, in each state, a State Level Review and Coordination Committee on Credit Delivery Innovations (SLRCCDI) comprising senior officials of the RBI, banks, prominent NGOs and a few state government departments, with the officer-in-charge of the bank's regional office acting as chairman-cum-convenor. These committees review the progress periodically in various credit delivery innovations to improve the access of the rural poor to credit. The Union Finance Minister, in his Union Budget 1998–99 speech asked NABARD to extend the coverage of the SHG-Bank Linkage Scheme so that two lakh SHGs covering 40 lakh families could be assisted over the next five years.

The Role of Non-institutional Agencies

Non-institutional agencies which supply credit to farmers and other rural people include professional moneylenders, agricultural moneylenders, landlords, traders, commission agents and friends and relatives. Traditionally, these agencies have played an important role in meeting the credit requirements of villagers. Most of the money advanced by them used to be, and still is, spent on household consumption and social and religious ceremonies and very little, if any, on production activities.

The interest rates were very high, usually ranging from 24 to 60 per cent per annum. The incidence of indebtedness was very high, and most of the rural poor were 'born in debt, lived in debt and died in debt'. According to the All-India Rural Credit Survey Committee Report (1951–52), non-institutional sources supplied 91.27 per cent of the total rural credit advanced in 1951–52. In 1961–62, their share declined to 81.3 per cent and in 1995–96, it was estimated to be about 65 per cent. Although there has been a marked decline in the share of non-institutional sources in the total rural credit advanced over the period 1951–52 to 1995–96, due partly to growing competition from institutional sources and partly to various agrarian reforms implemented since Independence, they still continue to be in business. Notwithstanding the criticism that has been levelled against them, these sources do provide valuable service, which is not available from any other alternative sources, and for which they are amply rewarded.

Deficit Financing or Controlled Inflation

Some economists have suggested that the simplest way to finance development in developing countries is to print money or borrow from the banking system—in short by deficit financing or controlled inflation. In this fashion, it is maintained that the population will be 'forced' to save, since the rise in prices will necessitate a reduction in the volume of physical consumption.

As we have already mentioned in Chapter 5, inflation is also a form of taxation. It is really a tax on cash balances, since those individuals and organisations in the economy who hold cash balances see their purchasing power eroded by inflation. There is, thus, a transfer of wealth from those who hold money in the form of cash balances to those (in this case the government) who obtain the resources through money creation. The government borrows heavily to finance spending, including that for rural development programmes. The GOI's rupee debt was Rs 7,18,299 crore at the beginning of 1998–99. Suppose inflation increases by three percentage points, then in real terms the value of debt decreases by 3 per cent, which is a whopping sum of Rs 22,000 crore. This is more than double the record levy of Rs 9,000 crore of fresh taxes announced by the Union Finance Minister in his Union Budget 1998–99 speech. Similarly, a government payment of interest on its debt now (in 1998) estimated at Rs 75,000 crore will also go down to Rs 2,250 crore if the inflation rate goes up by 3 per cent. Thus, inflation is an invisible tax on those the government borrows from, in the sense that it erodes the value of their capital and their interest payment. So inflation tax affects hundreds of millions of people, yet very few of them realise it. Most people value their investment and income without adjusting it for inflation. This is what is called money illusion in economics. Hence inflation is a politically easier way of taxing people than direct taxes.

According to Bronfenbrenner (1966: 465–66) there are two ways in which inflation may prove beneficial. First, it may permit 'the authorities ... to raise the relative prices of the types of labour and capital goods required for development projects without imposing on other sectors of the economy the reductions in money wages and prices which would otherwise be required'. This device (which was deliberately used by the Canadian government in the first two years of World War II) permits reallocation of resources, in a manner conducive to development, in relatively painless fashion. Second, and more important to Professor Bronfenbrenner's argument, is the money illusion.

A slow inflation, or even a rapid one, in its early stages induces labourers to work more intensively for real incomes which are no higher and which may be lower than their previous level. To a lesser extent, owners of land and capital may be induced to put their property to work more intensively in the same way when money incomes rise.

Thus, judicious inflation may result in increased output, which, if properly allocated, could significantly accelerate development. The accompanying forced saving helps to reallocate demand from consumer goods to capital goods. Beyond a certain point, however, further inflation will reduce output, partly because investment shifts to speculative hoarding of inventories, and partly because supply curves of various factors of production turn backwards as higher incomes are reached (workers prefer more leisure to more income, investors more safety and liquidity to more income).

But we would like to mention that even controlled inflation can have grave consequences for a developing country like India, which still suffers from a tendency on the part of investors to go in for speculative holding of inventories, rather than for the establishment or expansion of productive enterprises. A constantly rising price level tends to aggravate this tendency, by making speculation all the more profitable. Moreover, export industries, whose prices are determined in the world market, are confronted with constantly rising costs, and thus become increasingly unprofitable, leading to aggravation of balance of payments difficulties on one hand, and increasing demand for export subsidies on the other.

Inflationary (deficit) financing of the regular budget in the hope that a rising price level will in itself provide incentive for private investment in development projects is unlikely to be successful. However, if the government undertakes a large scale development programme, recognising that the level of deficit financing is in itself inflationary and mops up increases in income through tax policy, monetary policy, and direct controls, then mild inflation can have a positive impact on economic development.

Foreign Sources of Funds

As we mentioned earlier in this chapter, foreign sources of funds for rural development include a variety of institutional and non-institutional agencies. The funds are given in the form of grants, loans, and investment. Table 15.2 lists the major foreign development agencies/donors who provide assistance for rural development and other purposes.

Besides, there are four major international NGOs, namely, the Aga Khan Foundation, CARE India, the Ford Foundation, and the Save the

Table 15.2
External Sources of Development Assistance to India

Bilateral partners	Multilateral partners
Canada/Canadian International Development Agency (CIDA)	Asian Development Bank (ADB)
Canada/International Development Research Centre (IDRC)	European Union (EU)
Denmark	Food and Agriculture Organisation (FAO)
France	International Fund for Agricultural Development (IFAD)
Germany	International Labour Organisation (ILO)
Japan/Japan International Cooperation Agency (JICA)	United Nations International Children's Emergency Fund
Japan/Overseas Economic Cooperation Fund (OECF)	United Nations Development Fund for Women
Netherlands	United Nations Development Programme (UNDP)
New Zealand	United Nations Educational, Scientific and Cultural Organisation (UNESCO)
Norway	United Nations High Commissioner for Refugees
Sweden	United Nations Industrial Development Organisation
Switzerland	United Nations International Drug Control Programme
United Kingdom	United Nations Population Fund
United States of America	World Bank/International Bank for Reconstruction and Development (IBRD)
	World Bank/International Development Association (IDA)
	World Bank/International Finance Corporation (IFC)
	World Food Programme (WFP)
	World Health Organisation (WHO)

Source: UNDP. 1996. 'India's External Development Partners: Profiles of Cooperation Programmes'. September. New Delhi: United Nations Development Programme.

Children Fund (UK), that provide substantial assistance to India for various rural development projects.

We now briefly discuss the role of foreign investment and foreign aid in rural development.

The Role of Foreign Investment

Foreign investment is almost indispensable for promoting vigorous economic growth in developing countries. This is because many of them cannot raise the additional capital resources they need for the purpose. If a developing country wants to bring about economic development depending only on its own resources, it will have to wait for decades to be able to do so. Even if a country is fortunate enough to be able to meet its total capital requirements from domestic savings and taxes, it may nevertheless face a foreign exchange problem. As total outlays for development increase, foreign exchange requirements also go up.

In India, foreign exchange is required to import modern technologies, heavy machinery and equipment, fertilisers, fighter planes, missiles, computers, fossil fuels etc. The foreign exchange needed for development must be obtained by: (a) restricting imports of other goods and services; (b) increasing exports; and (c) obtaining loans and grants from foreigners. Reducing imports, in and of itself, is inflationary; it reduces the availability of goods and releases cash to be spent in other ways. Therefore, whereas it is good for a poor, developing country to have an austere import policy, it offers no panacea for financing its development.

There can be no argument against a policy to increase exports. However, four observations may be made about the role of expanding exports in financing development. First, the volume of exports depends very much on the world market conditions, on which individual developing countries have little control. Second, measures to increase exports are for the most part likely to operate rather slowly. Third, an export surplus, no less than a cut in imports, involves sacrifices; an export surplus means sending more goods abroad than one gets in return. Last, an export surplus is in itself inflationary; it reduces the supply of goods and services and increases the supply of money. It is not, therefore, a substitute for increased savings/taxes at home.

The third alternative for a developing country to secure needed foreign exchange is obtaining loans or grants from foreigners—foreign private investors, foreign governments, or international agencies. It is better for a developing country to obtain part of its additional requirements from each of the three sources, rather than from only any one of them. Certain development projects can be more easily organised and more efficiently managed if carried out on a private enterprise basis, with assistance from a foreign private investor. Other development projects which are highly beneficial to the country, but which do not attract any private investors, may be better handled through government channels, either on a bilateral basis or on a multilateral basis through an international agency like the World Bank.

Many people in developing countries still believe that a huge flood of foreign capital is waiting to inundate their lands if the gates are opened. This is very far from the truth. There is a lot of competition for capital amongst both the developed as well as developing countries. Furthermore, the prospective investor wants to be sure about the climate for foreign investments in the receiving countries. Certain elements constitute just such a favourable climate from the investor's point of view (ECAFE 1950: 4–5).

1. Political stability and freedom from external aggression.
2. Security of life and property.
3. Availability of opportunities for earning profits.
4. Prompt payment of fair compensation and its remittance to the country of origin in the event of compulsory acquisition of a foreign enterprise.
5. Facilities for the remittance of profits, dividends, interest, etc.
6. Facilities for the immigration and employment of foreign technical and administrative personnel.
7. A system of taxation that does not impose a crushing burden on private enterprise.
8. Freedom from double taxation.
9. Absence of vexatious controls.
10. Non-discriminatory treatment of foreigners in the administration of controls.
11. Absence of competition of state-owned enterprises with private capital.
12. A general spirit of friendliness for foreign investors.

It is unlikely that even highly favourable laws governing foreign investment will encourage sufficient inflow of private capital to meet a large share of the requirements of developing countries. Therefore, foreign aid has a substantial role to play in financing economic development in

Table 15.3
Inflow of Foreign Aid, Commercial Borrowing and Direct Investment in India
($ millions)

Particular	1990–91	1993–94	1994–95	1995–96	1996–97	1997–98[1]
A. Foreign capital inflow (net)	8,402	9,882	8,013	2,963	9,548	8,200
Foreign aid (net)	2,210	1,901	1,526	883	1,133	1,500
External commercial borrowing	2,249	607	1,030	1,275	227	500
Foreign direct investment	97	586	1,314	2,133	2,696	3,500
FII net investment	NA	1,665	1,503	2,009	1,926	1,500
NRI deposits (net)	1,536	1,205	172	1,103	3,439	1,500
Global deposit receipts	NA	1,602	1,839	149	650	500
B. Debt servicing	8,982	8,598	11,009	12,038	14,140	12,600
Repayments	5,028	5,067	6,963	7,670	9,416	NA
Interest payments	3,954	3,531	4,073	4,368	4,724	NA
C. Outstanding external debt	83,801	92,695	99,008	92,199	90,852	NA
D. Debt service ratio (%)	35.3	25.6	26.2	24.3	25.4	22.0

Source: Centre for Monitoring India's Economy. 1998. *Monthly Review of Indian Economy.*
Bombay: CMIE. p. 8.
Note: 1. Projected.

developing countries. Table 15.3 presents data on the inflow of foreign
aid, direct investment, foreign debt and the debt service ratio for selected
years from 1990–91 to 1997–98. As shown in the table, foreign direct
investment has been increasing over the period, thanks largely to the
opening up of India's economy in the wake of its new economic policy.

The Role of Foreign Aid

So-called 'aid' for development is provided by so-called 'donors' to so-
called 'recipients'. Perhaps it would be appropriate to refer to 'aid' as
'involvement' of the more developed countries in the economic, political,
military and social sectors of developing countries, either directly or
through international agencies.

'Donors' may be foreign governments, corporations, individuals, international organisations or private foundations. 'Aid' may be people serving

as actual workers, or just advisors endeavouring to impart knowledge, techniques and institutions or in the form of commodities, tools and machines. These items may be provided as gifts, loans or investments. Loans and investments comprise the great bulk of 'aid'.

What are the objectives of the aid policies of donors? They are a mixed bag, mainly economic and political, with a dash of the humanitarian. One of the most general facts of human nature and conduct is a 'tendency to assume that things which are associated in the society we know must necessarily be associated in all other societies' (Lewis 1968).

The United Nations Panel on Foreign Investments in Developing Countries in its meeting in Amsterdam in February 1969 called for a massive increase in the flow of foreign capital to developing countries, in order to provide a reasonable rate of per capita growth (SID 1969). These conclusions, though they may be false, have been accepted, more or less voluntarily by many of the developing countries, resulting in heavy obligations not only to foreign governments and international lending agencies, but also to private investors who have acquired the privilege of exploiting mineral, forest and land resources to produce commodities for export and the privilege of building electric power, communication and transportation facilities and industrial plants. In this way, the 'donors' promote their own exports, obtain raw materials and make very substantial profits. These operations are assumed to be in the national interest of both the 'donors' and the 'recipients'. What is good for the donors must be good for the recipients! This concept of the national interest rests on the further assumption that the way to better living for the people of all nations is in the direction of integrating their economies with those of other countries, so that they can maximise their access to the markets and resources of the world.

The governments of developed countries, in order to protect their foreign loans and the investments of their citizens, help recipient governments stay in power by strengthening their military and police forces. This arrangement leaves the large landowners, the military, the industrial and mining interests, the traders and the government bureaucracy, in firm control of a country. Any change, social, economic, or political, which threatens this power structure is deemed 'subversive' and dealt with accordingly. Should a government which attempts significant reforms come into power, there is always a military coup at hand to remove it from the scene.

As a consequence of a mutuality of interests between the dominant power groups in the donor and recipient countries, substantial 'aid' and indigenous resources have been used for the construction of luxury hotels, apartments, and office buildings, and for the manufacture of luxury consumer goods and services, as well as for obtaining resources for the establishment of capital-intensive industries. In agriculture, the more affluent landowners have been the first to obtain the benefits accruing from the introduction of high yielding varieties of rice and wheat. However, foreign aid has undeniably contributed substantially to present and potential progress in some sectors of the economies of the recipient countries, including the agricultural sector. Most of the infrastructural projects, such as roads, dams, electric power generation and transmission facilities, and some of the education programmes, such as the strengthening of medical, agricultural and public administration schools, have furnished a foundation for further economic and social progress.

Nevertheless, certain major aspects of foreign aid have helped create conditions which give little promise of dealing effectively with the need to advance a technology which will be suited to small farms, and the need to create non-farm employment opportunities for a rapidly growing rural labour force. Insofar as aid is responsible for maintaining governments in power which are unwilling to carry through meaningful land tenure reforms, or devise a tax system which provides sufficient revenue to support really adequate education and health programmes, or to accept responsibility for the creation of sufficient employment opportunities in rural areas, then aid has been inimical to agricultural development.

Insofar as aid has contributed to an emphasis on the expansion of capital-intensive industries in urban areas, and has given priority to the larger landowners in programmes to increase the output of food and export products, it has served to create islands of affluence, still leaving the bulk of the people with a traditional technology and at a subsistence level of well-being. A country with a dual society of this nature can never build a domestic consumption base to ensure the full realisation of its technological potential, either in agriculture or in industry. It leaves a major portion of its human resources untapped.

Rising pressures to produce for export distorts the allocation of resources in agriculture, causing production to increase regardless of export prices. The terms of trade worsen for the recipient, making still greater production for export imperative. More and more resources which might have been used to produce for domestic consumption must be allocated to produce for export, as debt and profit service requirements grow. Food production may have to be sacrificed to produce exportable products. Existing land tenure systems will remain entrenched, because they will most effectively produce surpluses for export. Unless there are drastic changes in the concept and direction of foreign aid and in the strategy for achieving goals in the developing nations, the standard of living of cultivator families will not be improved much.

It is intriguing to contemplate what might have happened if these poor countries with colonial and feudal backgrounds had been permitted to exercise a greater measure of responsibility for the development of their respective societies without external intervention or, indeed, what could happen even now, if they relied more on themselves.

A very minimal amount of loan and investment and a very minimal number of 'technicians' from external sources would best serve the national interest of these countries. In discussing the contribution of 'aid' to development, Mikesell (1968) concludes that

as a general proposition, external capital or aid is neither a necessary nor a sufficient condition for development . . . . By and large countries that are not making satisfactory progress, regardless of their per capita income, have failed to realise the potential returns from their own resources. What is required are policies and programs for mobilising, adapting and reallocating those resources, including the training of human resources for the operations of modern economy.

The foreign aid which a developing nation needed, and still needs, is the kind that would enable its citizens to utilise their own natural resources, accumulate their own capital, and operate their own economy by themselves, and exclusively for themselves, even though the process would be gradual, over a considerable period of time.

Table 15.3 presented data on inflow of net foreign aid, net direct investment and commercial borrowings for selected years for the period 1990–91 to 1997–98. As is evident from the table, net foreign aid has been declining over that period: it was $2,210 million in 1990–91 as compared to a projected figure of $1,500 million for 1997–98. A large chunk of the inflow of foreign capital is utilised to pay instalments and interest (debt servicing) on the outstanding loans: in 1997–98, as much as 22 per cent of the gross inflow was used for these purposes.

India's total outstanding foreign debt has been increasing over time: in 1997–98, it was estimated to be around $90,852 million. All these trends indicate that we have yet to go a long way before we reach our proclaimed goal of self-reliance. Another important observation which we would like to make in this connection is that the bulk of the foreign capital inflow is comprised of foreign direct investment and commercial borrowings.

Concluding Remarks

The government in the past has been, still is, and in future will remain the most important source of funds for rural development in India. Unpalatable though it may be to the government, it is true that there are no primrose paths to national development. Without a certain amount of national sacrifice, economic development will not occur. The sacrifice may be in terms of involuntary savings, or high taxes, or foreign aid and investment with strings.

Whereas it is necessary for the government to raise needed capital through various means to finance agricultural and rural development, it is equally necessary for the government to create an appropriate network of financial institutions which can absorb, mobilise, and canalise savings to finance development. Although both the RBI and NABARD have played important roles in making cheap credit available to rural people through cooperative banks, commercial banks and RRBs, the needs of the rural poor still continue to be unfulfilled.

Availability of credit at the right time and in adequate amount on appropriate terms has a bearing on production, productivity and diversification of economic activities. In the process of widening and deepening of credit, the health of the rural credit institutions has been increasingly strained. Non-adherence to credit discipline and non-viability of operations have been the bane of the rural credit institutions, in general, and of the cooperatives and RRBs, in particular. There is urgent need for revamping sick credit cooperatives and RRBs, if they are to survive in the wake of the new era of liberalisation and privatisation.

Self-help measures are more basic than external aid as means of financing development. Without them, no amount of external aid will bring about development. With strong self-help, however, foreign aid can be highly productive, as it was in Japan, Taiwan, Thailand, and South Korea.

Technical assistance is the most productive form of external aid. Transfer of knowledge, skills, and productive know-how from a developed to a developing country can permanently raise the productivity of labour, and make land and capital fruitful.

●

16

Implementation, Monitoring and Evaluation

Introduction

Implementation, monitoring and evaluation are all subsumed in the broader function of project management. Implementation may be regarded as a process by which a set of predetermined activities is carried out in a planned manner, with a view to achieving certain established objectives. As we mentioned in Chapter 13, a programme is usually implemented through a series of well-defined projects. This means that a programme usually consists of a number of projects, the implementation of which is supposed to eventually culminate in its execution. The scope of a plan is still broader, in the sense that it usually comprises a number of programmes. Thus, for its implementation, a plan has to be broken down into a number of programmes, each of which in turn is broken down into a number of projects. A project treats the questions, what, who, when and how, more specifically than does a programme.

Monitoring is a process of keeping a watch on the progress of a project vis-à-vis its targets and time schedule. The main objective of monitoring is to find out whether there are any deviations of actual physical and financial achievements from the planned/targeted ones, and to help the project authority take necessary corrective measures in time. Evaluation of a project is concerned with the assessment of the impact(s) of the project.

The failure of agricultural and rural development programmes in India, as also in other developing countries, can, in large measure, be traced to the difficulties which hinder their effective implementation. Clearly, a

programme is no better than its implementation. Emphasising the importance of implementation, the late Prime Minister Jawaharlal Nehru, who
had an unusual grasp of planning problems, once pointedly remarked,
'We in the Planning Commission and others concerned have grown more
experienced and more expert in planning. But the real question is not
planning, but implementing the plans. . . . I fear we are not quite so expert
at implementation as at planning' (quoted in Waterston 1970: 403). This
statement is notable because it recognises that the problems of plan implementation are more difficult than those of plan formulation. But the statement seems to imply that planning and implementation are two different
and unrelated functions. As a matter of fact, they are highly interrelated,
and therefore should be considered as an integral whole. Planners cannot
limit themselves to saying *what* is to be achieved, without showing *how*
and by *whom* it is to be done. Every target must be accompanied by
policies and measures which have been devised specifically to fulfil it,
otherwise it becomes only a forecast or projection.

Monitoring is an important aid to effective and smooth implementation
of a project. Concurrent evaluation can help the implementing agency
make mid-course corrections in the project, and thereby enhance its positive impacts and minimise its (unintended) negative effects. Therefore,
both monitoring and evaluation are necessary for the success of rural
development projects.

Massive investments have been made in rural development projects
since the beginning of the planning era, and will continue to be made
in the near future. Apart from several flaws in planning, there have
been numerous operational problems in the implementation of the programmes. The policy makers, the implementing agencies and the beneficiaries have all to be constantly vigilant, and watch closely the progress of
implementation of rural development projects. This can be done through
an appropriate system of monitoring built into the project design itself.
Effective monitoring can cut down the wastage of a lot of resources,
and help achieve project goals more effectively and efficiently. The
Percentage Progress Technique is a commonly used approach adopted
to assess the progress of a project. In this approach, the percentage
of physical work completed, and the percentage of project outlay expended, are used to review the progress of the project. The other aids to
monitoring include: (*a*) Network Analysis; (*b*) Objective-Oriented
Project Planning, also known as ZOPP; (*c*) Master Schedule; and
(*d*) Management Summary Reports (Gopalakrishnan and Ramamoorthy
1993: 332–37).

This chapter is devoted to an elaboration and discussion of the methods and processes of implementation, monitoring and evaluation of rural development programmes.

Project Implementation

We can distinguish between two approaches to implementation, namely, the traditional approach, and the open approach. The traditional approach is characterised by a mechanical view of planning and development, in which implementation is simply a tool of the powerful (donors, planners, politicians). Employees are seen variously as cogs in a machine, or troublesome but necessary raw materials. Project beneficiaries are seen either as clients (to be 'sold' an idea), or employees (to be instructed).

On the other hand, the open approach attempts to make people important, thinking in terms of 'instigators' and 'actors', rather than as planners and clients. It recognises that implementation is about the communication of meaning, and that it is concerned with power and influence. Implementation becomes more important and is seen as the education of both planners and clients to their mutual benefit. It is still a means of getting things done, but it is also concerned with how things are done and the desirable and undesirable consequences that accrue. As a result, it becomes much more an integral part of the planning process and influences the technical, financial and economic aspects of the process.

In the context of rural development, an approach is needed which encourages and fosters decreasing dependence and increasing self-reliance, and the open approach is suited to this. The traditional approach, on the other hand, can cause dependence and alienation, rather than reducing it. But it is still the predominant approach to implementation and is used by the majority of rural development agencies. The open approach is pragmatic and flexible and is suited to learning and adapting from experience. It leans heavily on the one great resource which the traditional approach has ignored, the people themselves, their motivation, experience and common sense. Furthermore, the open view would suggest that implementation cannot be separated from politics; to think of implementation purely in terms of the acquisition of finance, planning of expenditure, acquisition of inputs, budgetary control and other mechanics of management, is to miss the basic point. Implementation is concerned with action—who plans it, who does it, whom it is done to and why, who has the power, and how the power is organised for action.

Planning for Implementation

Some planning is required for plan implementation as well. A plan for implementation should, at the minimum, specify what is to be done, who is to do it, when it is to be done and how it is to be done. To begin with, the plan should be broken up into a number of projects, and then for every project an implementation system should be developed. Clearly, every project will require a unique implementation system tailor-made to suit its peculiar requirements and characteristics. It is not possible to develop universally applicable implementation systems. But a broad frame for implementation systems can be specified as follows (Kohli 1979: 13–17):

Plan for Physical Work Effort

The plan for physical work should include the following:

- Estimation of requirements of supplies, equipment and implements, labour, power, credit, managerial and technical staff.
- Recruitment, orientation and posting of the staff.
- Surveys, studies, investigations and reports.
- Procurement of supplies, equipment and implements, credit, etc.
- Arrangements for marketing the produce of the target beneficiaries.
- Allocation and distribution of supplies, equipment, credit, etc.
- Physical works.
- Decision making and administrative activities at different levels and stages.

All these activities should be clearly defined along with their sequence and interdependence.

Time Plan

First, the estimated time required for each activity assuming the availability of staff and other resources as planned should be decided, as also the dates when each item of work should begin and finish. Techniques such as bar charts, flow charts, Programme Evaluation and Review Technique (PERT), and Critical Path Method (CPM) could be used to develop a time plan for the project (Gopalakrishnan and Ramamoorthy 1993: Chs. 5 and 6). Care should be taken to match requirement with availability in each time period, both in terms of quantum and pattern.

Input Resource Planning

Input resource planning should include the following:

- Identification of scarce inputs, which would require detailed planning and matching with availability.
- Determination of total requirement of each category of inputs.
- Breaking the total requirement into period-wise components, in line with the time plan formulated.
- Realistic forecasts of likely availability of inputs for each period, and specification of assumptions underlying these forecasts.
- Comparison of requirements with availability for each period.
- Reworking of the time plan, whenever necessary, so that the revised requirements correspond to the availability.

After the time plan and the input resource plan have been thus integrated, the resultant implementation plan can be termed as realistic or implementable, depending upon how realistically the future conditions have been foreseen.

Equipment Order Planning

Separate lists of equipment and other items to be purchased should be prepared, and orders placed accordingly. The purchase plan and implementation plan should be synchronised.

Project Organisation

Both for preparing the implementation plan, as well as for executing the project, proper project organisation is to be developed, responsibilities for various tasks clearly assigned, and proper use of scientific equipment and tools ensured. Filling key positions with adequately skilled and experienced persons on time is also important. It is also better to spell out the monitoring and management information systems to be used during implementation, and to develop the necessary report formats.

Building Interlinkages

This is necessary to complete the project in time and to derive full benefits from the interrelated projects, e.g., bridges and roads, irrigation and crop development projects, production, processing and marketing projects, power and industry, etc. Both backward and forward linkages with other projects should be built and strengthened.

Drawing eclectically on several sources of ideas, Robert Chambers and his colleagues have developed a system for programming and controlling the implementation of rural development programmes and projects. It is called the Programming and Implementation (PIM) system. The pilot system has been tested in the Special Rural Development Programme (SRDP) in Kenya. The system has the following three main components (Chambers 1974: Ch. 2):

1. A programming exercise, which in the SRDP was annual, and held just before or just after the beginning of the financial year. This is a meeting attended by all those directly concerned with implementation, at which they jointly and freely draw up a phased work programme for the year.

2. A management meeting, which in the SRDP was usually monthly. At this meeting, attended by those concerned directly with implementation, progress is reviewed against the phased work programme, bottlenecks are identified, and remedial action agreed upon.

3. An action report, which in the SRDP was described as a monthly management report, summarising briefly the progress made and problems encountered, naming those responsible for action, and sent quickly and simultaneously to those concerned at different levels in the government.

The main principles incorporated in the system are as follows:

- A procedure requiring joint programming by all those responsible for implementation.
- Staff taking part in setting their own work targets.
- Collegial sanctions against poor work.
- Lean and functional reports.
- Communication direct from the implementer to the point of bottleneck or delay.
- Functional meetings used sparingly.
- Sophistication in simplicity.

These principles might be used in devising other implementation and management systems for other situations, as in India and other developing countries. A number of technical, economic, financial, commercial, sociocultural, and institutional-organisational factors affect the implementation of a rural and agricultural development programme. Knowledge about the nature and magnitude of the effect of each of these factors is necessary for rural development managers, to be able to implement and manage the programme efficiently and effectively. Similar knowledge is also essential for rural development policy makers and planners in order to formulate realistic policies and plans for rural development. It is the lack or inadequacy of knowledge about some or all of these factors, on the part of both development policy makers and administrators, that explains, to a large extent, the failure of India's development programmes.

Project Control

The functions of management and control are linked together because there is no generally agreed definition of them. Indeed, the words are often used interchangeably. However, I prefer to regard them as separate, though linked, functions. Control is concerned with maintaining project operations to meet changing circumstances, particularly those exogenous to the project, such as markets, input and product prices, government policy changes, and so on.

In practice, the control function of rural development projects is frequently so preoccupied with financial accountability, the prevention of fraud and the policing of project activities, that it tends towards a centralised, rigid and non-motivating structure. This preoccupation reflects the attitude of the operating ministries, which are spending, and not business institutions. The result is that project control is seen as the major function at the cost of project management, and this accounts for the inflexibility of project operations observed so frequently. Rural development projects rarely operate under static circumstances, and, therefore, project management should have the capacity to adjust project operations to change.

Regarding management structures and methods of control, these should be closely related to the basic physical, technical, social and economic characteristics of a project. In the early stages of project operation, strong technical and administrative control is likely to be beneficial, but over time, increasing benefits are likely to come from decentralisation of decision making and greater farmer participation.

Project management performance depends not only on a staffing structure appropriate to the type and size of the project, but also on the quality of staff—this refers to all levels of management. A shortage of high quality, well-motivated manpower is a common characteristic of developing countries, but it is particularly marked in the rural sector, where projects are often isolated and sometimes located in unattractive situations, which makes it difficult to attract people to work on them. Perhaps even more important is the fact that the wages and salaries of project employees, as well as access to urban amenities, are often unattractive and inadequate when compared with other sectors.

Integration and Coordination

Given the multi-disciplinary nature of rural development, and the multitude of governmental and non-governmental agencies engaged in the implementation of diverse agricultural and rural development programmes with different, and often conflicting, objectives, it is absolutely essential that the different development programmes in operation in an area be integrated and coordinated for optimum results. In the absence of requisite integration and coordination among various development programmes at present, there is a great deal of unnecessary overlapping, duplication and wastage of scarce resources. The main reason for the lack of integration and coordination among various development agencies can be traced to India's Constitution, which, until the 73rd Amendment to it in 1992, did not define the relationship between the state and the district and other lower tiers, with reference to planning.

A review of the experience of panchayati raj institutions prior to the 73rd Amendment, revealed that they had not been successful in achieving the desired integration of the political and administrative systems, and in enlisting people's participation in development plans and programmes. The development administration at the district and tehsil/taluka levels still faces the twin problems of horizontal and vertical coordination, and integration of the political and administrative systems. In order to solve these problems, and to bring together all the administrative operations under effective control of a single agency, it would be necessary to evolve a unified administrative structure at the district level, integrating the functions of the zila parishad and district rural development agencies.

The structure may have the collector, or some other generalist functionary, acting as the overall coordinator, whose authority should be reinforced through local people's institutions brought into the administrative process, with adequate powers and well-defined functions, and which can enforce their policy decisions on the functionaries operating within their jurisdiction.

People's Participation in Implementation

The implementation of any rural development project on a national scale cannot be possible without the active and widespread participation of its clientele. This is why a rural development project authority, to be effective, must know how to make the project's clientele see themselves as partners in the effort, and how to encourage the individual initiative dormant in the people. In other words, the project authority must be capable of maintaining a proper balance between public intervention and private initiative; the former will be greater in the early stage of development, and the latter in the advanced stage of development.

It is the task of the project authority to discover the active elements in the local population, to awaken their interest and to mobilise their initiative. The active elements may be found in the educated middle class, rural leaders, political parties, or in other groups. Their successful activation requires first hand knowledge of the population, their customs and traditions, and is often based more on perceptiveness and intuition, than on direct rules and principles.

Many different factors may motivate people to participate, or refrain from participating in, a rural development project. Therefore, it is necessary for those responsible for project implementation to find out the factors that motivate the local people to participate in a project and to formulate, on the basis of this first hand knowledge, a specific strategy to enlist their participation. A review of India's past efforts in involving people in the processes of plan formulation and implementation would reveal that decentralisation of planning and administrative functions through the panchayati raj institutions has not brought about the desired results. It is hoped that now, after the introduction of the Constitution (73rd Amendment) Act, 1992, people's participation in planning and implementation of rural development projects will improve.

In a few areas, some voluntary agencies have been successful in enlisting the support and participation of local people in the implementation of their development projects. But that is more because of the charismatic personality of the project leader, and less because of any institutional innovations that can be replicated on a large scale elsewhere in the country. The Anand pattern cooperative structure seems to be an appropriate instrument for enlisting people's participation in rural development projects. This has been amply demonstrated under the Operation Flood programme. (See Ch. 11 for details.)

Weitz (1971: Ch. 9) has distilled, from experience with various development projects, the following simple rules of thumb for enlisting people's participation in development projects:

- Create a human relationship, on the basis of equality, between the project clientele and the project employees, and institutionalise it.
- Know the traditions and social customs of the project's clientele.
- Introduce programmes gradually, and adapt them to the ability of the target population, to enable it to absorb the changes involved.
- Get yourself a partner from amongst the local leaders.
- Encourage and promote development leadership among both the project employees and the local people.

Project Monitoring

Monitoring is undertaken to fulfil the following purposes:

- To provide the information required for improving the selection, performance and cost-effectiveness of projects.
- To provide the information required by funding agencies and local level agencies interested in the project.
- To ensure effective vertical and horizontal information flows between different levels and agencies associated with the projects.

The major components of project monitoring are as follows:

1. Project Progress Reports.
   - Summary.
   - Progress of physical implementation compared to targets.
   - Financial performance compared to targets.
   - Performance of principal inputs and services.
2. Special Diagnostic Studies.
3. Project Completion Reports.
4. Project Sustainability.

Practically every major agricultural and rural development programme provides for monitoring of both the achievement of its physical and financial targets, and the benefits actually accruing to its target group. Usually, a family-based approach is used for monitoring the impact of a programme on its clientele. For example, IRDP provides for monitoring of incremental income of its beneficiary families, and for comparing it with their baseline incomes as assessed at the time of conducting household surveys for selection of beneficiaries. For this purpose, an identity-cum-monitoring card has been issued to each beneficiary family.

From the management perspective, it is necessary to differentiate between information needed for control, and information needed for purposes other than control. Therefore, management needs two types of reports—a control report, and an information report. For the purpose of control, what is needed is essentially a comparison of actual performance with planned performance and reasons for the deviations, if any. There-fore, a control report should be very brief and precise. The information report tells the management what is going on in the organisation. Such reports may or may not lead to action.

The format and frequency of a monitoring or control report will depend on the nature, size, complexity and structure of the organisation/programme which is to be monitored and controlled. But, in general, a monitoring system should be linked with the responsibility centres in the organisation concerned. A responsibility centre is simply a unit or a subsystem in an organisation headed by a responsible manager, who is accountable for the work done by his unit. The manager in-charge of a responsibility centre should be provided with the information which is relevant for his needs of planning, decision making, control and reme-dial action. The relevant information should, therefore, be identified for each responsibility centre, and the control report format designed accordingly.

The Union Ministry of Rural Areas and Employment has been giving special emphasis on monitoring and evaluation of rural development programmes in general, and poverty alleviation programmes in particular, being implemented in various states. To ensure this, the ministry has evolved a comprehensive system of monitoring and evaluation, the salient features of which are as follows (GOI 1997b: 101):

- Periodical progress reports.
- Financial returns/audit reports.
- Intensive inspections.
- Area officers scheme.
- Review by various committees.
- Concurrent evaluation reports.

Monitoring of rural development programmes at state level is the responsibility of the State Level Coordination Committee (SLCC) for rural development programmes. A representative of the Union Department of Rural Development is also invited to participate in the meetings of the SLCC. The chief ministers of the states also review, from time to time, the progress of various programmes with Members of Parliament (MPs) and Members of Legislative Assemblies (MLAs) and senior officers of the state governments concerned. At the central level, sanctioning and screening committees critically review the overall performance of rural development programmes, and suggest necessary measures to effect improvements in their implementation.

Apart from the monitoring mechanisms stated above, the standing committee and the consultative committee of parliament also take stock of implementation of various rural development programmes at periodical intervals. The shortcomings/lacunae observed by local MPs in the implementation of the programmes are looked into, and quick remedial measures taken to improve the programme, wherever required.

Project Evaluation

By evaluation we mean assessment. We distinguish between three types of evaluation, namely, *ex ante* evaluation, concurrent evaluation, and *ex post* evaluation. In *ex ante* evaluation, a project is assessed before it is executed; in concurrent evaluation, assessment is made while the project is underway; in *ex post* evaluation, assessment is made after the project is completed. This section is confined to concurrent and *ex post* evaluation.

Objectives of Evaluation

The main objectives of *ex post* evaluation are to find out whether, and to what extent, the programme has been successful in achieving its objectives and at what cost, to investigate the reasons of both good as well as bad performance, and to bring out the lessons learnt. A secondary objective of evaluation could be to suggest appropriate measures to improve the performance of the programme. The main objective of concurrent evaluation is to find out whether the programme is progressing as per the plan (and if not, why) and what its impacts are.

Methodological Issues

Evaluation of a rural development programme is beset with a number of conceptual and empirical problems. First, there are conceptual problems of devising a composite index of rural development, which can capture its multidimensional nature. Then, there are problems of quantifying all the programme interventions and measures that directly and/or indirectly seek to promote rural development, and recording and monitoring their values at the beginning, at the end, as also during the course of the programme. These problems are further complicated by the fact that the causal variables or determinants of development keep changing simultaneously, rendering it very difficult to isolate and measure the effect of any one of them. It is difficult—and if at all possible, extravagant in resources—to apply a classical experimental design of studies with random samples, controls, treatments, measurement of effects and attribution of effects, to programme measures. Also, a long period may be needed to identify and observe the 'after' effects of a rural development programme, given the slow diffusion of its effects.

Setting targets is an important management tool which is commonly used in rural development programmes to control and improve the performance, and evaluation is invariably geared towards measuring achievement against the targets. This form of evaluation is liable to bias activity and effort towards achieving outputs which are quantifiable and measurable, to the neglect of those which may be more important, but which are less easy to quantify and measure. For instance, the eradication of poverty is the ultimate goal of IRDP, but its performance is evaluated in terms of achievement of its physical and financial targets. This is mainly because monitoring changes in the magnitude of poverty is more difficult than reporting the progress achieved in fulfilling the physical (number of beneficiaries covered) and financial (amount of subsidy and loans disbursed) targets. It is important, therefore, that programme administrators and evaluators take care in choosing evaluation criteria, and see the causal links between the programme measures, sub-goals and main goals.

Rural development projects and their outcomes can be seen as long, causal chains of the following type.

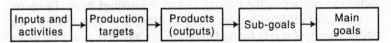

An evaluation system has to select points along the chain at which observations and measurements can be carried out. Evaluation could be done at any or all the points along the chain.

Rural development programmes usually have multiple effects, only a few of which will be specified in an evaluation plan. Some of the effects may be anticipated, others unanticipated or spillovers. Of the unanticipated effects, some may be harmful, and some may be beneficial. For instance, a shortage of good quality milch animals, and the consequent hike in their price, may be an unanticipated harmful effect of provision of milch animals under IRDP, and fostering of managerial capacity of the beneficiaries may be an unanticipated beneficial effect of the same programme. Unless an evaluation design is open to change, and unless perceptive and open-ended research is undertaken concurrently with evaluation, significant unanticipated effects may be missed.

Evaluation is also vulnerable to political insecurity and pressures. External evaluation is usually called upon for three reasons, or for combinations of them: to be quasi-judicial; to be supportive; or to improve performance. Consequently, the evaluator may be regarded as a spy, an investigator, or an enemy; but it is quite likely that he will be co-opted into the system. Co-opted evaluators resemble parasites in their concern not to kill their hosts, and there is a danger that their reports will be muted in criticism, and over-lavish in praise, in order to secure their continued employment or the chance of another job.

Besides external evaluation, much informal and unsystematic evaluation takes place within departments/organisations, through the experience gained with implementation, through personal impressions, and through the feedback of internal reporting systems. An external evaluator may contribute a lot by examining the reporting and evaluation systems which already operate within the organisation, and trying to improve them and link them up functionally with remedial action and with future resource allocations.

Criteria for Evaluation

The criteria for evaluation of a programme should be related to the major goals of the programme and should be operational. For example, a simple criterion for evaluating IRDP could be the number of people helped to rise above the poverty line on a sustained basis. To operationalise this criterion, we will need to define a poverty line for each state, district, or maybe for the block also, separately at some base year's price, and then keep updating this year after year to neutralise the effect of inflation. Once this is done, the next thing required is to develop a system to determine and report the annual per capita income for each beneficiary household every year. This way, we may, at the end of each year, see how many poor families have been helped to rise above the poverty line.

Determining the area-specific poverty line, updating it, and assessing per capita income for each and every beneficiary household are all very difficult tasks, and would require expertise and resources that are not available at present at the block and district levels anywhere in the country. Unless requisite resources and expertise are made available, nothing more or better than the existing system of reporting progress in terms of physical and financial targets can be expected. Universities and research institutes could help in determining poverty lines, updating these, and assessing per capita incomes in a few blocks and districts, but the major brunt of the task will have to be borne by the programme itself.

'Before and After' and 'With and Without' Approaches

Most evaluation studies have used either the 'Before and After' or 'With and Without' approach to isolate and measure programme impacts. Ideally, both these approaches should be used together. The 'Before and After' approach purges the programme impact of the cumulated effect of past programmes, and the 'With and Without' approach eliminates the effects of the natural process of development, as well as of other development programmes under way in the area of study. But the 'Before and After' approach can be used only when the baseline data for the year immediately preceding the year when the programme to be evaluated was launched are available.

Under IRDP, baseline household surveys were conducted in all the villages selected for the programme, and the incomes of the eligible beneficiaries determined. Assuming that this information is readily available at the block headquarters, one could use both these approaches to evaluate the impact of IRDP. For the 'With and Without' approach, the households who are otherwise eligible for assistance under the programme, but were excluded because of the limited target, constitute the 'control' (without programme) group, and the beneficiaries would constitute the 'project' (with programme) group.

In the 'With and Without' method, an attempt is made to identify and value the costs and benefits that have arisen from the programme, and to compare them with the costs and benefits in the situation which would have prevailed without the programme. The difference is the incremental net benefit that can be attributed to the programme. The 'Before and After' method, if used alone, fails to take into account the changes in income, employment, or any other performance indicator that may occur autonomously without the programme, and thus may lead to an erroneous estimate of the benefits attributable to the programme.

Figure 16.1
Mechanics of Impact Assessment of a Programme like Operation Flood

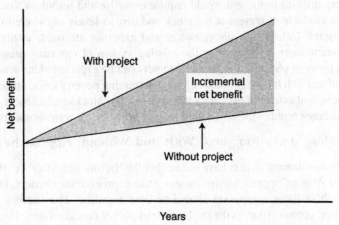

Generally speaking, one may encounter one of three situations in which the programme which is to be evaluated may be operating (Gittinger 1982: 47–50):

1. A situation in which output or income, or any other performance indicator has been growing, but at a slow rate, say, 5 per cent per annum, even without the programme. With the programme, the rate of growth may increase to, say, 10 per cent per annum. So, the incremental effect is $10-5 = 5$ per cent per annum. This situation is represented in Figure 16.1. This kind of situation prevailed in India in the dairy sector before Operation Flood I was launched.

2. A situation in which output has been declining, say, at a rate of 5 per cent per annum naturally, but with the programme, the decrease in output may be checked and output may be stabilised at the normal level. In this case, the benefit from the programme is in the form of prevention of loss in output. In agriculture, this kind of situation may arise in areas which are prone to droughts, floods and wind erosion. This situation is represented in Figure 16.2.

3. A situation in which no change in output is expected without the programme, but with the programme the output is expected to increase, say, at the rate of 5 per cent per annum. In this case, all the increase (5 per cent) may be attributed to the

Figure 16.2
Mechanics of Impact Assessment of a Flood Control Project

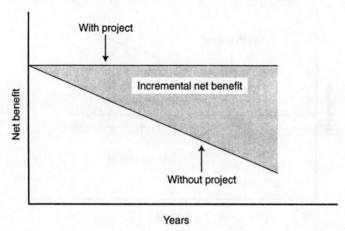

programme. In this situation, the use of 'Before and After' and 'With and Without' methods would yield the same results. In this kind of situation, one may use either of these methods. This situation (depicted in Figure 16.3) may prevail in new settlement project areas where, without the project, the productivity of land and other resources is almost stagnant or negligible, but after the project it starts increasing.

The conceptual design that we can use for impact evaluation may be presented as follows:

	Before the Project	*After the Project*
Beneficiary group (With the project)	I_{PB}	I_{PA}
Non-beneficiary group (Without the project)	I_{CB}	I_{CA}

In the above,

$I_{PB} =$ the level of a selected impact indicator for the beneficiary group before the project was launched;

$I_{PA} =$ the level of a selected impact indicator for the beneficiary group after the project is over, or is still under way;

$I_{CB} =$ the level of a selected impact indicator for the non-beneficiary group before the project was launched; and

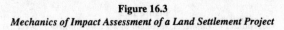

Figure 16.3
Mechanics of Impact Assessment of a Land Settlement Project

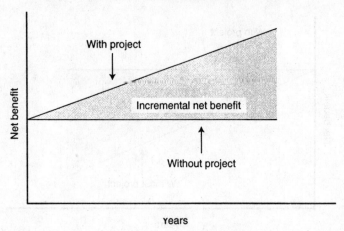

$I_{CA} =$ the level of a selected impact indicator for the nonbeneficiary group after the project is over, or is still under way.

The net effect of the project is given as:

Net Effect $= (I_{PA} - I_{PB}) - (I_{CA} - I_{CB})$

Alternatively,

Net Effect $= (I_{PA} - I_{CA}) - (I_{PB} - I_{CB})$.

$(I_{PA} - I_{PB})$ gives an estimate of the gross effect on the level of an impact indicator over the duration of the project due to the project and non-project activities, and $(E_{CA} - E_{CB})$ indicates the change in the level of an impact indicator due to the non-project activities alone.

Uses of Evaluation

The results of evaluation studies could be used as feedback to policy makers, planners, administrators, implementers, bankers, researchers and to other agencies directly or indirectly associated with the programme. Evaluation could make policy makers and implementers aware of the inadequacies of the 'blueprint' approach to planning and implementation of rural development programmes. To be of any use, the results of evaluation should be presented in simple and non-technical language, and should be made available to the potential users in time.

The lessons derived from evaluation studies, including the reasons for good and bad performance, should be discussed with both the programme planners and administrators, as well as with the beneficiaries.

Any systematic but simple procedure requiring staff to evaluate the projects on which they are working is likely to be beneficial in heightening their awareness, and in communicating their problems to levels at which some of them can be tackled. In the context of IRDP, this means that the assistant project officers, EOs and even VLWs should be encouraged to undertake some simple but systematic evaluation of their activities, and present their findings at annual staff meetings at the block and district levels. Of course, some training in how to conduct scientific evaluation would be necessary before they are asked to do the job.

At the end, we would like to caution that it is asking a lot of a social scientist, whether he be in a university or in the government, to make programme recommendations which require an assessment of the organisational and management aspects of implementation, unless he is trained in management also, or has relevant managerial experience. This is perhaps one reason why so many of the proposals which are made by social scientists not trained/experienced in management are never implemented. One way of improving the chances that recommendations are implementable is to give priority to discussion and exchange of ideas between the evaluator who will make the recommendations, and the manager who will be faced with implementing them (Chambers 1974: 124).

In order to assess the impact of various rural development programmes, the Union Ministry of Rural Areas and Employment undertakes concurrent evaluation studies from time to time with the help of reputed and independent research institutions/organisations. The main aim of the evaluation studies is to identify the strengths and weaknesses of various programmes, to enable the Ministry to apply corrective measures for improving their implementation. The evaluation studies are quite comprehensive, and the survey schedules designed for the purpose cover a wide range of questions for eliciting information from the sample respondents. So far, five rounds of concurrent evaluation of IRDP, two rounds of JRY, and one round each of the Million Wells Scheme and Indira Awas Yojana have been completed. The findings of the reports of all concurrent evaluation studies are sent to state governments for taking suitable remedial actions to remove the bottlenecks/weaknesses as revealed in the findings of the studies. Besides regular concurrent evaluation of programmes, the monitoring division of the Ministry also carries out research studies from time to time (GOI 1997a: 101–3).

Concluding Remarks

A review of the failure of a number of rural development programmes in India reveals that there are significant gaps in the application of requisite management tools, techniques and skills in the implementation, monitoring and evaluation of these programmes. There is a credibility gap between the highly prestigious and sophisticated Planning Commission, which is responsible for plan formulation, and the lowly paid and highly demotivated village level worker who is responsible for plan implementation. Given the existing salary structure and punishment and reward system, there is very little hope of improving the implementation of rural development projects with the existing staff, who, by and large, are a frustrated lot, who have no motivation or initiative to improve the existing state of affairs.

In view of this, there is urgent need to professionalise rural development administration and rename it as 'rural development management'. To professionalise rural development management, it will be necessary to induct fresh, professionally trained rural managers at all levels, and to reorient the existing staff engaged in rural development administration through short-term training courses in rural development management. Unfortunately, at present, the supply of professionally trained rural managers and the facilities for in-service training of existing rural development staff in rural development management are both extremely limited. There is, therefore, need to establish many more institutes of rural development management in the country, and to reorient the existing institutes of public administration to focus on rural development management.

We conclude this chapter and book by asserting that for effective implementation, the development projects should basically be *people's projects* with government's and/or other agencies' participation, and *not government projects* with people's participation. Every project should have a well-thought plan of implementation, and its activities properly coordinated and controlled by the project authority. Project beneficiaries should be closely involved in implementation, monitoring and evaluation of the project. The roles of governmental and non-governmental organisations should be limited to that of catalysts. Both concurrent and *ex post* evaluations are necessary for efficient and effective implementation of a rural development programme. Both 'With and Without' and 'Before and After' approaches should be used to assess the impacts of a project on its clientele and other persons. An external evaluator can contribute a lot by examining the systems of reporting and evaluation which already exist within the organisation, and trying to improve them and link them functionally with remedial action. Besides, an internal evaluation based on personal impressions and the feedback of internal reporting systems can also be very useful, if it is done objectively and used constructively. Internal evaluation should not be used as an espionage system, and the internal evaluator should not be allowed to become a power-wielding centre.

•

References and Select Bibliography

Acharya, S. S. 1997. 'Agricultural Price Policy and Development: Some Facts and Emerging Issues', in the *Indian Journal of Agricultural Economics*, 52(1): 1–47.

Adelman, Irma and **C. T. Morris.** 1967. *Society, Politics and Economic Development.* Baltimore: Johns Hopkins University Press.

Agrawal, A. N. and **S. P. Singh** (eds). 1975. *The Economics of Under Development.* Delhi: Oxford University Press.

Aiyar, Ankleshwar and **S. Swaminathan.** 1995. 'Encouraging News About Poverty', in *The Economic Times*, 14 December.

Alavi, Hamza and **Teodar Shanin** (eds). 1982. *Introduction to the Sociology of 'Developing Societies'.* London: Macmillan.

Alderman, Harold, George Mergos and **Roger Slade.** 1987. 'Cooperatives and the Commercialisation of Milk Production in India: A literature Review', IFPRI Working Paper on Commercialisation of Agriculture and Nutrition, No. 2, Washington, D.C.

Alex, Alexander V. 1983. *Human Capital Approach to Economic Development.* New Delhi: Metropolitan.

Alvares, Claude. 1985. *Another Revolution Fails.* Delhi: Ajanta Publications.

Anonymous. 1968. *Webster's Dictionary*, Third New International Edition, Springfield (Massachusetts): G. & C. Merriam Co.

———. 1978. 'Mahatma Gandhi on Rural Development', in *Indian Farming*, October–November.

Ansoff, Igor H., Roger P. Declerck and **Robert L. Hayes.** (eds). 1976. *From Strategic Planning to Strategic Management.* London: John Wiley and Sons.

Atkinson, Anthony B. 1970. 'On the Measurement of Equality', in the *Journal of Economic Theory*, 2. February: 253–54.

Bandyopadhyay, D. 1988. 'Direct Intervention Programmes for Poverty Alleviation: An Appraisal', *Economic and Political Weekly*, 25 June: A77-A88.

Barnett, T. 1988. *Sociology and Development.* London: Hutchinson.

Basu, D. N. and **G. S. Guha.** 1996. *Agro-Climatic Regional Planning in India, Vol. I: Concepts and Application.* New Delhi: Concept Publishing Co.

Basu, D. N. and **S. P. Kashyap.** 1996. *Agro-Climatic Regional Planning in India, Vol. II: Themes and Cases.* New Delhi: Concept Publishing Co.

Bauer, Peter. 1991. *The Development Frontier.* Cambridge: Harvard University Press.

Berger, Peter L. and Richard John Neuhaus. 1977. *To Empower People: The Role of Mediating Structures in Public Policy*. Washington (DC): American Enterprise Institute for Public Policy Research.

Boeke, J. H. 1953. *Economics and Economic Policy of Dual Societies*. New York.

Bronfenbrenner, Martin. 1966. 'The High Cost of Economic Development', in *Land Economics*, August 1953, quoted in Benjamin Higgins, *Economic Development: Principles, Problems and Policies*. Allahabad: Central Book Depot.

Bryant, Coralee and Louise G. White. 1980. *Managing Rural Development: Peasant Participation in Rural Development*. New Hartford (Connecticut): Kumarian Press.

Buckley, Walter. 1967. *Sociology and Modern Systems Theory*. Englewood Cliffs (New Jersey): Prentice Hall, Inc.

CMIE. 1997. *Approach Paper to Ninth Five Year Plan*. Bombay: Centre for Monitoring Indian Economy, February.

Chambers, Robert. 1974. *Managing Rural Development, Ideas and Experience From East Africa*. Uppsala: Scandinavian Institute of African Studies.

———. 1983. *Rural Development: Putting the Last First*. London: Longman.

———. 1987. 'Sustainable Rural Livelihoods: A Strategy for People, Environment and Development', Commissioned Study No. 7, Institute of Development Studies at the University of Sussex, Brighton, England.

Chand, Ramesh. 1997. 'Import Liberalisation and Indian Agriculture: The Challenge and Strategy'. New Delhi: National Centre for Agricultural Economics and Policy Research, Policy Paper 6.

Cochrane, Willard W. 1969. *The World Food Problem: A Guardedly Optimistic View*. New York: Thomas Y. Crowell Company, Inc.

Dandekar, V. M. and Nilakanth Rath. 1971. *Poverty in India*. Pune: Indian School of Political Economy.

Dandekar, V. M. 1972. 'Effectiveness in Agricultural Planning', in *Teaching Forum: Development Processes and Planning*, 19. July. New York: The Agricultural Development Council.

Dantwala, M. L. 1970. 'From Stagnation to Growth', in the *Indian Economic Journal*, 18. October–December: 165–92.

Das Gupta, A. K. 1978. 'Plan Priorities: Some Basic Issue', in *Yojana*, 12. 26 January: 16–18.

Desai, D. K. 1983. *Management in Rural Development*. New Delhi: Oxford and IBH.

Deshpande, D. V., M. K. Mudgal and K. K. Gupta. 1996. 'Regional Rural Banks at Cross Roads', Working Paper 9. Lucknow: Bankers Institute of Rural Development.

Doornbos, Martin and Liana Gertsch. 1994. 'Sustainability, Technology and Corporate Interest: Resource Strategies in India's Modern Dairy Sector', in *Journal of Development Studies*, 30(3): 918.

Doornbos, Martin, Pietrvan Stuijvenberg and Piet Terhal. 1987. 'Operation Flood: Impact and Issues', in *Food Policy*, 12(4): 376–83.

Doornbos, Martin, Frank van Dorsten, Manoshi Mitra and Piet Terhal. 1990. *Dairy Aid and Development: India's Operation Flood*, Indo-Dutch Studies on Development Alternatives, 3. New Delhi/Newbury Park/London: Sage Publications.

Dorner, Peter. 1973. 'Institutions as Aids to Development', paper presented at the 15th International Conference of Agricultural Economists, Sao Paulo (Brazil), 19–30 August.

Dulfer, E. 1974. 'Operational Efficiency of Agricultural Cooperatives in Developing Countries', FAO Development Paper No. 96. Rome: Food and Agriculture Organisation, United Nations Organisation.

Dunn, Edgar S. 1971. *Economic and Social Development: A Process of Social Learning*. Baltimore: The Johns Hopkins University Press.

ECAFE. 1950. *Foreign Investment Laws and Regulations in the ECAFE Region*. Bangkok: United Nations Economic Commission for Asia and the Far East, Committee on Industry and Trade.

Ekaus, Richard S. and **Kirit S. Parikh.** 1968. *Planning for Growth: Multisectoral, Intertemporal Models Applied to India*. Cambridge (Massachusetts): The MIT Press.

Ensminger, Douglas. 1968. *An Evolving Strategy for India's Agricultural Development*. New Delhi: The Ford Foundation.

———. 1972. *Rural India in Transition*. New Delhi: All-India Panchayat Parishad.

FAO. 1996. *Production Year Book, 1995, Vol. 49*. Rome: Food and Agriculture Organisation, United Nations Organisation.

Fox, Karl A., Jati K. Sengupta and **Erik Thorbecke.** 1966. *The Theory of Quantitative Economic Policy with Applications to Economic Growth and Stabilisation*. Amsterdam: North Holland Publishing Company.

Fei, John C.H. and **Gustay Ranis.** 1964. *Development of the Labour Surplus Economy: Theory and Policy*. Homewood (Illinois): Richard D. Irwin Inc.

Gaikwad, V. R., Gunvant M. Desai, Paul Mampilly and **V. S. Vyas.** 1977. *Development of Intensive Agriculture: Lessons from IADP*. Ahmedabad: Centre for Management in Agriculture, Indian Institute of Management.

Gangrade, K. D. 1997. 'Power to Powerless: A Silent Revolution through Panchayat Raj System', in the *Journal of Rural Development*. 6(4): 755–56.

Ghosh, A. 1968. *Planning, Programming, and Input-Output Models: Selected Papers on Indian Planning*. Cambridge: Cambridge University Press.

George, Shanti. 1987. 'Stemming Operation Flood: Towards an Alternative Dairy Policy for India', in *Economic and Political Weekly*, 26 September.

George, Shanti. 1988. 'Cooperatives and Indian Dairy Policy: More Anand than Pattern', in D. W. Attwood and B. S. Baviskar (eds), *Who Shares? Cooperatives and Rural Development*, Delhi: Oxford University Press.

Gibbons, David. 1997. 'Targetting the Poor and Covering Costs', a paper presented at the Micro-Credit Summit and communicated to the author via e-mail by Robert Gailey, Research Director, Micro-Credit Summit Secretariat, under the auspices of the 'Poverty Discussion Group' programme.

Gittinger, J. Price. 1982. *Economic Analysis of Agricultural Projects*, Second edition. Baltimore: The Johns Hopkins University Press.

GOI. 1961. *Towards a Self Reliant Economy: India's Third Plan, 1961–66*. New Delhi: Planning Commission, Government of India.

———. 1963. *Intensive Agricultural District Programme: Report (1961–63)*. New Delhi: Expert Committee on Assessment and Evaluation, Ministry of Food and Agriculture, Government of India.

———. 1968. *Modernizing Indian Agriculture (1960–68)*. Vol. 1. New Delhi: Expert Committee on Assessment and Evaluation, Ministry of Food and Agriculture, C. D. and Cooperation, Government of India.

GOI. 1975. *Report on Evaluation Study of Small Farmers, Marginal Farmers and Agricultural Labourers Project, 1974–75.* New Delhi: Planning Commission, Government of India. Chapter 6.

———. 1976. *Report of the National Commission on Agriculture 1976, Part II: Policy and Strategy.* New Delhi: Ministry of Agriculture and Irrigation, Government of India.

———. 1977. *Report of the Review Committe on Pilot Intensive Rural Employment Project (PIREP).* New Delhi: Ministry of Irrigation and Agriculture, Government of India. pp. 11–19.

———. 1978a. *Report of the Finance Commission.* New Delhi: Government of India.

———. 1978b. *Report of the Working Group on Block Level Planning (1978).* New Delhi: Planning Commission, Government of India.

———. 1979. *Study of CSRE 1971–74.* New Delhi: Planning Commission, Government of India.

———. 1980. *Manual on Integrated Rural Development Programme.* New Delhi: Ministry of Rural Reconstruction, Government of India, January.

———. 1984. *Report of the Evaluation Committee on Operation Flood II.* New Delhi: Government of India, Ministry of Agriculture, Department of Agriculture and Co-operation.

———. 1997a. *Annual Report 1996–97.* New Delhi: Ministry of Rural Areas and Employment, Government of India.

———. 1997b. *Economic Survey 1996–97.* New Delhi: Ministry of Finance, Government of India.

———. 1998a. *India 1998.* New Delhi: Ministry of Information and Broadcasting, Publications Division.

———. 1998b. *Economic Survey 1997–98.* New Delhi: Ministry of Finance, Government of India.

Gopalakrishnan, P. and **V. E. Rama Moorthy.** 1993. *Text Book of Project Management.* New Delhi: Macmillan India Ltd.

Gould, Julius and **W. L. Kolb.** 1967. *A Dictionary of Social Sciences*, 4th Printing. UNRS. Co. Paris: UNESCO.

Gouldner, Alvin. 1959. 'Organisational Analysis', in Robert K. Merton (ed), *Sociology Today.* New York: Basic Books Inc.

Gran, Guy. 1983. *Development by People: Citizens Construction of a Just World.* New York: Praeger.

Gulati, Ashok. 1989. 'Input Subsidies in Indian Agriculture: A State-wise Analysis', in the *Economic and Political Weekly.* 24(25), June, pp. A–57–65.

Gulati, Ashok and **A. N. Sharma.** 1992. 'Subsidising Agriculture: A Cross Country View', in the *Economic and Political Weekly*, 27(39), September, pp. A–106–111.

Gupta, K. R. 1976. *Economics of Development and Planning.* Delhi: Atma Ram and Sons.

Gupta, S. P. 1995. 'Economic Reform and its Impact on Poor', in the *Economic and Political Weekly*, 3 June. 1295–1313.

Halite, Graham. 1968. *The Economics of Agricultural Policy.* Oxford: Basil.

Hamza, Alavi and **Teodor Shanin** (eds). 1982. *Introduction to the Sociology of Developing Societies.* London: Macmillan.

Harold, Alderman, George Mergos and **Roger Slade.** 1987. 'Cooperatives and the Commercialisation of Milk Production in India: A Literature Review', IFPRI Working Paper on Commercialisation of Agriculture and Nutrition, No. 2, Washington DC.

Hayami, Yujiro and **V. W. Ruttan.** 1970. 'Agricultural Productivity Differences Among Countries'. *The American Economic Review*, 60(5). December: 895–911.

──────. 1971. *Agricultural Development: An International Perspective.* Baltimore: The Johns Hopkins University Press.

Heady, Earl O. 1965. *Agricultural Policy Under Economic Development.* Ames (Iowa): Iowa State University Press.

Hickman, Bert G. (ed). 1965. *Quantitative Economic Policy.* Washington: The Brookings Institution.

Higgins, Benjamin. 1966. *Economic Development: Principles, Problems and Policies.* Allahabad: Central Book Depot.

Hirway, Indira. 1988. 'Reshaping IRDP: Some Issues', in the *Economic and Political Weekly*, 25 June: A89–A95.

Honadle, George and **Rudi Klauss** (eds). 1979. *International Development Administration: Implementation Analysis for Development Projects.* New York: Praeger Publishers.

Hunter, Guy. 1970. *The Administration of Agricultural Development: Lessons from India.* London: Oxford University Press.

Ickis, John C. 1983. 'Structural Response to New Rural Development Strategies', in David C. Korten and Falipe B. Alfonso (eds), *Bureaucracy and the Poor: Closing the Gap.* West Hartford (Connecticut): Kumarian Press.

Indian Dairy Corporation. 1982. *Eleventh Annual Report, 1980–81.*

Jesus, Ed C. De. 1984. 'Learning About Bureaucratic Reorientation', paper presented at the 4th International Conference of Management Institutes Working Group on Social Development Management, Ahmedabad, 23–27 January.

Johnston, Bruce F. and **William C. Clark.** 1982. *Redesigning Rural Development: A Strategic Perspective.* Baltimore: The Johns Hopkins University Press.

Kakwani, N. C. and **N. Poddar.** 1976. 'Efficiency Estimation of the Lorenz Curve and Associated Inequality Measures From Grouped Observations', in *Econometrica.* 44(1): 137–48.

Khera, S. S. 1977. *Government in Business.* New Delhi: National Publishing House.

Kirschen, E. S., J. Benard, H. Besters, F. Blackaby, O. Eckstein, J. Faaland, F. Hartog, L. L. Morissons and **E. Tosco.** 1964. *Economic Policy in Our Time*, I. Amsterdam: North Holland Publishing Company.

Kohli, Uddesh. 1979. 'Implementation Planning', in *Yojana*, 23(11), June: 13–17.

Korten, David C. (ed). 1980. 'Community, Organization and Rural Development: A Learning, Process Approach', in *Public Administration Review*, September–October.

Korten, David C. 1981. 'The Management of Social Transformation', in the *Public Administration Review*, November/December: 610.

Korten, David C. and **Felipe B. Alfonso.** (eds). 1983. *Bureaucracy and the Poor: Closing the Gap.* West Hartford (Connecticut): Kumarian Press.

Korten, David C. and **Rudi Klauss** (eds). 1984. *People Centred Development.* West Hartford (Connecticut): Kumarian Press.

Krishnaji, N. 1997. 'Human Poverty Index: A Critique', in the *Economic and Political Weekly*, 30 August: 2202–5.

Kumar, Nalini. 1997. 'Operation Flood: Literature Review and Reconciliation', Occasional Publication No. 13. Anand: Institute of Rural Management.

Kumar, Pradeep and **S. P. Pal.** 1998. 'Delivery Makes the Difference', in *The Economic Times*, 16 May.

Kurien, V. 1978. 'Food Aid in the Form of Dairy Products', speech delivered at the 20th International Dairy Congress, Paris, 26–30 June. Anand: National Dairy Development Board.

———. 1992. 'Food Aid for Dairy Development', in *Dairy India 1992*. 4th Annual Edition. Delhi.

Leibenstein, Harvey. 1957. *Economic Backwardness and Economic Growth.* New York: John Wiley.

Lewis, W. Arthur. 1955. *The Theory of Economic Growth.* London: George Allen and Unwin Ltd.

———. 1954. 'Economic Development with Unlimited Supplies of Labour', in *The Manchester School*, 22. May: 139–92.

Littrell, W. Boyd. 1980. 'Bureaucracy in the Eighties: Introduction', in *The Journal of Applied Behavioural Science*, 16(3), July–September: 560–61.

Lorsch, Jay W. and **Paul R. Lawrence.** 1972. *Organisation Planning: Cases and Concepts.* Homewood (Illinois): Richard D. Irwin Inc.

MIT. 1957. 'The Objectives of United States Economic Assistance Programmes'. Washington: Massachusetts Institute of Technology, Centre for International Studies.

Macy, Joanna. 1983. *Dharma and Development: Religion as Resource in the Sarvodaya Self-Help Movement.* West Hartford (Connecticut): Kumarian Press.

Maheshwari, Shriram. 1987. 'Voluntary Action in Rural Development in India', in the *Indian Journal of Public Administration*, July–September: 560–61.

March, James G. and **Herbert A. Simon.** 1958. *Organizations.* New York: John Wiley and Sons Inc.

Mascarenhas, R. C. 1988. *A Strategy for Rural Development: Dairy Cooperatives in India.* New Delhi: Sage Publications.

McKay, John. 1990. 'The Development Model', *Development, Journal of the Society for International Development*, Vol. 33, No. 3/4, p. 55.

Mehta, Shiv R. 1984. *Rural Development Policies and Programmes.* New Delhi: Sage Publications.

Meier, Gerald M. 1976. *Leading Issues in Economic Development,* Third Edition. New York: Oxford University Press.

Meier, Gerald M. and **R. E. Baldwin.** 1957. *Economic Development: Theory, History, and Policy.* New York: Wiley.

Mellor, John W. 1966. *The Economics of Agricultural Development.* Ithaca: Cornell University Press.

Mergos, George and **Roger Slade.** 1987. 'Dairy Development and Milk Cooperatives: The Effect of a Dairy Project in India', World Bank, Discussion Paper No. 15, Washington DC.

Mikesell, Raymond F. 1968. *The Economics of Foreign Aid.* Chicago: Aldine Publishing Company.

Minhas, B. S. 1974. *Planning and the Poor.* New Delhi: S. Chand and Company Limited.

Minhas, B. S, L. R. Jain and **S. D. Tendulkar** 1991. 'Declining Incidence of Poverty into the 1980s: Evidence vs Artefacts', in the *Economic and Political Weekly*, July.

Morgan, Theodore and **George W. Betz** (eds). 1970. *Economic Development: Readings in Theory and Practice.* Belmont (California): Wadsworth Publishing Company Inc.

Moris, Jone. 1981. *Managing Induced Rural Development.* Bloomington: Indiana University, International Development Institute.

Morris, David Morris and **Michelle B. McAlpin.** 1982. *Measuring the Condition of India's Poor: The Physical Quality of Life Index.* New Delhi: Promilla and Company Publishers.

Mosher, A.T. 1966. *Getting Agriculture Moving.* New York: Frederick A. Praeger Inc.

———. 1976. *Thinking About Rural Development.* New York: Agricultural Development Council.

Murdick, Robert G. and **Joel E. Ross.** 1971. *Information Systems for Modern Management,* Second Edition. New Delhi: Prentice-Hall of India Pvt Ltd.

Myrdal, Gunnar. 1957. *Economic Theory and Under-developed Regions.* Bombay: Vora and Co. Publishers Pvt Ltd.

NABARD. 1997. *Annual Report 1996–97.* Mumbai: National Bank for Agriculture and Rural Development.

NDDB. 1997. *Annual Report 1996–97.* Anand: National Dairy Development Board.

NIRD. 1996. *Rural Development Statistics 1994–95.* Hyderabad: National Institute of Rural Development.

Owens, Edgar and **Robert Shaw.** 1972. *Development Reconsidered.* New Delhi: Oxford and IBH Publishing Company.

Pal, Suresh and **Alka Singh.** 1997. 'Agricultural Research and Extension in India: Institutional Structure and Investments', Policy Paper 7. New Delhi: National Centre for Agricultural Economics and Policy Research.

Panda, Snehlata. 1997. 'Political Empowerment of Women: A Case of Orissa', in the *Journal of Rural Development.* 6(4): 663.

Patel, Amrita. 1996. 'Operation Flood: The Next Step', in *Dairy India 1997.* Delhi.

Paul, Samuel. 1982. *Managing Development Programs: The Lessons of Success.* Boulder, (Colorado): Westview Press.

Prasad, Brahmanand. 1968. 'Foreign Technology and India's Economic Development', *International Development Review.* Washington: Society for International Development. June.

Ramakrishnaih, D. 1980. 'Area Development Planning for Agriculture in Naurar Watershed, Almora (U.P.): A Multi-period Programming Approach', Unpublished Ph.D. Thesis, G.B. Pant University of Agriculture and Technology, Pantnagar, Nainital (U.P). 90–131.

Ranis, Gustav and **John C. H. Fei.** 1970. 'A Theory of Economic Development' in Theodore Morgan and George W. Betz (eds), *Economic Development: Readings in Theory and Practice.* Belmont (California): Wadsworth Publishing Company Inc.

Rath, Nilakanth. 1985. 'Garibi Hatao: Can IRDP Do It?', T.A. Pai Memorial Lecture-2. Also in *Economic and Political Weekly,* 9 February: 20–21.

Raymond, Susan. 1996. 'Corporate Voluntarism: Private Support for Social Policy', in *Economic Reform Today,* 4. Washington: Centre for International Private Enterprise.

Rosenstein, Rodan, P. N. 1970. 'Notes on the Theory of the "Big Flush"', in Theodore Morgan and George W. Betz (eds) *Economic Development: Readings in Theory and Practice.* Belmont (California): Wadsworth Publishing Company Inc.

Schickele, Rainer. 1954. *Agricultural Policy: Farm Programmes and National Welfare.* Lincoln: University of Nebraska Press.

Schultz, W. Theodore. 1964. *Transforming Traditional Agriculture.* Ludhiana: Lyall Book Depot.

Seers, Dudley. 1969. 'The Meaning of Development', paper presented at the Eleventh World Conference of the Society for International Development, New Delhi.

Shah, Dilip R. 1992. *Dairy Cooperativisation: An Instrument of Social Change.* New Delhi & Jaipur: Rawat Publications.

Sharma, Miriam and **Urmila Vanjani.** 1993. 'When More Means Less: Assessing the Impact of Dairy Development on the Lives and Health of Women in Rural Rajasthan (India)', in *Social Science Medicine*, 37:11.

SID. 1969. *United Nations Panel on Flow of Foreign Capital to Developing Countries.* Society for International Development. March.

Singh, Hoshiar. (ed). 1985. *Rural Development in India: Evaluative Studies in Policies and Programmes.* Jaipur: Printwell Publishers.

Singh, Katar. 1973. 'The Impact of New Agricultural Technology on Farm Income Distribution in the Aligarh District of Uttar Pradesh', in the *Indian Journal of Agricultural Economics*. 28(2) April–June: 4.

———. 1994. *Managing Common Pool Resources: Principles and Case Studies.* Delhi: Oxford University Press.

———. 1997. 'Property Rights and Tenures in Natural Resources', in John Kerr, Dinesh K. Marothia, Katar Singh, C. Ramasamy and William R. Bentley (eds), *Natural Resource Economics: Theory and Application in India.* New Delhi: Oxford and IBH Publishing Co.

Singh, Katar and **J. Acharya.** 1986. 'The Impact of the Madhya Pradesh Dairy Development Project', Research Report. June. Institute of Rural Management, Anand.

Singh, Katar and **V. Mukunda Das.** 1982. 'Impact of Operation Flood at the Village Level', IRMA Research Report I. Anand: Institute of Rural Management.

Singh, Katar, P. Durgaprasad and **K. Vengama Raju.** 1985. 'Impact of Milch Animals Programme of IRDP in Sabarkantha District, Gujarat', Research Report, Institute of Rural Management, Anand. June.

Singh, Katar and **Anil Shishodia.** 1992. 'Irrigation Management in India: Need for Reforms', in *Indian Economic Panorama*, 2(1): 39–41.

Somjee, Geeta and **A. H. Somjee.** 1989. *Reaching Out to the Poor: The Unfinished Rural Revolution.* London: Macmillan.

Tinbergen, Jan. 1952. *On the Theory of Economic Policy.* Amsterdam: North Holland Publishing Company.

———. 1966. *Economic Policy: Principles and Design.* Amsterdam: North Holland Publishing Company.

———. 1968. *Central Planning.* New Haven: Yale University Press.

Todaro, Michael P. 1977. *Economic Development in the Third World.* London: Longman.

Toffler, Alvin. 1980. *The Third Wave.* New York: William Morrow and Company Inc.

UN/FAO. 1972. *Interim Evaluation Report of the Inter-Agency (FAO/WFP 1972) Mission on Operation Flood (India-618).*

———. 1976. Detailed Report of the Second UN/FAO World Food Programme Evaluation Mission on Operation Flood (India-WFP-618).

UN/FAO World Food Programme. 1981. Terminal Evaluation Report on Project India 618. 'Milk Marketing and Dairy Development', (Operation Flood-I), prepared by an Inter-Agency Mission which visited India from 9 February to 8 March 1981.

UNDP. 1990. *Human Development Report 1990.* New York: Oxford University Press.

———. 1994. *Human Development Report 1994.* New York. Oxford University Press.

———. 1996. *Human Development Report 1996.* New York: Oxford University Press.

———. 1997. *Human Development Report 1997.* New York: Oxford University Press.

Uphoff, Norman T. (ed). 1983. *Rural Development and Local Organisations in Asia - 3: South East Asia.* Delhi: Macmillan India Limited.

Uphoff, Norman T. and **Milton J. Esman.** 1983. *Local Organisation for Rural Development: Analysis of Asian Experience.* Ithaca (New York): Cornell University, Rural Development Committee, Centre for International Studies.

Vaishnav, P. H. and **K. V. Sundaram.** 1978. 'Integrating Development Administration at the Area Level', a note incorporated in the *Report of the Working Group on Block Level Planning.* New Delhi: Planning Commission, Government of India.

Waterston, Albert. 1965. *Development Planning: Lessons of Experience.* Baltimore: The Johns Hopkins University Press.

———. 1970. 'A Hard Look at Development Planning', in Theodore Morgan and George W. Betz (eds), *Economic Development, Readings in Theory and Practice.* Belmont (California): Wadsworth Publishing Company Inc.

———. 1974. Quoted in Robert Chambers, *Managing Rural Development: Ideas and Experience From East Africa.* Uppsala: The Scandinavian Institute of African Studies.

WCED. 1987. *Our Common Future, Report of World Commission on Environment and Development.* Delhi: Oxford University Press.

Weitz, Raanan. 1971. *From Peasant to Farmer: A Revolutionary Strategy for Development.* New York: Columbia University Press.

WFP. 1981. UN/FAO, *World Food Programme Terminal Evaluation Report on Project India 618-'Milk Marketing and Dairy Development' (Operation Flood I).* Rome: World Food Programme, FAO.

Wharton Jr, Clifton, R. 1970. 'Stages in Agricultural Development', in Theodore Morgan and George W. Betz. (eds).

World Bank. 1997. *World Bank Development Report 1997.* Delhi: Oxford University Press.

Yotopoulos, Pan A. and **J. B. Nugent.** 1976. *Economics of Development: Empirical Investigation.* New York: Harper and Row Publishers.

Index

About the Author

Katar Singh is currently Director and Reserve Bank of India Chair Professor, Institute of Rural Management, Anand (IRMA). Prior to this, he has been Associate Professor at the Department of Agricultural Economics, G.B. Pant University of Agriculture and Technology, Pantnagar; Professor at IRMA; and Director, Bankers Institute of Rural Development, Lucknow. Professor Singh is a life member of numerous bodies including the Indian Society of Agricultural Economics and the Indian Association of Public Administration, and is the Founder Chairman of the India Natural Resource Economics and Management (INREM) Foundation. In recognition of his outstanding research in agriculture and rural development, he was awarded the Sir Chhotu Ram National Award for the year 1996–97. Professor Singh has to his credit a large number of publications including seven books and several essays in contributed volumes.

●

Of related interest

Rural Credit and Self-help Groups

Micro-finance needs and concepts in India

K.G. Karmakar

In an increasingly expanding market-driven economy, the rural sector of India has often been marginalised with regard to its economic empowerment. Premised on a model of development that is largely titled in favour of the urban elite, the Indian economy is a picture of growth with a dim and often wavering focus on the primary sector, namely-agriculture. K.G. Karmakar emphasises the need to strengthen and restructure the existing credit systems for alleviating rural poverty. It was India that pioneered the involvement of the banking network in the assault on rural poverty and in providing adequate credit for agricultural operations. Dr Karmakar points to the unfortunate result of this exercise in the form of the creation of a vast and complex multiagency system which is beset with many problems.

This study enumerates the various factors which have been instrumental in weakening rural credit agencies. These range from a poor resource base, low income margins and a high default rate to frequent shifts in policy, narrow bureaucratic and political interests, and poor implementation. Dr. Karmakar illustrates his study with examples of several self-help groups, like BAAC in Thailand and the Grameen Bank in Bangladesh, engaged in innovative efforts at improving the present scenario. The author suggests management strategies in credit delivery (especially at the micro level) to enhance rural productivity.

This book will be of interest to those in the fields of economics, banking, finance, rural development, commercial banking, and those involved with co-operative banks, NGOs as well as management, planning or rural development policy formulation.

220mm x 140mm/370pp (tent.)/Hb/Pb/1999

Sage Publications
New Delhi □ Thousand Oaks □ London